JESUS: A BIOGRAPHY

by

HUGH J. SCHONFIELD

Jesus a Biography

Hugh J. Schonfield

Published by Texianer Verlag

for

The Hugh & Helene Schonfield World Service Trust

www.texianer.com

Editor: Stephen A. Engelking

ISBN: 978-3-949197-02-4

Front Cover: Christ in the desert by I.N. Kramskoi (1837-1887)

"If you venture to wonder how Christ would have looked... or whether he laughed over the repartees by which he baffled the priests when they tried to trap him into sedition and blasphemy ... you will have made the picture come out of its frame, the statue descend from its pedestal, the story become real, with all the incalculable consequences that may flow from this terrifying miracle."

George Bernard Shaw

Preface to *Androcles and the Lion*

Table of Contents

Preface

This book was first published in 1939 and yet still contains ideas fundamental to an understanding of the person of Jesus in his historical setting.

In his preface to the second edition published in 1948, Hugh Schonfield wrote:

'Since this book was first published I have received many letters from unknown friends telling me that I had enabled them for the first time to appreciate that Jesus was a "real person." I am naturally grateful if to that extent I have succeeded in my task; but it is somewhat surprising and illuminating to discover for how many people the Prophet of Nazareth has been little more than a theological concept with a semblance of humanity.

Owing to the war this Biography could not be reprinted sooner; so that unfortunately numbers had to complain that they could not obtain a copy. I have shared their disappointment, as even advertising failed to produce a single volume secondhand. I am therefore most appreciative that my Publisher has made the book once more available, so that all who wish may become intimately acquainted with the character and the circumstances of the life of this Man of the People, and of the Ages.

I have now been permitted to complete the trilogy I had designed, and in the two volumes *The Jew of Tarsus* and *Saints Against Caesar* the reader will find the rest of the story of the beginnings of Christianity as seen from the viewpoint of the independent historian.'

Stephen A. Engelking (Editor of this edition)

To the Reader

I have chosen the ambitious description of biography for this life of Jesus, because that is the class of writing to which it is intended to belong. My book is not designed to serve any theological or propagandist purpose whatsoever. I have attempted to take the subject out of the domain of purely religious literature, though I know how difficult it is—and has been for myself—to acquire the unbiased and detached viewpoint which is vital to such an experiment. I cannot pretend that I have always succeeded; but I believe that I have gone further in this direction than any of my predecessors. The name of Jesus is so intimately bound up with an exalted faith, which is daily operative for thousands, that the task of him who would remember only that his function is to relate the story of a Galilean Jew, who lived nearly two millenniums ago and claimed to be his people's Messiah, is no enviable one.

There are several grounds, however, on which I think my description can be justified. I have utilized all the available sources, and not only those contained in the New Testament. I have sought to understand, and to do full justice to, the position of the opponents of Jesus as well as his own position. I have tried, and how arduously, to introduce myself into the mind of Jesus, so as to comprehend his character, conceptions, feelings, motives, mannerisms, and even disabilities and shortcomings. Can I say, in all sincerity, that I have striven to live the part as if I had to play it? I have made myself intimately acquainted with the circumstances of his life, the country in which he lived, the times in which he lived, the people among whom he lived, and the conditions under which he lived, recreating that bygone age in all its essential aspects.

The practical equipment for a work of this sort is much heavier than a devotional or homiletic life of Jesus would require. I have had to complete and publish over the past twelve years a series of scholarly treatises affecting a variety of problems in Christian origins research. I have had to translate from Hebrew, Greek, Latin and Aramaic, to investigate at first-hand the masses of cognate material from the first seven centuries of our era preserved by Christian, Jew, Mohammedan and Heathen. The writing of other biographies has also formed part of the necessary education. I only hope, profoundly, as my book is intended for the reading of every man and woman, that I have not allowed any of these labours to appear too obviously in the body of the volume. I also hope that no one will think me wise in my own conceits. They must be aware that these qualifications have to be stated, and appreciate that without them I could have had no prospect of succeeding in my undertaking. It has needed at all points the very opposite of conceit to set aside my own preconceptions and to handle difficulty after difficulty which arose, patiently and on its own merits, with the ever present thought that I was running contrary to many cherished convictions. The heart was too deeply engaged for any selfish considerations.

I must convey the warning that there is much that is novel in my presentation—though friends have wondered whether there could be anything new to say. The biographer is quite naturally proud when he can claim that he has employed previously neglected or fresh material. That pride can be mine. But even in the documents which have long been familiar some things emerged, which were novel to me when I first apprehended them. The burden, indeed, has been eased continually by the joys of discovery. I am glad to know that Bible students will find special pleasure and profit in coming across a number of incidental revelations, which others will pass over without recognizing their significance. There is in any case nothing of weight set down which is unsupported by ample testimony. Interpretations may be criticized, conclusions attacked; but the records which gave rise to them cannot be impeached by any impartial authority.

To those who may be offended at my treatment I wish to say that this biography has been compiled, as I imagine will be evident on every page, in no spirit of levity. Let them consider that the name of Jesus is being used today as a peg on which to hang all kinds of political and social theories. There seemed to me to be a very real justification for a book which, instead of attempting to work the oracle, provided the proper criteria by which the truth of any of these theories might fairly be tested. The sayings of Jesus have been retained firmly within their historical and contemporary setting. They can only be removed out of them, in my opinion, at the peril of the doctrine which they are advanced to support. I may add, in passing, that I have been deeply impressed by the authenticity of the portrait which the Gospels furnish, and with the general trustworthiness of the accounts transmitted, both canonical and uncanonical.

Wherever the sense is clear I have kept largely to the language of the Authorized Version for Biblical quotations; but I have not hesitated to retranslate from the Greek where an obscurity exists, or where the rendering, in my view, exhibits prejudice. I have, however, frequently used my translation of an ancient Hebrew manuscript of the *Gospel of Matthew*, because it better reflects the actual diction of Jesus, and restores some of the poetry, word-play, and force of utterance, lost in the Greek version. I have also brought in sayings from the *Gospel of the Hebrews* and several early Gospel manuscripts. A few appropriate remarks by minor characters are fictitious; but these can readily be distinguished by their modem style.

The popular aim of the book made it undesirable to crowd the pages with footnotes. All the sources employed will be known to specialist scholars; but for the less instructed, and those who might otherwise be tempted to think that some of the propositions have been invented, I have provided the essential minimum of explanatory notes and non-Biblical references as an appendix.

I have not included everything recorded to have been said or done by Jesus. I have reserved the same right as

the Evangelists to select my material; but I have con-
sciously excluded nothing which represented a problem
which I ought to have faced, and omission does not imply that the saying or incident has been thought un-his-
torical. Manifestly there must have been many things in
the life of Jesus of which we have no record.

If I have anything left to say, it is this. Laying aside all
matters of creed, the life of Jesus surely teaches that if a
man has a great vision, and is faithful to it, though he
grow old or die young without seeing it realized—and the
world, perhaps even he, thinks that he has failed—yet he
has unleashed mighty forces which ultimately will bring
it to fruition.

H. J. S.

Prologue in Galilee

A tortuous road rising and falling among the verdant foothills brought the traveller of King Herod's time, coming from the newly-built haven of Caesarea, into a region distinctive both in physical features and in the character of its inhabitants. From the Great Plain of Esdraelon the land rose in successive ridges running east and west in an ascending scale towards the north. It was a populous country, at least in its southern part. In the valleys and the shelter of the hills clustered hundreds of hamlets, and, as if standing guard over them, a strange rounded mountain lifted its tree-clad slopes in majestic isolation. The name of the mountain was labor, but the natives commonly spoke of it as the holy mount, for, as far back as folk-memory would carry, the forces of nature had been worshipped with strange rites on its summit.

As the traveller followed the road in a north-easterly direction, he hardly needed the evidence of its physical aspect to make him aware that he had crossed a boundary into a different country. At the very first village where he stopped for refreshment he would realize unmistakably that he was among people of another race. His requests, made to them in the prevailing Aramaic tongue, would be answered in a barbarous dialect of that language, hard to be understood because of the slurring of the gutturals. If he made a purchase he would find that the weights and measures were not the same as in the south. There was something also a little queer and forbidding about the people themselves. It was not that they were inhospitable or lacking in friendly welcome; but they seemed abrupt, uncommunicative, and rather puritanical. In features, too, they were unlike the Judeans, or even Samaritans, a ruder folk evidently of mixed origin, the surviving synthesis of ancient tribes which had held tenaciously to their highlands while their fellows in less favoured regions had become extinct. Jews they were by religion, but if the traveller had occasion to sojourn for any length of time among them he could not fail to notice that many of their customs and practices were distinctive, and that they were highly superstitious.

The region which the traveller had entered had been called from of old the Girdle of the Nations, Galilee of the Gentiles. Here had lingered on, and mingled their blood, the remnants of once mighty races. These were now forgotten, and the generic name of Syrians covered all the mountain dwellers who were not of the community of Israel. But if time had obliterated the distinctions between the several peoples it had not healed the ancient enmity which had its origin when the intruding tribes of the Hebrews under Joshua mercilessly dispossessed the heathen of their inheritance. The emergence of the Jewish Commonwealth after the Babylonian Exile, and especially the political events of the second century B. C., had only served to fan the still glowing embers of hatred into a fierce flame. There was a feud between the Jewish Galileans and the Syrians, which for bitterness and active hostility made the differences between the Jews and Samaritans pale into insignificance.

The traveller, except in conversation, would nor realize the full strength of this feeling while he continued among the peaceful villages of Lower Galilee. But let him journey on into the highlands of Upper Galilee, and there the tale would be constant of retributive burnings and slayings. Once it had seemed as if Syria would settle all its scores when the megalomaniac Antiochus Epiphanes overran the country with his remorseless soldiery. Then had arisen the Maccabean warrior priests, and had slowly won back the land from its conquerors. In those days of national faiths, God One, or gods many, had been the opposing and challenging creeds. A man might humble his enemy in the dust, but there could be no final victory so long as he clung to his ancestral belief. So the Seleucid Syrians imposed Paganism on the stricken Jews, and the Hasmoneans in their turn forced Judaism on the unwilling Syrians. The horrors of warfare were lent by this policy the false attributes of righteousness and holiness, and on either side religion was debased by concomitant fanaticism. Thus it came about that of all Jews the most uncompromising in their faith were the Galileans, and the neighbouring Gentiles were hardly less rigid in their own belief.

For some decades now the mutual animosity had been restricted in expression to contemptuous talk and incessant petty raiding, for Rome had effectively reduced the land of Syrian and Jew alike to a state of dependency on her sovereign power.

By the favour of Rome, Herod, son of the converted Idumean Antipater, had been made king of a Judea which included the larger part of Galilee, with further extensions granted to him in the course of his reign by Augustus Caesar. There was no love lost between the monarch and his Galilean subjects. They detested him as a foreigner, and utilized to the full the oriental power of invective to asperse his origin. It was a national insult that such a man, professing Jew though he was, should reign over them. The king in turn, ambitious, religiously indifferent, anxious to be esteemed by Pagan and Jew alike throughout the Near East, was impatient of the strict monotheism and national prejudices of his people, which hampered him in his grandiose schemes. In Galilee, he knew from long and bitter experience, dwelt the most pitiless of the elements opposed to him, capable of inflaming the rest of his realm with their bigoted hostility. He could have no certainty of peace at home, nor assure himself of favour abroad, until he had brought Galilee into a state of abject submission.

The enmity between the Galileans and their king was of long standing. It dated back to the time when Herod, then a young man of twenty-five, was created Governor of Galilee by Antipater his father. At that time the future king had attacked the Galilean terrorist bands commanded by their chief Hezekiah, who had been earning what they believed was a commendable livelihood by swooping down from their highlands and plundering the rich Syrian cities of the coastal region. Hezekiah and many of his men had been killed, to the great comfort of the Syrians, who sang songs in Herod's praise in their towns and villages.

This unauthorized action, involving the slaughter of fellow Jews, was abominated by the Galileans and reprehended even in Jerusalem, where the principal men appeared before the weak King Hyrcanus and insisted that he order Herod to stand his trial before the Sanhedrin. The bereaved mothers also came wailing and clamouring into the Temple demanding vengeance on the murderer. Yielding against his inclination to popular pressure, for he had a great liking for Herod, Hyrcanus summoned him to come up for trial. Herod came; but advised by his father he brought a strong bodyguard. Surrounded by his men-at-arms he presented himself insolently before his judges. In face of this display of force no one dared to accuse him, until Sameas or Shemaiah, an eminent religious legislator, broke the spell of silence in burning words. The Sanhedrin was aroused to do its duty, and was ready to pass a death sentence, when the king, seeing how the verdict would go, adjourned the proceedings, and persuaded Herod to use the interval to make good his escape. Like a certain Saul of Tarsus, nearly a century later, the erstwhile Governor of Galilee, yet breathing out threatenings and slaughter, took the road to Damascus. There he purchased from Sextus Caesar the generalship of the armies of Coelesyria, and was only with difficulty prevented from assaulting Jerusalem.

Baulked of his vengeance at this time, Herod, after he had been made king, did not long delay to rout out the Galilean brigands from their fastnesses. His action then was partly dictated by political necessity; for though the hardy and fanatical Galileans had little sympathy with the effeminate and Hellenized members of the Hasmonean dynasty, they preferred them infinitely as rulers to the Idumean usurper. Antigonus, last of the Maccabean priest-kings, held a number of places in Galilee with his garrisons, and it was essential that these should be subdued.

Herod first seized on the prominent fortified city of Sepphoris, which was abandoned without a struggle by its defenders. He then sent a skirmishing party eastward to Arbel, a village lying in a fertile valley close by the Lake of Chinnereth, the Sea of Galilee, and followed it up with his main army some days later. A pitched battle was fought in the neighbourhood of Arbel in which Herod was ultimately victorious, and the forces of Antigonus were scattered among the mountains and beyond the Jordan. Galilee was quelled, except for the brigand bands in their rocky retreats.

A little to the north of the scene of the battle, and not far from the town of Magdala, noted for its dye-works, is the fearsome gorge of pigeons. The precipitous cliffs which rise on either side are studded with deep caves and fissures. In these almost inaccessible strongholds the Galilean Zealots well-furnished with fuel and provisions had long been able to maintain themselves and their families. But Herod was not to be daunted by physical obstacles. From the top of the cliffs he caused iron-bound chests filled with his men to be let down by chains to the mouths of the caves. The soldiers were equipped with hooks with which to drag out the defenders and tumble them down to their death. And when the wretched troglodytes retired into the inner recesses of their rocky habitations, they were burnt or smoked out by flaming darts shot into the brushwood piled in the caves for fuel. Herod offered a free pardon to all who would give themselves up; but few took advantage of the amnesty, and one proud old man, rather than allow his sons to save themselves by surrender, slew them one by one, and then his wife, casting their bodies down the cliff. Finally, reviling the king for his mean descent, he himself plunged into the gulf below. Thus Herod had his revenge.

But the Galileans, though beaten, were by no means conquered. No sooner had Herod left the country and entrusted his army there to Ptolemy, his general, than the bands mysteriously reformed, attacked the king's troops, and as mysteriously dispersed among the mountains and waste places with which they were familiar. Herod had to return and conduct another punitive campaign, and levied a fine of a hundred talents upon the disaffected cities.

Even this did not terminate the struggle. The Roman mercenaries commanded by Joseph, Herod's brother, in the south, and consisting largely of recruited Syrians, were defeated by the soldiers of Antigonus, and Joseph himself was slain. When the news reached Galilee, there was no restraining even those Galileans who had been forced to serve in Herod's garrisons. They broke out in open mutiny, and proceeded to drown the Herodians in the lake.

So it came about that Herod, by his actions, became identified with the Syrians by the men of Galilee, and the feud was extended to include the person and authority of the king.

With the capture and execution of Antigonus, the last king of the Hasmonean line, there was a temporary lull in the conflict which had destroyed the flower of Galilean manhood. During this lull Herod, instead of trying to placate his subjects and gain their goodwill, went out of his way further to alienate them by paganizing and romanizing Palestine. He built theatres, and staged costly games, while everywhere Caesar was honoured by inscriptions and the exhibition of trophies. New towns adorned with palaces and temples filled with heathen statuary rose at his command, each testifying to his Roman loyalty. Strato's Tower became the port of Caesarea. Sebaste could barely be recognized as the ancient Samaria. Such a policy might have resulted in a national revolution had it not happened that prolonged droughts just at this time occasioned a terrible famine.

Deprived of sustenance, the boldest of them lost courage, and thousands perished from want and disease. Galilee the fruitful became Galilee the barren, and in their misery and desperation the people turned to the king for relief. Herod could not fail to listen to their pleas for his own sake., He had exhausted his money in his lavish building schemes, and there was no prospect of raising more from an impoverished population whose sun-baked fields could not produce the crops to yield the means of paying taxes. In this emergency there was only one thing to be done; to melt down the gold and the silver in his palaces and to purchase with it com from Egypt. So driven by very necessity the king fed and clothed his people as much as he was able, and bought with his charity a measure of goodwill. He also remitted to them a third of the taxes, which in any case they were in no position to pay.

But Herod knew well enough the transient character of this stomach loyalty, and he was on the alert for signs of recrudescence of the old disaffection. His officers had orders to see that the people were kept constantly at work so that the opportunity for hatching plots was denied to them. He also interdicted public meetings, and instituted an elaborate spy system so that he might have prompt information of any secret gatherings or expressions of antagonism towards his authority. It is said that he even sought first-hand knowledge by mingling with the populace in disguise. There were mysterious disappearances of prominent citizens, who were never heard of again. The fortresses and the galleys preserved their secrets. Galilee endured sullenly. No wonder then that the traveller found the hill folk taciturn and uncommunicative.

The effect of this policy, however, was not to eliminate revolutionary propaganda, but to drive it underground. Resourceful zealots contrived somehow to communicate with one another, and to prepare for the great day of vengeance. Many left all their possessions and joined the outlaws in their caves. Judas, son of the slain chieftain Hezekiah, steadily reorganized the guerrilla bands with tested recruits. A new Herodian edict added greatly to the number of desperate characters on whom he could call. The prevailing want and distress had increased the crime of burglary. The king had therefore decreed, contrary to Jewish usage, that all found guilty of housebreaking should be sold into slavery to foreigners, thus condemning them both to exile and to a life religiously intolerable.

Galilee, however fair and peaceful in outward seeming, was seething with unrest. Beggary had multiplied to an inconceivable extent even in a country where the mendicant was a familiar figure. Robbery with violence was so common that the courts had difficulty in dealing with the cases. Disease was rampant. A physician visiting the cities and villages could not hope to treat the enormous number of nerve-cases, the blind, the deaf, the dumb, lepers, epileptics and paralytics, the majority of them sufferers who owed their miserable state to the political and economic conditions. Women were hysterical, men frightened at shadows. The land was ridden with a great fear of the Evil One and his demons. Superstition and religiosity flourished. Many resorted to magical practices. Many made pilgrimages to the shrines of saints and to holy springs. There were those who gave themselves up to agonized prayer and severe fasting, and poor souls who ran wild and naked in the waste places and sheltered themselves in tombs in the rocks. Surely the Redemption could not long be delayed.

Word went round, and Herod's informers reported it, that a Deliverer was expected to free the oppressed people from alien tyranny. It was whispered in Nazareth and Cana. The report, inspired by prophecies and the expositions of synagogue preachers amplified by popular desire, ran up hill and down dale. Magdala heard it, and Kefar-Naum, Chorazin, Bethsaida, and scores of other towns and villages. The Messiah is coming, he is coming soon, he is coming in Galilee. In the Vale of Arbel, the scene of the great defeat, he will raise the standard of victory. One cannot lay hands on a rumour: one cannot imprison and torture it: one can only discredit it. The agents of Herod busied themselves to prove that there could be no Messiah except the king. Had he not enlarged the borders of Israel, rebuilt the Temple, dealt bread to the hungry, clothed the naked? The Galileans listened in stony silence; but back in their own homes, with no stranger by, tongues were loosed, imagination took wings, and a great hope was bom.

All these things the traveller would learn, if he succeeded in gaining the confidence of the people in his northward journey.

Passing by Nazareth, set on the slope of a hill, the road ran on to Kefar-Kenna, Cana of Galilee. On the mountain opposite was a famed holy place to which there was a constant stream of pilgrims. It was the tomb of the Prophet Jonah; he who had prophesied the restoration of Israel and brought the Ninevites to repentance. Further on, the road began to dip down and, between the hills, the traveller caught his first glimpse of the Lake of Chinnereth, the Sea of Galilee, hundreds of feet beneath him. There it lay, a sapphire jewel in a setting of old gold, one of the loveliest scenes upon which the eye of man can rest. As the road descended in a succession of bends so the temperature rose steadily to tropical heat; for the lake lay nearly seven hundred feet below sea level. Lush vegetation flourished in profusion. The date palm reared its stately head. On either side of the road were to be seen plantations of olives, fig-trees, and vines, while the increase of traffic and the distant prospect of buildings gave evidence of a populous area.

The road turned north along the lakeside, but a branch to the right led down to the city of Rakkath and the Hot Springs, and on to the Ford of Jordan. Near the site of Rakkath the tetrarch Herod Antipas would afterwards build his city of Tiberias. In summer the region was plagued with insects, which suggested to some Galilean the two-edged witticism, "Baal-Zebub (Lord of Flies) hath his seat at Tiberias." Chammath, or Emmaus, the place of the hot springs, was also traditionally associated with the demons. It was said that King Solomon had sent them there to heat the water, and had afflicted them with deafness so that they might never learn of his death and cease to perform their appointed function. Bathing in the waters was believed to bring certain relief to sufferers from rheumatism, boils, and even leprosy, and at this sad time there was always a large crowd waiting on the means of health.

The lake itself was dotted with craft, while on the strand were fishermen repairing their boats and mending their nets. Some stood knee-deep in the water, their robes girt about their middle, exposing their brown legs and thighs. Others sat at the opening of their tents on the waterfront while the women scoured their utensils with fine sand and rinsed them in the limpid water. Much of the fish caught was landed higher up the lake at the city called by the Greeks Tarichaea, there to be pickled in brine and sold for distribution in all parts of the country.

The fishermen, like those of the same calling in many other lands, were simple, direct folk, with an assured faith in God and a no less assured belief in demons and malignant spirits, who could raise a sudden storm and keep the fish away from their nets. It was largely they who carried momentous news and gossip to the various cities and villages bordering on the lake, and they were the link between the outlaws and their secret sympathizers. On dark nights dangerous messages and even political refugees were conveyed over the water. From the Galilean fishermen the Messianic hope received its most enthusiastic endorsement.

On the far side of the lake the mountains of Gaulan showed up harshly as a high and arid plateau pouring itself into the water in plum-coloured lumps intersected by clefts and gorges. This too was Herod's territory, the traveller would be told, but they were mainly foreigners and pig-breeders on that unpromising coast.

The road swung out from the shore and back again to industrious Magdala. The mountains on the left, seeming higher for the deep depression in which the blue lake glistened, were pierced with valleys, notably that of Arbel, dark with foliage. But presently the highlands receded, and the traveller came out on the fruitful Plain of Gennesareth, greatly favoured because of its temperate climate and extreme fertility. Its manifold delights, with the consequent situation here of the estates of the rich and noble, originated a play on its name, so that Gennesareth was interpreted as "The Garden of Princes." But the great drought had not excepted even Gennesareth, and at this time its returning fruitfulness was heavily fenced and guarded against thieves. Beyond the plain, away to the north-west, could be seen a city set on a hill, the fortified town of Zefat. Nearer at hand were the ravines of the robbers, while to the north-east in the far distance rose up the snow-clad glory of Hermon.

Traversing the edge of the plain, threading its way through groves and orchards, the road turned again to the lake, and reached it at the busy mart and customs-station of Kefar-Naum. There it was joined by another road coming across the mountains from the Syrian seaboard at Acco (Ptolemais). A large foreign element was to be found at lordly Kefar-Naum, and for this reason the Jews there tended to be more lax in their religious observances. The poorer and, by contrast, more devout Jewish folk found a home in the fishing village of Bethsaida, a little to the south and almost a suburb of Kefar-Naum.

Resuming his northward journey the traveller was not long in reaching the head of the lake, and here he could turn and look back on the nearly thirteen miles of its length. At his feet the young Jordan, strengthened by its passage through the Waters of Merom, entered the expanse of waters to emerge again adult and powerful at the distant end, to tumble down, as its name described, on its long course to the grave in the Dead Sea. Crossing the river he came shortly to the other Bethsaida, a frontier city afterwards renamed Julias by the tetrarch Philip, and by easy stages he continued along the road to his ultimate destination at old Damascus.

At this point we may leave our traveller to pursue his way out of the Land of Israel and out of this history. He has served us well in introducing us to Galilee and its inhabitants in the critical days when Herod reigned and a certain Jesus of Nazareth was born.

CHAPTER I

The Sure Mercies of David

The Court of King Herod was filled with plotters. The life of the monarch was made miserable to him by the schemes and machinations of the sons of his several wives and their kindred, and latterly of his favourite son, Antipater. The common fate of tyrants was fast overtaking him. Through blood he had secured himself on the throne,' and now his declining years were stained with the blood of his offspring whom he was forced to slay lest their real or fancied treason should deprive him untimely of a life which day by day grew more burdensome. Well might Augustus exclaim in punning Greek: "It would be better to be one of Herod's *swine* than one of his *sons!*"

Late in July, the twentieth of the Hebrew month Tammuz, was the date assigned to the descendants of the House of David for bringing to the Temple their gift of fuel for the altar. But none of the heirs of Herod, pitting their wits against one another to obtain the succession, dreamed of any threat from one of the ancient blood royal to his chances of becoming King of the Jews.

There seemed, indeed, no likelihood of a challenge from this quarter. Among the risings which Herod had been compelled to suppress not one had been led by a Davidic claimant to the throne. Those who could trace their ancestry back to the shepherd-king were content with the small traditional privileges which testified to their noble origin. From the worthy Hillel, Doctor of the Law, and by trade a wood-cutter, down to the most obscure representative of the family, there was no sign of any pretensions to sovereignty. Even when Herod had rifled the tomb of David in search of gold not one descendant had lifted his voice in public protest.

But if the Herodians saw no menace in the Davidians, and the Davidians themselves were satisfied with private citizenship, there were devout men among the priests and scribes who began to use the name of David, at first cautiously and in secret, but gradually with less restraint, as a symbol of coming deliverance. The spiritual and political degradation of the nation set them to studying the sacred scrolls for light on what they felt must indeed be the last days of human folly and transgression. And in the writings of the Prophets they found many indications that a scion of the stock of David would be the ultimate saviour of his people. There were others also, believing no less in the final salvation, whose minds were obsessed with the thought of wrath and judgment upon the wicked. On these pietists fell the spirit of prophecy, which had seemed to have departed from Israel, and manifested itself in a literary form characteristic of the period.

And so began the age of apocalypse, or revelation.

An age which believed that upon itself had fallen the ends of all the ages, that it was to witness the consummation, the catastrophic curtain to the drama of humanity, must be something of a phenomenon in history. No other age that we know, unless indeed it be our own, has been so much impressed with its own finality, so greatly preoccupied with its own imminent disintegration. There was nothing of senility in the idea; rather was it the kind of clairvoyance which comes in times of great crisis. One may liken the situation to that of a ship which has struck a submerged rock and is slowly settling down into the waters, with all its passengers conscious that the end is near and reacting in their own way to the threat of impending dissolution; some souls frenzied and driven near to madness, some attempting to banish fear by jests and laughter, some affecting a stoical indifference, others betaking themselves to prayer and self-examination. Prophets before this age had had apocalyptic moments, but never in the known traditions of man had there been such an outburst of religio-political ecstasy, which penetrated the guarded gates of heaven by its own intensity, and saw the fate of humanity mirrored in the crystal sea that surrounded the Throne.

No one who has read the apocalyptic writings can doubt the urge, the compulsion put upon the authors. "What thou seest, write in a book!" is the barest statement of a command that would brook no refusal. They felt themselves pressed into service to convey the final warnings of God. Some of them question the justice of the Divine action, as if to find excuse for requesting a stay of execution of the sentence passed upon the world. Like Abraham

Seeking to save Sodom, they bargain down to the smallest shred of merit. But none of the writers doubts the terrible reality of the Wrath to Come. The emotional stress under which they laboured by the very urgency and desperation of their calling defies calculating analysis. The visions tumble over one another; there are abrupt transitions, for the action is continuous and one scene gives place to another with kinematic rapidity. There was a double strain both on heart and hand. Numerology is only one of the scribe's devices to record purposefully as well as rapidly: he employed appropriate round figures, meaningful abbreviations, but without occult significance unless so stated. The same principle applies to the theriology, the menagerie of queer beasts presented as typical of the qualities of men and kingdoms. The visions were subjective, the writing in a sense automatic, the phraseology and imagery often borrowed, but it is fitness rather than previous association that usually dictates their use.

The apocalypses were of necessity pseudonymous, put forth in the names of ancient seers and patriarchs of Israel, and on that very account importing a sense of the miraculous and the revealed presence of God into an age of sophistication, worldliness and agnosticism. With a stroke of the pen the past was telescoped into the present, and what was once possible became possible again, because with God all things are possible.

These writings, circulating among the more spiritually minded of the intelligentsia, inspired for the first time a real belief in the advent of a Messiah. Previously the doctrine had been both vague and indecisive. The great secret could not long remain imprisoned in the assemblies of the holy brotherhood of the Essenes, nor confined in the conclaves of the schoolmen: it pressed to come forth. The pious priests and scribes began to impart something of their knowledge to the people. Up and down the land, when the citizens and villagers gathered in the synagogues for worship and to hear the reading of the prescribed portion of the books of Moses, local or visiting teachers added a messianic discourse. In burning words, but careful to make much use of metaphor and hyperbole, they expounded the prophetic writings. There was little that was definite, except the urge to repentance. No Herodian spy could glean when it was expected that the Messiah would come, who he would be, or in what way he would make himself known. But now it was not concealed that the Redeemer would be of the House of David, and the people were exhorted to return to the Lord that the Day of Deliverance might be hastened.

Thus a strange shadow, mysterious and awe-inspiring, spread over the Land of Israel, affecting the populace in varying degrees with exaltation and dread. Its intangible presence was realized in Judea, and Samaria, and Galilee alike. It was the shadow of the Lord Messiah. The peaceful descendants of the House of David, with the rest of the people, could not fail to become conscious of it. Even the old and morbid king was sensible of it before death claimed his disease-ridden body. Who and What was this Son of David who was coming? There was something more than mortal about his approach. One thing was certain, the shadow was there, and the shadow was alive. There was a general preparedness to see it take form and substance at any moment; but the outline was too indistinct for anyone to be able to say with assurance what the reality would be like.

Of all the forms which the messianic expectation assumed in the imaginations of the Palestinians that which prevailed in Galilee was the most human and natural. It was by no means divested of the miraculous and the prodigious: this aspect was even accentuated by the superstitious highlanders; but it was relieved of the otherworldliness of the dwellers in the wilderness, and the theatricality of the southerners. In Galilee the Messiah would be recognized as a man of the people: no one looked to see him drop from the skies. It was this difference in outlook which made it inevitable that the Son of David should manifest himself in Galilee. There he would find friends and willing helpers; elsewhere he must remain a solitary figure wrapped in impenetrable and insupportable glory.

It was expedient, therefore, that the Messiah should be a Galilean, although this might be unacceptable to the wise men of Jerusalem. As a consequence something could be known of his origin and the circumstances of his birth. Had Judea claimed him he would have been like the remote Melchisedec, king of Salem, "without father, without mother, without pedigree, having neither beginning of days, nor end of life."

It is to the Galileans that we owe our knowledge of the parents of Jesus, his ancestry, and the reminiscences of his infancy and childhood. This information, however, has not come down to us in a cold statement of facts, for that would have been foreign to the Galilean temperament. These highlanders are famed in Jewish literature for their fertility in the creation of pious legends. They delighted in folk tales; and few of the great stories of the Bible, especially those dealing with the old Israelitish heroes, have not been embellished by their fancy. In the story of the messianic advent they had a subject worthy of the best that they could give, and they responded wonderfully to the opportunity.

Substantially, the nativity narratives which have thrilled and gladdened generations of readers are Galilee's tribute to her King. Loving hearts have adorned the simple truth with a robe of such majesty, dignity, and charm, that the mind accepts with joyful emotion the idealized realities. The native legends of the great departed have been ransacked for jewels to set upon the royal brow; the angelic annunciation comes from the legend of Samson, the heralding star and the astrologers from the legend of Abraham, the light in the cave and the persecution of the child from the legend of Moses. Other precious elements derive from the legends of Isaac and Samuel. Sometimes two or more legends supply precious stones that match one another, though all have been recut by cunning hands for their final exalted purpose. But if the jewels are Hebrew heirlooms, the diadem in which they are so perfectly set is pure gold from the mines of contemporary information, pointed with the pinnacles of prophecy. Every gift has been willingly offered that our eyes "may see the king in his beauty."[1]

And who could fail to identify the object of such loyal homage, when the sacred tongue itself proclaims him, *Notzer* the craftsman, of *Natzrath* the city of Galilee, *Netzer* the scion of David, *Nazir* dedicated to the service of God, and crowned with the royal diadem *Nezer*? By such indications we are directed to Nazareth, a township of Lower Galilee straggling up the western slopes of a natural amphitheatre of gentle hills, and are sent to seek among its habitations for the home of a craftsman of the lineage of David, whose wife has recently presented him with a firstborn son. Almost anyone will tell us that the man for whom we are looking is Joseph the Carpenter, whose wife Mary has borne a son called Jesus. The gossips will supply us with further information, for they know the family well; and the sum of their knowledge is this:

"Master Joseph bar Jacob! Oh, yes, a very pious and God-fearing man. You will not find a better. No, not a young man, nor yet very old. Both his parents died many years ago. His wife was the only child of old Master Joachim the farmer and Hannah his wife, likewise dead now, peace be upon them! Yes, both families are of the House of David, may Heaven cause his horn to flourish!

Mary was hardly more than a child when her father betrothed her to Joseph. But old Joachim knew what he was doing, for he did not long survive. Master Joseph was often at the farmer's house on business; he makes ploughs and yokes: it was in this way that he came to know him. You may imagine that the wedding was a quiet one, everyone remembers it, so sad, the bride having lost her father, and then her mother soon after, poor girl, may the All Merciful comfort the mourners in Zion! Quite a tragedy, never to have seen their grandchild, a fine boy too. Their circumstances? Many fare worse. But who is rich in these evil times? She brought him some property, not much, you know, the awful drought and the taxes of the Edomite, may his memory be blotted out! Ah! Excuse my cursed tongue, sir, that wags too freely. Perchance you are of the Herodians?"[2]

After this fashion we may imagine a native of Nazareth replying to our questions. But there are strange and intimate matters connected with the birth of the carpenter's son, some of which his mother may have related long afterwards, but which at this time would have been known to no one except the master and mistress of the house. Whatever they were, we can only become acquainted with them now through the medium of the later Galilean wonder-tales, where truth is woven into the traditional design with such superlative artifice that it cannot by any means be separated and exhibited as a connected whole.

The tales will stand for all time unique in their simple grandeur, and it does not make our homage less sincere if we discern beneath the robe of glory the plain garment of the countryman. A story is there, a vibrant story, of two very human souls, a man and his wife, natural in their hopes and fears, their tenderness and jealousy, behaving as we should expect real and sentient beings to behave. There is the young woman flushed with youth's vast dreams and imaginings. There is the man already settled in sober God-fearing ways. They, of the family of David, look for a king of their lineage, for a son of their love. And, behold, her dreams and his desires have coalesced, and their son has. become the king.

The record was never meant to content the historian, but to rejoice the humble. That is why they that dwell like the Galileans among hills and dales, who know "seed-time and harvest, cold and heat," will always prefer to believe that "the birth of Jesus the Messiah was on this wise."

Those Galilean country folk have credited themselves with the knowledge of the manner of the birth of the Deliverer before Joseph and Mary plighted their troth. They can tell the story of the advent of Moses with a wealth of detail not found in the book of Exodus and give an account of the coming of Samson with embellishments undiscoverable in the book of *Judges*. Some of this material may still be read in the legends of the Jews, and its extraordinary likeness to the Gospel records need occasion no surprise. The angelic annunciation to the woman, the man's suspicion of her unfaithfulness, the dream that sets his mind at rest, they are all there. We may tell a Galilean peasant of King Herod's time about the quite normal birth of So-and-so the son of So-and-so, and he will be prepared to believe us; but if we suggest that this is how the Messiah will be bom, he will smilingly shake his head. And then we shall find ourselves listening to another tale.

The mother of the Messiah will be a beautiful young woman, whose husband is a very righteous man, and learned in the Law. They will both of them be of the lineage of David.

Now they have no children. But one day the woman goes to the well to draw water; and while she is there alone, suddenly there appears before her a handsome young man; and this is the angel Gabriel. And when she is afraid at his presence, for she is virtuous, the young man bids her not to fear, because he is the angel of the Lord, and he has been sent to tell her that she will bear a son. "He shall be great," says the angel, "and shall be called the son of the Most High; and the Lord God shall give unto him the throne of his father David: and he shall reign over the house of Jacob for ever, and of his kingdom there shall be no end."

And when the woman wishes further to inquire how this may be, the angel answers that the power of the Most High will overshadow her. And the woman says, "Behold the handmaiden of the Lord; be it unto me according to thy word." Then the angel departs from her.

And the woman comes and informs her husband. When he hears of the beauty of the young man, he does not believe that he is an angel, but supposes that his wife has been seduced by an evil man professing to be a messenger of God. Being a just man, he will not make her a public example, but determines to divorce her privately.[3]

Nevertheless his conscience vexes him, lest, after all, his wife be innocent and he should be found fighting against God. That very night, while he meditates on these things, the angel of the Lord appears to him in a dream, and says to him, "Thou son of David, fear not to take unto thee thy wife, for through the Holy Spirit of God she has conceived, and she shall bear thee a son, who shall save his people from their enemies." And the man awakes from sleep, and gives thanks to God, and takes unto him his wife. And when her time is fulfilled she brings forth her firstborn son, who is the Lord Messiah.

"That, sir," our Galilean assures us, "is how our Messiah will come into the world."

It is a strange tale, we think, but in face of such simple faith we dare not suggest that it puts a great strain on our credulity.

Yet, afterwards we may begin to wonder whether we were justified in our disbelief. Is not this a most apt and charming way of representing so significant an event, hallowed as it is by the folkconsciousness of the Hebrew race? And so, when we read such tales of the origin of Jesus told in almost the selfsame words, we too may find ourselves proclaiming that "the birth of the Messiah was on this wise."

CHAPTER II

Unto Us a Son is Given

There were in Jerusalem two famous Doctors of the Law, Judas the son of Saripha and Matthias the son of Margaloth. These men, encouraged by the reports of Herod's sickness to believe that his days were numbered, determined to begin the cleansing of Jerusalem from its heathen adornments. And where could such a beginning best be made if not at the House of God? There, over the great gate of the Temple, in blatant violation of the Mosaic prohibition of the making of images, a massive golden eagle was poised with outspread wings. This had been the king's personal votive gift, erected in defiance of the sentiments of his subjects, a reminder that the dread shadow of Roman sovereignty readied even to the Sanctuary.

When the students assembled in the lecture-hall it was to find their reverend seniors aroused out of their normal placidity. The atmosphere was electric. In place of the anticipated exposition the Doctors Judas and Matthias began to address them in burning words that quickly kindled an answering fire in the young men's breasts.

"It is not enough to know the Law," the sages cried: "you must be prepared to observe it, and to maintain its observation, even at the risk of your lives. While you study here the Law of God is being broken every day, and every day His Holy Name is profaned. The Lawless man has filled Jerusalem with his idols, and he has not been afraid to defile the Holy Place. And we have done nothing! But God has not forgotten: His judgments are sure. Even now He has smitten that man so that he is dying the terrible death of the wicked, and worms devour his body. The torments of Gehenna still await him. But what of us? Shall we share in the same condemnation, because we are parties to his sin? Unless we act, we cannot escape the guilt. All of us must die one day. Is it not better to die at once, if need be, for the sake of holiness, and to attain to the World to Come, than to go down to the grave in dishonour?"

Inflamed by the passionate speeches of their tutors a hundred eager voices demanded: "What shall we do?"

The answer came with assurance: "Cut down the eagle from the Temple gateway."

In the midst of the resultant commotion someone brought the tidings that Herod was dead. "The king is dead!" "Dead and damned!" Excitement rose to fever heat. The voice of the teachers shrilled above the din: "To the Temple! Follow us to the Temple!" The throng of students pressed and jostled each other to reach the door in a stampede of maddened zeal. "To the Temple!" "Bring axes!" "Down with the eagle!"

The midday peace of the Sanctuary was shattered as the yelling mob rushed up the steps, and startled worshippers scuttled hastily into the shelter of the colonnades. It was the work of a moment to clamber up the walls. Reaching the top of the gateway eager hands let down improvised cradles of rope, while some sitting in the nooses tore and hacked at the golden image and cast its fragments on to the pavement below.

The destruction was far advanced before the alarm was raised, and the captain of the Temple came running with the guard. The more timid fled at the approach of the officers, but above forty of the students, glorying in what they had done, remained and were captured. With them were the rabbis Judas and Matthias, who calmly stood and awaited arrest.

When news was brought to Herod, who despite the rumour was still in the land of the living, he worked himself up into such a fury as temporarily to overcome the advances of his fatal disease. By his orders the principal men of the city were summoned to the theatre to which he had himself conveyed on a couch, and there he conducted the prosecution in person. In passionate words he inveighed against the rioters as impious wretches, who, under pretence of upholding the Law, were only intent on committing sacrilege. With that impressive piety which he so well knew how to assume when it served him, he denounced the desecration as being an insult not to himself but to Almighty God, and prayed for a verdict of guilty from all right-thinking men.

Seeing the king's temper, the judges thought it better to let him have his way, lest if he were baulked of his revenge many more might perish than those who had taken part in the disturbance.

It was a craven decision; but the terror inspired by Herod was so deep-seated that none dared to oppose him. The officials declared that the action of the students had neither their sanction nor their approval, and they besought the king's clemency after he had dealt as he would with the perpetrators, who, they conceded, were deserving of punishment. But they could hardly restrain their horror when the tyrant ordered the two rabbis, and those caught in the act of cutting down the eagle, to be burnt alive, while the remaining prisoners, who had assisted, were to be slain with the sword. Having appeased his wrath by this barbarous sentence, the king consented to be merciful to others whom he suspected of having a hand in the affair, and contented himself with depriving the highpriest, Matthias, of his office and bestowing it on his brother-in- law, Joazar.

"That night," reports the historian Josephus, to show the Divine cognizance of this cruelty, "there was an eclipse of the moon."[4]

It seems probable that about this time Jesus of Nazareth was bom. But where he was born can by no means be stated with certainty. Like travellers mutually agreed on a meeting-place; all the traditions converge on Bethlehem of Judea. There, according to the prophecy, "he should come forth, the ruler in Israel." Poetically, the fitness of Bethlehem to be the city of the nativity cannot be disputed, for it was the home of the shepherd-king; and it is this consideration, rather than the messianic necessity, that popularized the belief that the Son of David would be bom in the city of David. In face of the evidence, however, which points to Galilee, and particularly to Nazareth, as the birth-place of Jesus, it would be difficult to uphold the claims of Bethlehem on purely historic grounds. On the other hand, it must be conceded that tradition makes the parents of Jesus undertake the long and trying journey to Bethlehem from their own city of Nazareth, not because it was prophetically proper that the child of destiny should be bom there, but because of a decree of Caesar Augustus that the population be registered for the purpose of taxation, each family in its ancestral home. In this statement, however, we may see if we will a device based on a knowledge of the periodic census for purposes of taxation carried out in Judea for the first time some years later when Quirinius was Governor of

Syria. If the record is one of fact, then the shadow of the Roman eagle, hacked in effigy from the Temple portal, fell across the cradle of the Christ.

In an inscription of the period Augustus is addressed as "Caesar, who reigns over the seas and continents, Jupiter, who holds from Jupiter his father the title of liberator, master of Europe and Asia, star of all Greece, who lifts himself up with the glory of great Jupiter, saviour."

To the proud proclamation of the Roman Goliath is returned the piping challenge of another David, whose titles also are saviour and liberator, king of kings, lord of lords, star of Judah, son of the Most High God. From this moment it becomes possible to personify opposing spiritual principles. There are no other alternatives. Mankind must choose its allegiance. It is Christ or Caesar!

The conflict, brilliantly dramatized by the author of the Book of Revelation, is subtly reflected in the details of the nativity stories. The recorders of these traditions show a continual awareness of the larger issues in their descriptions. They know of the war that has been waged since Eden, and it is with obvious deliberation that they borrow the likeness of the legendary past and apply it to the present. What are their tales but the refurbished armour of former battles? One by one the Jewish heroes of old are made to offer for the service of the Lord's anointed the saga of their own victorious contests. There was no need of acknowledgment, for each source could readily be distinguished by the reader. The intention to reproduce ancient episodes in terms of the life-story of Jesus, which can be discerned in many places in the Gospels, should rightly be attributed to the recognition by the evangelists of the eternal redemptive struggle which had now received its supreme exemplification, and attained its most powerful climax in the crucifixion, when the cry was raised, "We have no king but Caesar!"

The same consciousness of the true nature of the conflict is responsible for the rending of the veil between heaven and earth, so that there is a mingling of the two spheres, and the voices of angels and the thunders provide a commentary on the progress of events.

This insight into the redemptive course of history, and the fulfilment of the Scriptures in the Messiah, is part of the self-revelation of Jesus to his disciples, and the riches of the teaching are the legacy of his spirit. With this gold the evangelists have traded profitably, though sometimes in strange markets, and we are become the inheritors and also the assessors of the relative value of their acquisitions.

It is a Jewish and an Eastern inheritance, and on this account it is doubly in need of interpretation to the literally-minded occidental, who will have a three-dimensional doctrine of inspiration where the oriental recognizes a fourth dimension.

If, then, we agree with the evangelists to transfer the scene of the nativity from Nazareth to Bethlehem it is because we see with them the tremendous import of the change. Nazareth has no associations, while Bethlehem is full of significance. There is a curious elation about the legends which we are about to consider, a keen expectancy, a child-like anticipation of amazing discoveries. It is as if a group of eager cherubs up aloft were saying, "Let us put Mary upon an ass, and give the rein into the hand of Joseph, and set them on the way to Bethlehem, and wonderful things are sure to happen." And, indeed, as soon as husband and wife enter the enchanted region, things do begin to happen.

The road to Bethlehem wound past the tomb of Rachel. On the right the hills slid gently down into the maritime plain, while on the left they rose up more steeply, terraced almost to the top with plantations of vines guarded by watch-towers. Fields of barley were to be seen on the lower slopes and in the valleys, the unripe grain standing out in green relief from the natural greyness of the rocky soil. Many a summit was crowned with a village, and some with grim fortifications. Further east the hills became more rugged, and impressively beyond them there was a clear prospect of the mountains of Moab.

It was David's country, where as a boy he had pastured the flocks of Jesse, and where later he had led the life of a hunted outlaw. The road itself had memories; for it was the road of exile. Along it, hundreds of years before, had struggled a confused and disheartened mass of Jewish refugees fleeing from the sack of Jerusalem. Mary, sensitive and highly impressionable, heard the story of these events from the lips of Joseph as they pursued their way. Presently they fell silent, until Joseph, turning to inform bis wife that it wanted only three miles to their destination, noticed a swift change of emotions in her features. And he asked her with concern, "Mary, what aileth thee that I see thy face at one time laughing and at another sad?" And she answered, "It is because I behold two peoples with mine eyes, the one weeping and lamenting and the other rejoicing and exulting." And Joseph knew that a vision had been given to her of the exile and restoration of Israel.[5]

And when they had gone a little further, while they were yet some way from the city, Mary's time came that she should be delivered. So Joseph lifted her gently down from the ass and brought her into a cave near by, while he went in quest of a midwife. And as he hastened on his errand it seemed to him that suddenly all Nature stood still. For a few moments there was a great silence, and then it was past, and life resumed its normal course. Presently, he fell in with a woman named Salome coming down from the hill-country, to whom he explained his need, and who expressed her willingness to perform the office. But when they returned to the cave the child was already bom, and, behold, a shining cloud overshadowed the cave. Slowly the glory withdrew itself, and the wondering eyes that watched saw for the first time the infant Deliverer.[6]

The more familiar account relates that Joseph and Mary came indeed to Bethlehem, but there was no accommodation for them in the crowded caravanserai. So perforce they had to abide, as the poor and latecomer usually did, in the place where the beasts were tethered. Here, not in silence, but amidst the noise and bustle of living things, with only the night for a screen, the Redeemer was ushered into the world, and wrapped in swaddling clothes was laid in a manger for a cradle.

But that same night out on the hills shepherds were keeping watch over their flocks. And lo, the angel of the Lord appeared to them, and the glory of the Lord shone about them; and they were sore afraid. "Fear not," the angel said, "for, behold, I bring you tidings of great joy, which shall be to all people. For unto you is born this day, in the city of David, a saviour, who is the Lord Messiah. And let this be a sign unto you: ye shall find the baby wrapped in swaddling clothes, lying in a manger." And suddenly there was with the angel a multitude of the heavenly host praising God, and saying,

> "Glory to God in the highest,
> And on earth peace
> Unto them that please Him."

And when the appearance had vanished, the shepherds came in haste to Bethlehem, and they found it even as they were told. And they proclaimed the news to the wondering citizens, and returned to their flocks, glorifying God.

On the eighth day Joseph made a feast for the circumcision of his son. And when the seal of the covenant with Abraham had been set in the child's flesh, he that circumcised him prayed, "Our God, and God of our fathers, preserve this child to his father and to his mother, and let his name be called in Israel Jeshua ben Joseph. Let the father rejoice in the issue of his loins, and let the mother be glad with the fruit of her womb.... This little one, Jeshua, may he become great. Even as he has entered into the covenant, so may he enter into the Law, and into the marriage canopy, and into good deeds."

It is further related that Joseph and Mary brought their firstborn to the Temple at Jerusalem to accomplish the ceremony of redemption of the firstborn at the hand of a priest, and to pay the Lord's ransom of five shekels of the Sanctuary. There also the mother offered the sacrifice for her purification from the Levitical defilement of childbirth.

And while they were about these services there drew near an aged teacher named Simeon, whose devout life and study of the Law of God made him worthy, in Jewish parlance, that the Holy Spirit should rest upon him. He was one of those earnest souls who waited patiently for the consolation of Israel, enduring the bitterness of the Roman-Edomite domination, and having the assurance that God would mercifully permit him to see His anointed before he passed away. Coming into the court of the Temple the eyes of the old sage were drawn towards the little group, and with simple courtesy the saintly man honoured the humble parents by taking the child in his arms and blessing him in such words as these: "God make thee as Ephraim and Manasseh!" But as he held the infant, whose name he learnt spoke of God's salvation, the Spirit came upon him, his hands shook, and his old eyes grew moist and dim. Providence had guided his footsteps here to-day. This baby, cradled peacefully in his arms, was none other than the one for whom he waited. In quavering tones of joy he chanted:

> "Lord of the Universe, now dismiss Thy servant In
> peace, according to Thy word;
> For mine eyes have beheld Thy salvation,
> Prepared in the presence of all people;
> A light to give light to the Gentiles,
> And the glory of Thy people Israel."

And Joseph and Mary marvelled as they heard him. And Simeon blessed them. And as he returned the infant to its mother, he said: "He is set for the fall and the rising again of many in Israel, and for a sign which shall be denied—yea, a sword shall pierce through thy own soul also—that the reasoning of many hearts may be revealed."

There was also an aged widow, Hannah daughter of Phanuel, who frequented the Temple and gave herself up to a life of prayer and fasting, petitioning God that He would have mercy upon Zion. She, coming at this juncture, saw the child and likewise gave thanks to God, and spoke of him to all that looked for redemption in Jerusalem. But the local worshippers were too familiar with the old woman and her strange talk to pay much attention to her tidings. Only the parents of the child, their minds bemused and wondering, were impressed by her appearance immediately after the previous incident.

According to this story, Joseph and Mary then returned to their home in Nazareth of Galilee. But there is another story, which would detain them still at Bethlehem.

At this time there came a party of Arabian magi to Jerusalem, inquiring, "Where is he, the king of the Jews that is bom? For we in the East have seen his star, and are come to do him homage." Now the Arabians were famed astrologers, and, moreover, they had almost as great a detestation of Herod as the Jews themselves. So that this embassage in any case was a subtle insult to the king. But Herod was superstitious, and though he was exceedingly angry at the news of the mission, he nevertheless called together the chief priests and elders and demanded to know where the Messiah should be bom. And they informed him that the place was Bethlehem of Judah, according to an ancient prophecy. Herod, therefore, dissimulating his anger, sent for the Arabians privately, and examined them strictly as to the time when the celestial phenomenon had been seen. He then directed them to Bethlehem, and commanded them, "Go, and search diligently for the young child; and when you have found him, bring me word again, that I too may come and do him homage."

The magi heard the king, and forthwith departed. And when they were come to the region of Bethlehem they rejoiced greatly when they discerned the royal star riding high in the heavens. And they came into the house where the family was now lodged, and saw the child with Mary his mother: and when they had opened their baggage they offered him their gifts, gold, and frankincense, and myrrh. And, having been warned in a dream that they should not return to Herod, they departed into their own country by another way.

And the angel of the Lord appeared also to Joseph in a dream, saying, "Arise, and take the young child and his mother, and flee into Egypt, and be thou there until I bring thee word: for Herod will seek the young child to destroy him."

So Joseph rose in haste, and saddled the ass, and took the child and his mother, and set forth for Egypt that very night.

When there came no news of the return of the Arabians, Herod was forced to conclude that he had been mocked, and his rage knew no bounds. The whole business might be a silly trick played on him by his enemies. On the other hand there might be something in it. In any case he could secure himself from any preposterous pretender by killing all the male children in Bethlehem and its environs, from two years old and under, according to the time that the magi had stated that they first saw the star.

The fruitless massacre was carried out, and shortly after this the tyrant himself went to his account. Again the angel of the Lord appeared to Joseph in sleep, saying, "Arise, and take the young child and his mother, and go into the land of Israel: for they are dead which sought the young child's life." Joseph therefore returned with his family from their temporary exile; but, learning that Archelaus was now ruler of Judea in succession to his father Herod, he was afraid to go there, and journeyed on by the coast road into Galilee, and came and dwelt in the city of Nazareth.

Such are the enchanted tales which follow from the association of the birth of Jesus with Bethlehem. They arise in large measure out of a series of fulfilments of prophetic sayings, and also from the heroic legends of Israel. We should not expect these tales to be consistent with each other, and any attempt at harmonizing them must necessarily fail. But we do expect them to be genuine products of their age in their colouring and detail, and here there can be no question of their faithfulness, which is borne out by the manner in which small "period" elaborations offer themselves naturally and spontaneously in the retelling. Indeed, it would have been possible to stress other contemporary references of a purely incidental character.

These nativity records, therefore, cannot rightly be dismissed as simply fiction, even with the qualification pious fiction. We do not know how much is true, and there is a sense, which we have tried to explain, in which they are tremendously true as a whole. It is as if, on another plane of consciousness, in a Bethlehem which is above, these messianic events were taking place coincidental with the normal circumstances attending the birth of the baby at Nazareth. In the one condition Joseph and Mary are wonderingly aware that their child is the Lord Messiah, while in the other they have no glimmering of knowledge that their firstborn is more than a very dear, but quite unremarkable infant.

The capacity for simultaneous citizenship of two worlds exemplified by this literature is itself an indication of the period; for it is in Palestine at this time that we find what may be termed a messianic school of thought treating of events with a certain approximation to this curious duality. It is one of those circumstances which the old Christian divines liked to think of as *Preparations for the Gospel.* And how momentous does this mode of presenting history become when, as in the person of Herod, the two worlds meet, and history can exhibit in actuality the tyrant king which the mystic drama demands!

We are dimly in contact here with a viewpoint, at once intimate and detached, of the entire terrestrial scheme from the beginning to the end of time, that God-outlook which has made the Chosen People, and the Messiah as its head, the embodiment of the historic present. It is in this sense that the apostle Paul can speak of Jesus as "the same yesterday, and to-day, and for ever," and Jesus himself can say, "Before Abraham was, I am." The tyrant, who persecutes the Messiah and his people, may have many names through the ages, but essentially he too is the same, the eternal opponent of the Divine plan. The end, perhaps, will only come, not with the fall but with the conversion of the tyrant.

CHAPTER III

Out of a Dry Ground

"Herod is dead! The Tyrant is dead!" This was the most important news that had been heard in the Land of Israel for many a day, and it was doubly welcome in Galilee.

There were few outward demonstrations of joy, just as there were few expressions of regret. But the popular relief was sufficiently indicated by an almost simultaneous upheaval as of languishing captives suddenly released from their bonds. Herod, well knowing the sentiments of his subjects towards him, had evolved in his diseased mind a plot whereby he proposed to make sure that if they did not mourn his own passing they should nevertheless have that for which to mourn on their own account. He commanded the attendance of the principal men of each village, and when they were assembled in the Hippodrome, he had them shut up there. He then gave private instructions to his sister Salome and her husband Alexas for a general massacre of the imprisoned men immediately upon his death, "and then all Judea, and every family of them," he explained with grim humour, "will weep at it whether they will or no."[7]

Mercifully, Herod's relatives would be no party to this brutal scheme, and dismissed the incarcerated company to their homes. Despite the abhorrence of the tyrant's

rule, however, it was widely recognized that he had conferred many benefits on the nation, and consequently
the day of his death does not appear in the ancient *Scroll
of Fasts,* which lists memorable occasions of deliverance,
when fasting, and sometimes mourning, is forbidden.

The new reign, that of Archelaus, began far from auspi-
ciously. The king designate, for he would not assume the
title until it was confirmed to him by Caesar, was surrounded by importunate crowds in the Temple when he
first attended at the evening sacrifice. There was a clamour about him to remit taxes, to depose the present high
priest, to give a public funeral to the victims in the affair
of the golden eagle, and to punish the friends of Herod.
The clamour developed into a riot when it was seen that
these wholesale demands would not be granted; and
when Archelaus sent envoys to parley with the people
and to pacify them they were received with a fusillade of
stones. It was the season of the Passover, and the population of Jerusalem was swollen to several times its normal size by the thousands who came up out of the
country and from foreign lands to observe the festival.
Among the more turbulent elements the Galilean highlanders could readily be distinguished, who cheerfully
set about stoning the cohort of soldiers which Archelaus
found it necessary to send to enforce order.

There was no obvious organization about the disturbance. It appeared to be an emotional outbreak which had
spent itself in its first violence, and the people immediately proceeded to the sacrifice of the paschal lambs as if

no untoward incident had occurred. Archelaus, however, saw in the situation a real threat to his government, and unwisely dispatched all the troops at his command, who fell upon the unarmed crowds and slaughtered about three thousand of them as they endeavoured to escape among the neighbouring hills. Heralds followed up the fleeing multitudes, ordering all to retire to their homes. Abandoning the celebration of the festival, the parties of pilgrims streamed away from the city carrying the direful news to the most distant parts of the country. There was hardly a company that was not lamenting its dead and calling down vengeance on the son of Herod.[8]

The event marked the end of years of sullen endurance. In a hundred towns and hamlets in Judea, and Galilee, and beyond Jordan, there were risings of embittered citizens determined that there should be an end to the Edomite domination. As the Jewish envoys afterwards stated to Caesar: "they had borne more calamities from Herod, in a few years, than had their forefathers during the whole of the period that had elapsed since the return from the Babylonian Exile," and if now under Archelaus they were to undergo further miseries, "they would oppose themselves like warriors to receive those stripes on their faces, and not on their backs like slaves as hitherto."[9]

Most of the sporadic outbreaks which followed the black Pass- over lacked both objective and leadership. They were demonstrations symptomatic of popular feeling; but they were not sufficiently coherent to prove in any way menacing. As usual, in such circumstances, there were opportunists who endeavoured to make capital out of the general unrest, petty kinglets who strutted their hour upon the stage, and troops of old soldiers who took to brigandage. They gave some trouble to the government forces, but were suppressed in the end without much bloodshed.

A more formidable threat to the Herodians and to their Roman sponsors was represented by the Zealot outlaws of the Galilean highlands. They had both a clear purpose and a responsible leader. Never fully subdued by Herod, they had continued in their northern fastnesses, quietly increasing their strength and preparing to strike a great blow for Jewish liberty and independence when the time should be ripe. They gave allegiance now to Judas, son of their former chief Hezekiah who had been slain by Herod. Judas of Galilee was a man of mature years, resourceful and courageous. As he read the situation, the prospects were not good enough yet to bring about a general revolt; but he noted with approval the growing unrest, and by sending members of his band to Jerusalem for the feasts he sought to foment dissatisfaction and to provoke disturbances. There can be little doubt that the massacre at the Passover would never have taken place if it had not been for the deliberate aggressiveness of Judas's Galileans.

This policy of inspiring sedition, enflaming the masses, and purposely magnifying every real or fancied infringement of civil or religious liberty, was carried on with increasing success by the Zealots for nearly forty years until it led, as had all along been intended, to war with Rome. Anyone who is familiar with the excitable and fanatical nature of the oriental will readily perceive the cleverness of these tactics, to which in our own day the activities of the Arabs in Palestine offer a remarkable parallel. We shall learn in due course how this policy affected the activities of Jesus, and was largely responsible for his death. It was always a difficult matter when a riot had taken place to discover the actual instigators, who had melted away in the crowd, or, when a secret assassination of a "moderate" leader was carried out, the perpetrators, who stood around and loudly lamented the victim.

But while Judas, through his agents, was fostering a spirit of revolt at Jerusalem on the convenient occasions of the festivals which brought large numbers of people together from all parts of the country, he was by no means neglecting his own forces.

Taking advantage of the uncertain political situation, he carried out a bold raid on Sepphoris, seized the palace, and looted the treasury and the arsenal in order to equip his men.

In the meantime, Archelaus had not been able to delay any longer his departure for Rome to secure the ratification of his kingship; but he had invited Quintilius Varus, Governor of Syria, to keep an eye on Jerusalem in his absence. Varus came down to Caesarea, where he found

Sabinus on the point of setting out for Jerusalem to secure Herod's effects on Caesar's behalf, and, fearing that this visit would only be provocative, he persuaded him to remain where he was for the present. He himself, finding all quiet in the capital, returned shortly to Antioch, leaving behind a legion to ensure the maintenance of peace. As soon as he was gone, however, Sabinus broke his word and hastened to Jerusalem. There he occupied Herod's palace, and would have taken possession of the citadels also if he could have persuaded the custodians to give them up to him. He immediately set about taking an inventory of all Herod's goods on the pretext of holding them for Caesar; but his private purpose was to juggle with the figures so as to secure a goodly sum for himself without anyone being the wiser. But he had reckoned without the populace and the Zealot agitators.

The crowds that assembled for the feast of Pentecost, seven weeks after the Passover, had come prepared for trouble. And when they found Sabinus and the Roman legion in occupation of the palace and its fortifications they were in an ugly mood. Little persuasion was wanted to induce a considerable body of determined men to invest the area closely, and Sabinus was justifiably alarmed when he discovered that he was hemmed in on three sides by a greatly superior and threatening force. He at once dispatched urgent messages to Varus to come to his aid; but thinking there was a chance that he might be able to break through the cordon he foolishly ordered his soldiers to attack the Jews on the side which was most open, the Temple area on the east of his position. A terrible hand-to-hand struggle developed in the outer court, in which the Romans, through better discipline, were likely to have proved victorious, until a number of Jews climbed on to the roof of the cloisters and from this vantage ground hurled down darts on their assailants. The Romans retaliated by firing the cloisters, which so affected the defenders that they left off fighting in order to prevent the spread of the flames. With the Temple proper left almost unguarded, the enraged legionaries broke into the Sacred Treasury and made off with about four hundred talents. But they could not get clear away, and were forced to retire again into the palace, where they were besieged in earnest by a more formidable force than before.

Cries were raised on every side that a new day of liberty had dawned, and Sabinus was given the choice of laying down his arms and leaving at once with his legion, or remaining to be cut to pieces when the palace was captured. Mistrustful of this offer of safe conduct, Sabinus thought it more prudent to stay where he was in the hope that relief from Varus would not long be delayed.

Varus, indeed, was already on his way, cursing the stupidity of his subordinate. So alarming did the situation appear to him that he took two legions and a host of auxiliary troops, including an army of horse and foot sent by the Arabian king Aretas. Advancing rapidly with his main body, he sent a large detachment to hold Galilee, in case the highlanders should show any inclination to march south to help their brethren. Sepphoris was sacked and burnt, and its inhabitants enslaved. Fire and sword were carried southward, the Arabians proving bad allies, as their hatred for Herod urged them to stop and plunder any place that belonged to his friends.

When Jerusalem was reached the besiegers scattered in face of this overwhelming force, and the siege was raised. Sabinus dared not face Varus and sneaked away to the coast. The day that was to be the day of liberty saw a forest of crosses set up round the walls of Jerusalem on which hung above two thousand Jewish sufferers.[10]

And while these expired in agony, envoys of the Jewish people at Rome were pleading with Caesar not to make Archelaus king over them, but to "have compassion on the poor remains of Judea" and to put the country under the Governor of Syria, that same Quintilius Varus.

Augustus eventually nominated Archelaus ruler of Judea, Idumaea and Samaria, with the title of ethnarch, promising him that he would be made king if he proved himself worthy. Antipas was given the tetrarchy of Galilee and Peraea, while another tetrarchy was created for Philip consisting of Batanaea, Trachonitis, Auranitis, and certain parts about Jamnia. Thus, with some minor provision for other members of Herod's family, was the kingdom divided between three of his surviving sons.

This scheme of partition was designed not only to do justice to the claims of the Herodian princes, but also to preserve peace; and in fact it was successful in giving the Land of Israel rest for about nine years. It is significant that Josephus, the Jewish historian, has no event of importance to report between 3 B.C. and A.D. 6. That period covered the childhood of Jesus.

We have no means of knowing whether Joseph was at Jerusalem at the Black Passover, and even blacker Pentecost; but it is not unlikely that he was one of the Galilean pilgrims. If so, he was an eye-witness of the terrible events which we have just described. But even if he had remained at home he must have been affected by the clash between the troops of Varus and the bands of Judas of Galilee. Sepphoris lay only two hours march to the north-west of Nazareth. Mary would have known fear for herself and her infant during those uncertain days when the little town listened with dread to the clank of mailed warriors and the blare of war trumpets, while the flames of destruction flickered fitfully on the northern heights.

But the danger passed. Life resumed its normal course. Joseph could return again to his craft, and Mary might freely make her daily journeys for water to the gushing spring which issued just beyond the borders of the township. Yet for many a day there would be a keen discussion of events, and much speculation as to what kind of ruler Herod Antipas would make, who now had taken up his abode in Sepphoris rising anew from its ashes.

It was a very circumscribed life that the family led. By western standards their home would be described as a hovel. It was entered by a low door, which gave little light within, and access was to a single room with an inner recess. A short flight of steps outside led up on to the flat roof which in summer made an extra room. Joseph had no separate workshop, and much of the limited space was taken up with the tools and impedimenta of his trade. His carpentry brought in a small but, for the family's simple needs, sufficient income. There was also the plot of land out on the hills, which had come to him as part of his wife's dowry and provided grain and vegetables.

From the time that he could toddle Jesus, the eldest son, was much more with his father than with his mother. Mary was burdened with the cares of her growing family. Four more boys, James, Jose, Simon and Judas, and at least two girls, arrived within almost as many years. The home was filled continuously with the clamour and prattle of infant voices. Under these conditions it was quite impossible for Mary to give much attention to her firstborn in his early years, and later events showed that they did not well understand each other. There are indications that Mary was strongly superstitious, like many of her countrywomen, and highly imaginative; and she may be excused if the responsibilities of her household, increased by early widowhood, inclined her to be somewhat domineering. Jesus inherited her vivid imagination and strength of character: his gentleness coupled with a certain reserve, his sense of justice and simplicity of religious belief, were legacies from his father. He must have remembered the mother of his boyhood chiefly as one who was always telling him to do things. Indeed, there was much to do in the house, and as soon as he could go alone he was expected to fetch the water from the spring.

Jesus loved to be with his father, and the rather severe and unbending man adored his son. While Joseph fashioned farming implements and other articles, Jesus would watch by the hour, offering to lend his childish help, and deeming it a red-letter day when first he was allowed to use the tools by himself. He also went with his father to the field, and was given a handful of seed to do his little bit in sowing the crops.[11] But most of all he loved to ask questions, and to have Joseph tell him about God, and about the history of Israel, and of the Messiah, and the golden age to come. Many a time must the father have been amused by some fancy, and have called to his wife or to a neighbour, "What do you think the child is saying now?" Jesus trusted his father implicitly, and there can be no doubt that Joseph was very indulgent with him. Already in those early formative years there was implanted in the young mind the belief that God was someone very like his father. At the seasonal festivals, when Joseph told the boy that he was going up to Jerusalem to God's House, Jesus thought of the Temple as a glittering palace where a glorified personification of his own parent had His dwelling-place, and he looked forward eagerly to the day when he should pay his first visit to the Sanctuary.

If Joseph favoured any school of thought in Judaism it was that of the Pharisees. He was a particularly observant Jew in all the practices of his faith, and being a Galilean he was more conservative in certain matters than the Judeans. He did not, however, set such store by the traditions of the elders. He accepted, without qualification, the doctrines of the resurrection of the dead, the

immortality of the soul, and the day of judgment. He no
doubt believed, as one would naturally expect of a descendant of David, in a Davidic Messiah, and he looked to
see the age of righteousness ushered in by a Divine
manifestation. In his opinion the redemption of Israel
would never be brought about by acts of violence. In this
he differed from his wife, whose family connections inclined her towards Zealotism. Her view was that if you
want to get anywhere you have to do tilings, while his attitude was that you must be deserving for God to do
things. The character of the man was typical of the best
of the Galileans, who were noted for their charitableness
and for setting honour above personal interest.

The influence of his father's religious instruction is apparent in the teaching put forth by Jesus himself. It is a
sturdy, homely, common-sense faith, getting to the heart
of the matter, the weightiest things in the Law, judgment, loving-kindness, and truth. Ceremonial observances, though obligatory, were of secondary importance.
On many an occasion Joseph's blunt way of putting first
things first stood his son in good stead, and out of his
personal experience Jesus could advise his disciples in a
more exalted sense: "It shall be put into your mouths
what ye shall answer; for it is not ye that shall speak, but
the Spirit of your Father shall speak in you."

The elements of religion were imparted as soon as the
child could speak. He learned to recite the *Shema'*, the
declaration of God's Unity, which the sages called taking
upon oneself the yoke of God's kingdom, and the Ten

Commandments, and also certain blessings to be said at mealtimes and at other appropriate occasions. These, and some further prayers, Jesus was taught in Hebrew; but much of his knowledge of Jewish observances was acquired in the clipped Galilean dialect of his native Aramaic. He did not go to school, for there was none at Nazareth at this time; yet he was better off than many of the local children, for a resident student of the Law, greatly impressed by the boy's eager interest in religious matters, offered to give him tuition. The lessons never proceeded to advanced studies, for Jesus seems to have been a difficult pupil, but at least they provided a basis which enabled him readily to understand the interpretations of the scribes, and later invested his message with an authority which surprised many of his contemporaries and made him to be regarded widely as a learned rabbi.

Jesus did not possess the type of mind which falls in easily with a curriculum. In another age he would hardly have satisfied an examiner. A teacher, for him, meant someone who could enlighten him about the things that he wanted to know, not someone who wished to confine his instruction to a familiar and approved course. It was not long, therefore, before good Master Zaccai, or whatever his name may have been, trained as he was in a system, gave up as hopeless a pupil who was always interposing an inconvenient "Why?" and urging him into bypaths of knowledge which had little or nothing to do with the matter in hand.[12]

Worship in the synagogue was to the boy a continual delight. Fervently he pronounced the benedictions, feeling the nearness of God, as near to him as the tall father at his side. The Law of Moses he was very familiar with through the vernacular translations which followed the readings of the set portions on market days and on the Sabbath. In the same way he came to know many passages from the Psalms and the Prophetic books. He particularly looked forward to the discourse given by a resident or visiting Doctor of the Law, for then he would hear fascinating parables and legends, and often about the Messiah and the coming Redemption. And when the preacher concluded his burning words with the regular Aramaic formula:

> "Magnified and hallowed be His great Name in the world which He hath created according to His will. May He establish His kingdom in your lifetime, and in your days, and in the lifetime of the whole house of Israel, speedily and at a near time......"

none of the congregation responded more earnestly, "Amen. May His great Name be blessed unto the remotest ages!" In after years that *Kaddish* prayer, with extracts from other prayers, would become peculiarly his own, a beautiful composition known to us as the Lord's Prayer.

Other observances of Judaism which Jesus grew to love centred upon the home and the field. Some of them are reflected in his teaching and in incidents of his life. There were occasions when, like other Jewish children, he broke the letter of the commandment ordaining Sabbath rest. It was, when the boy was rebuked by some busybody in the little community, his father, no doubt, who explained when the tale came home that the Sabbath was made for man and not man for the Sabbath.[13]

Of many childhood memories of a religious character we may select one which appears to have greatly impressed the boy.

In an agricultural country there was always the fear of drought, of mildew, and of a plague of locusts and caterpillars. When any of these calamities occurred it was customary to proclaim a fast, and such an event took place in the severe drought of A. D. 6.

Jesus was an eye-witness of the solemn procession which issued from the synagogue. In front walked the trumpeter, sounding an alarm on his instrument of ram's horn. Behind him followed the dignitaries of the synagogue, accompanied by an elder who was counted "worthy to fast and to pray" for the community. Then came other members of the synagogue, perhaps the father of Jesus among them, bearing the sacred chest containing the scroll of the Law. The company proceeded slowly to the open space, or market-square, of the township, where a crowd of men, women and children awaited them. Here the chest was set down, and fine dust was sprinkled upon it and upon the heads of the dignitaries. Then all the people sprinkled dust on their own heads. The elder, and leader of the prayers, stood forth and addressed the silent assembly. "My brethren," he said, "it is not written of the men of Nineveh, 'God saw their sackcloth and their fast,' but 'God saw their works, that they turned from their evil way.' And in the Prophets, what saith it? 'Rend your hearts and not your garments, and turn to the Lord your God.'" After this admonition, he led the community in the prescribed prayers. At the end, the chest was carried back into the synagogue; those with means distributed alms liberally to the poor, and the people dispersed to spend the rest of the day in fasting and supplication.[14] 8

What made the service of special interest to Jesus was the fact that the birthplace of Jonah at Gath-Hepher was only five miles from his home, and he had been there on visits to his mother's relatives at Cana. In after life he made use of the lesson of Jonah and the Ninevites, and called attention to the hypocritical abuse of the ceremony in his famous Sermon on the Mount.

It would be a mistake, however, to imagine that Jesus spent a great part of his time in religious duties, or even in meditating on spiritual things. He was quite a normal boy, with a bright intelligence and keen powers of observation. We have already noted that he had plenty to occupy him at home, looking after his young brothers and sisters and helping his parents. But he also had time for play. He was fond of the companionship of other children, and could sport with them on the house tops, dash about the narrow streets, and join in the games of make-believe. With them he would stand solemnly and stare at parties of strangers who passed through the little town, the merchants, the escort of a great lady or nobleman, troops of stradiots (soldiers). He may even have indulged in the children's pleasure of booing the tax-collector. What his fellows thought of him we do not know for certain, but there is some evidence that they found him rather masterful and inclined to fits of seriousness and abstraction. Jesus also seems, as happens with some children, to have had a curious capacity for being present at accidents. Once a boy fell off a flat roof and was killed, and it was suggested that Jesus had pushed him. At another time he was at hand when his brother James was stung by a viper. These incidents made him keen on first-aid as it was practised in those days, and at an early age he made the discovery that he possessed the gift of the healing touch.[15]

So passed those blessed and care-free years of childhood, when the great world beyond the closely surrounding hills intruded but little upon the consciousness of the growing lad. It was not until his tenth or eleventh year that a national event of shattering significance broke rudely upon the pastoral peace of Nazareth.

CHAPTER IV

The Days of the Taxing

The disturbing event which roused the whole land of Israel in violent protest, and which was to have the most far-reaching consequences, came about as the direct result of the conversion of Judea and Samaria into part of the Roman province of Syria. The event itself was the taking of a census as a preliminary to Roman taxation.

The Jews on their own responsibility, finding the Herodian government unbearable, had petitioned for this change of rule. But they cannot have realized the straits to which it would bring them. The change was already partially accomplished when Augustus, as Herod's testamentary executor, had confirmed the succession of Archelaus to a limited extent as ethnarch of Judea, Samaria and Idumaea, and had made his kingship conditional on his good behaviour. The Jewish representatives were well content with this arrangement, believing that it gave them a definite guarantee of the good conduct of their affairs, as they had only to complain to Caesar should Archelaus show any disposition to tyrannize. The ethnarch, forgetful of his dependent position, foolishly played into their hands by lording it over his subjects, with the inevitable result that the chief priests and elders kept a tally of his misdeeds, and when the evidence had accumulated over a period of years they laid an accusation against him at Rome.

Archelaus, feasting merrily with his friends one day in the tenth year of his rule, received a severe shock when suddenly his steward, supposed to be at Rome, appeared before him in Jerusalem bearing an imperious summons to the presence of Caesar. There was no alternative but to sail immediately. When he reached his destination it was to discover a lengthy indictment to which he could make no satisfactory reply. Augustus was implacable. Archelaus had had his chance, and he had failed. The sentence was banishment to Vienne in Gaul and the confiscation of his property. Without an effort, to all intents by invitation, no longer in effigy but in reality, the Roman eagle spread his wings over Mount Zion.[16]

The change of rule meant much more than a transference of a nominal allegiance; it involved a change in the system of government, and for this the common people of Judea had not bargained. Indeed, it was in direct conflict with the proud assertion, "We be Abraham's seed, and were never in bondage to any man." For the Imperial system of provincial government represented a kind of enslavement of the nation. The ruling class, which included the great hierarchical families, did, it is true, obtain privileges and a measure of authority which had been denied to them by the Herodians; but only as the creatures of the Emperor. They received Roman citizenship; a large number of them were given equitorial rank with the right to wear the narrow stripe on their tunics (*tunica augusticlavia*), and some were even raised to senatorial rank with the right to the broad purple stripe (tunica laticlavia). Below them, however, the middle-class, and still less the peasantry, had no civil status at all in the Roman sense, and no immunity from Imperial exactions.

Wliile the people had been heavily burdened by imposts under Herod and Archelaus, there had been no attempt to assess for taxation the worth of each individual. But the immediate consequence of Judea becoming a part of the Roman province of Syria was the institution of the periodic census, an exact register and valuation, for the purpose of imposing the land tax (*tributum soli*) and personal tax (*tributum capitis*). Caesar, diligently keeping his accounts at Rome, was to be put in a position to determine to what amount Judea could be mulcted. There was no haphazard assessment according to the Roman method.

The farming of the taxes was placed in the hands of the equites, who employed their own publicans, or tax-gatherers, to carry out the actual work of collection. In the case of Judea this was adding insult to injury; for the loyal Jew not only found himself subjected to an institution which violated the Divine injunction which forbade the numbering of the people, but he also found his own chief priests—the servants of God—converted into a Roman aristocracy, and made in part the agents responsible for the odious business of obtaining from him the Imperial dues.

From the Jewish viewpoint an altogether iniquitous situation arose out of the new domination, which all the people could barely stomach, and which many determined not to tolerate.

It was quickly realized that Roman rule differed from that of other foreigners in that it was possessed of a definite religious character. It was not a question of one nation imposing its gods on another nation; it was that Roman Imperialism was itself a cult, which all nations included in the Empire were expected to embrace alongside of and in addition to their national faith. Rome was not only a political mistress demanding allegiance, but a goddess demanding worship. Caesar himself was invested with divine attributes. New Year's Day was required to be a festival sacred to Rome in the religious calendar of every subject people, with the local priesthood officiating in its ceremonial.

To this arrangement Judea could not submit. In recognizing the Roman government the problem to be resolved was how to avoid a clash between two mutually exclusive theocracies. It was bad enough that the Romans, as successors to the Herods, had become the custodians of the vestments of the high priest. These were kept in a stone chamber under seal in the tower of Antonia adjoining the Temple and were handed out prior to the pilgrim festivals of Passover, Pentecost and Tabernacles, and the fast day of Atonement, and had to be returned immediately after use. But it was not possible that the Temple should be regarded in the remotest sense as a Roman cult centre. The limit of concession granted by the chief priests—and this was far too much for the mass of faithful Jews—was the acceptance of votive gifts, provided that they did not represent the image of any living creature and that they were displayed in the Court of the Gentiles only; the offering to the God of Israel at Caesar's expense of sacrifices twice daily for the welfare of the Emperor and the Roman people; and the permission to non-Jews generally to have sacrifices made on their behalf. The Jews on their own account offered sacrifices daily for all nations.

As to the internal government of the people, that rested nominally with the Sanhedrin; but this body was stripped of most of its authority, and persisted mainly to administer Jewish civil and religious law, and even here it ceased to be able to impose a death penalty unless ratified by the Roman procurator. On the other hand the great hierarchical families and the nobility were closely associated with the procurator in the conduct of the country's affairs and the collection of the revenues. This inevitably led to serious abuses, for the chief priests were enabled to amass enormous wealth and to dominate the Sanhedrin. Moreover, as the Roman governor exercised the right to appoint the high priest, the sacred office itself was sometimes secured by bribery.

It is important to realize that the radical changes, political, economic and religious, which came about as a result of Roman rule, forced the individual Jew to determine what his attitude was to be towards the new order. Both Jewish and Christian writers, who lived near to those times, agree that it was at this period that the people was split into parties. Most of these had, of course, existed for a great while previously; but it had never been necessary for the rank and file of the nation definitely to adhere to any one of them. Now it became extremely difficult not to do so, for the Judean certainly, and to some extent also for those Jews who resided in the tetrarchies of Antipas and Philip, and who were not so directly affected. Each party, from its peculiar religious viewpoint, represented one of the possible positions which a Jew might adopt in considering his future bearing towards the Roman domination.

The majority of the people sided with the *Pharisees* (the Compartmentalists). Their policy was to maintain a State within a State, and their attitude towards the Roman domination was one of passive endurance of a temporary affliction. They were prepared to submit to the decrees of the rulers, except when they interfered with Jewish observances, when every legitimate and non-violent method was to be employed to resist the innovation and to safeguard the religious life of the nation. Pharisaism sought to increase the spiritual stamina of the community, so that it became capable of surviving any and every attempt to weaken and disintegrate it. Just as a man would build a fence round his property to protect it from robbers, so Israel, the property of God, was to be fenced about with ordinances which offered an impregnable barrier to all disruptive influences. The pious Pharisee saw in the foreign government a punishment sent by God, which must be patiently borne, and from which deliverance would only come through sincere national repentance.

The policy of the Pharisees, however, was too negative and gentle for the more ardent spirits. They therefore sided with the *Kannaites* (the Zealots), whose programme was active opposition. Kannaism favoured an unqualified theocracy. There must be no acknowledgment of the foreign government, as God was their only Ruler and Lord, and every means must be pursued to secure political freedom, including violence. The Kannaites raised religious principle to the pitch of fanaticism. Their natural stronghold was in Galilee, where their ideas commanded the ready sympathy and support of the independent highlanders. They were ready to murder a Jew who married out of the faith; they would not handle a coin bearing an image, and would not enter a city if there were statues ornamenting the gateway. They objected even to the name of the foreign governor appearing with that of Moses on a divorce decree. Their animosity was directed especially at the chief priests and Jewish nobility, who not only tolerated, but supported the Romans. These were black traitors to God and to His people. Judas of Galilee was the present leader of this party, and with him was Zaddok, one of the more extreme Pharisees.

Completing the triangle of parties, which all derived ultimately from the Assidaeans (the Pietists) of the time of the Maccabees, were the *Essenes*. Their peculiar outlook prevented many of the people from joining them; for they neither tolerated the government nor opposed it. Instead, the principal groups among them withdrew from the ordinary life of the nation into the wilderness or into rugged regions where they set up an independent order almost monastic in its severity. There were grades of Essenes, however. Not all left the towns, and not ail were celibate; but the whole movement was strongly tinged with mysticism, which increased in isolation. Essenism was archaic in principle: it was an attempt at returning to the primitive life of the wandering tribes of Israel, the conditions under which it was believed the Law of Moses could more exactly be observed. Necessarily, therefore, Essenism played a more indirect part in the affairs of the nation. Its contribution lay in the circulation of fiery and, from the political angle, subversive literature, which was regarded with superstitious reverence and authority by the masses.

The fourth party was that of the *Sadducees*, the direct successors of the earlier and more moderate Hellenists. The Sadducees had found a way of coming to terms with the Gentile world while remaining Jews in religion. They were not less concerned to uphold the Law of Moses, but they refused to extend its discipline to circumstances and situations which it did not profess to cover. Consequently they were able to accept the Roman government without prejudice to their faith, and to give it the fullest co-operation so long as it did not interfere with the practice of their religious observances. There were Sadducees who became lax in their Judaism through this accommodation to changing conditions, but on the whole they were strongly conservative and keenly ritualistic. Sadduceeism appealed most strongly to the well-to-do classes, which included the chief priests, as it was they who suffered least and gained most from the Roman domination.

In these brief descriptions the doctrinal positions of the Jewish parties have been omitted as here irrelevant. We have been concerned only to indicate their attitude towards the new masters of Judea.

There were, of course, independents, who could declare for none of these parties, and outstanding among them one John (Johanan), a unique personality who stood at the very centre of the Assidaean triangle and enlisted a considerable following of his own.

The history of John is as mysterious as the man himself. He was a Levite, the son of a priest named Zacharias and his wife Elizabeth. In his generation, and even long afterwards he was regarded by many as the Messiah; for he seemed to fulfil the widespread expectation based on the words of Moses, "The Lord thy God will raise up unto thee a Prophet... like unto me; unto him ye shall hearken." To this promise both the Assidaeans and the Samaritans had clung. When the government of the Commonwealth of Israel was entrusted to the priest-prince Simon Maccabaeus his tenure of office was limited to the time preceding the coming of "that Prophet." With the later development of the messianic idea there was a tendency to regard the priestly Prophet and the Messiah as two distinct persons; but it must be admitted

that the doctrine of the advent of the one was as indefin-
ite as that of the other, and their respective functions
were easily confused. The ancient anointing had applied
to prophet, priest and king, and the current conceptions
of the Anointed One allowed, therefore, of an Elijah, a
Moses, and a David, as the instruments of Israel's deliverance. It is not, then, a matter for wonder that legends
surround the birth of John, just as they do the birth of
Jesus, and that it should be believed in time that they
were related to each other. Whether in fact there was any
kinship cannot be stated with certainty, but there can be
no question that John was much the elder man.

There is some evidence that the Baptist came of a line of
hereditary rain-makers, and we may bear that in mind in
thinking of the rite which accompanied his message.
Tradition relates that his fadier was a victim of Herod's
cruelty, being slain in the Temple for refusing to disclose
the whereabouts of his son, who, it was supposed, was
destined to become the saviour of the Jews. The mother
had fled with the child into the hill-country of Judea,
having received a heavenly warning of the approach of
the king's soldiers. He grew up in the fierce solitude of
the wilderness, a wild man, hairy of body, a silent,
brooding figure, wiry, agile as a mountain goat, clad in
raiment of camel's hair, and subsisting on carob pods
and wild honey. He was not only a strict Nazarite, ab-
staining from wine and strong drink, but he also refused
all animal food and would not touch bread, even the unleavened bread of the Passover. A terrifying sight he
must have presented on the few occasions when he was
seen, this man of the woods and rocks with his glowing

eyes, matted beard, and shaggy elf-locks, a satyr, something not quite human.[17]

But John now showed that he was no creature of the half-world. Suddenly he broke out from his retreat, and appeared before the starded people, a man with an urgent message to deliver. The word of the Lord had come to him.

Not within living memory, not indeed since the return from Babylon, had there appeared one like this. It seemed as if the sacred scroll of Scripture had suddenly unrolled of its own accord, to release as by the opening of two-leaved gates a being of another age as a sign and a portent. He could not be claimed as a Pharisee, a Kannaite, or an Essene, still less as a Sadducee. He fitted nowhere into the contemporary scheme. He denied that he was either the Messiah, or Elijah, or the Prophet. But he refused to dispel the mystery that surrounded him. When they asked, "Who then are you?" he replied, "I am a Voice, the voice of one crying, Prepare ye in the wilderness the way of the Lord: make straight in the desert a highway for our God." He would make no other concession to popular inquisitiveness. But if he would say little to satisfy curiosity concerning himself, he had much to say on other matters, without fear or favour. Standing on the banks of the Jordan he sent forth a great call to national repentance, and summoned all Israel to undergo the symbolic ritual of freeing their souls from defilement by bathing in the river. Only when they had been thus cleansed from every idol would God free them from the rule of tyrants and send them His own true king.

So it was that when the might and pomp of Rome entered Judea in the train of Quirinius, Governor of Syria, and Coponius, the newly appointed procurator, there was no eager welcome such as attends the coming of deliverers. The country folk stood stolidly, or sullenly, watching the legionaries go by. This impassive oriental reception was far more disconcerting than any expression of open hostility. The Romans felt that the tawny land itself was tensed like a young lion ready to spring, waiting for the first false move. It was not a pleasant sensation, and could best be overcome by loud jests and bawdy songs.

Yet the chances of active opposition were slight. They rested with a brigand chief in the north and a mad prophet in the east. If these two should unite.... But of that dangerous possibility there seemed to be no prospect. Even though the slogan was the same, "No lord but God!"Judas worked by fire and John by water, and they could no more mingle than the two elements which they represented. Thus the potentially perilous measure of the census was taken with little more than verbal outbursts of protest; the citizens of Jerusalem, in particular, yielding to the persuasions of Joazar the high priest.

Nevertheless it was easy to gauge the depths of feeling which might have been roused to the pitch of bloody resistance. The word kenas (census) passed into the language as a description of every kind of fine or financial punishment, and tax-collecting was stigmatized as an odious and immoral profession, placing any Jew that followed it outside the pale of religion.

In conservative and liberty-loving Galilee the question of revolt was hotly debated. Judas and his Zealots were ready and anxious to march at the first indication that the country would rise to support them. But the signal was never given. There was no strength nor heart in the people to face such an unequal struggle. The situation, however, was sufficiently critical to make Herod Antipas, tetrarch of Galilee, hasten the refortification of Sepphoris, which he surrounded with a great wall. He also built a wall around Betharamtha, which he renamed Julias to signify his loyalty to the Imperial family. His brother Philip followed suit, and enlarged Paneas at the springs of the River Jordan, and called it Caesarea Philippi. He likewise elevated the village of Bethsaida, at the head of the Sea of Galilee, to the dignity of a city, and called it Julias. While these building operations may have gratified the Herodian love of architecture, the places concerned occupied strategic positions, and it is apparent that they were intended to be defensive strongholds in the interests of Rome.

The radical change in Jewish affairs was momentous news even in secluded Nazareth. There too, as in every other village, town, and hamlet, there was keen discussion of the turn of events, their implications, and probable outcome. To the boy Jesus it was brought home that the times were big with decision. Waves of emotion flowed over him as he listened with strained attention to the various opinions expressed by the elders. Men talked bitterly of the national degradation. Some were in favour of the militant policy of the Kannaites. Others counselled the patience of the Pharisees. There was general agreement that the prolonged and increasing troubles were the woes that presaged the coming of the Messiah. "May he come speedily!" ejaculated one of the little group of Nazarenes, and the hope was echoed fervently. And then, as so often, the company fell to theorizing about the advent of the Deliverer, who he would be, what he would do. But it was all vague, all guesswork. No one really knew.

Jesus was profoundly dissatisfied. Here the honour of God and the existence of Israel were at stake, and there was no clear plan of salvation! They were all like sheep without a shepherd. He may have voiced his complaint in a boyish treble. "We shall know one day, my son," his father replied to an eager question. "But why can't we know now?" A friend of Joseph's smiled at the excited child. "Those learned doctors at Jerusalem, maybe they can tell him, eh!" Perhaps they could. "When am I going to Jerusalem, father? I'm twelve now." Joseph tweaked the flushed cheek. "God willing, you will go with us next Passover, my son." And with this Jesus had to be content.

In those grave days the boy grew old beyond his years, as children often will when the stem realities of life, and especially a national crisis, suddenly force upon their consciousness the contemplation of heavy responsibilities. Almost in a day the simple insouciance of childhood may be replaced by a portentous seriousness. Jesus was by nature thoughtful and observant; but now, facing fully for the first time the problems confronting his people, he became aloof and deeply introspective. In his own way he wrestled with issues which were proving too big for much more experienced heads, and probably for the first time also he was concerned about the part which he should play. He prayed earnestly that he might be found worthy to stand before the Messiah. Youth sees itself in heroic roles. Did there enter into his mind tentatively, speculatively, the frightening yet fascinating suggestion that he himself might be the Messiah? It is not unlikely. At first he would have rejected the idea as a temptation of the Evil One, and asked forgiveness of God for his sinful pride. But where was the wickedness? Was it wrong to think that he might be the instrument of his people's salvation? Once the purity of his purpose was conceded and given due weight, the seed could be safely received into fertile soil, tended as a secret and precious thing, nourished and watered in the night watches when silence reigned. The seed germinated, and put forth shoots; it gained strength with every remembrance of words of commendation addressed to him by visiting rabbis, by elders of the synagogue; it struck its roots into the knowledge of his own Davidic descent. He must study the Scriptures: he must prepare himself; for ahead of him there loomed a future fraught with the strangest possibilities.

These imaginings in a highly sensitive and spiritually receptive boy, living under such apocalyptic conditions, are
psychologically intelligible. Upon his soul beat like angel's pinions the creative force generated by thousands of
his suffering countrymen concentrated on this one expectation of a Saviour. If we have to state a rational case
for the growth in the boy Jesus of a messianic consciousness it is not difficult to do so.

How anxiously now he looked forward to going up to
Jerusalem. But it was no longer just the natural eagerness of the child to travel, to see new places, and to behold the glittering, almost mythical Temple. There was a
great truth which he must learn there. He had a rendezvous with God.

His parents were unaware of the tumult in the mind of
their eldest son. They were more immediately concerned
about the preparations for the journey, and arrangements for the care of the young ones left behind. For
weeks beforehand, even before the visit of the licensed
money-changer of the Sanctuary to exchange common
coin for the sacred half-shekel of the Temple tribute,
there were solemn conferences with relatives and
friends. For this was the first of the three pilgrim festivals under the new regime, and who could know what
might happen at Jerusalem when patriotic sentiment
was at fever heat? Would the Galilean Zealots choose
this opportunity to make trouble? It was devoutly to be
hoped that they would exercise restraint. An outbreak
just now could do no possible good.

It was agreed that it would be wiser not to take the direct road through Samaria, for that, too, involved the risk of a clash. The longer route would certainly be safest, crossing the Jordan at the ford below the Sea of Galilee, proceeding through Peraea, and recrossing near Jericho. This choice was fortunate for the boy Jesus, for it meant approaching Jerusalem from the east over the Mount of Olives, where the city and Temple, hidden from view during the steep ascent, suddenly revealed themselves in dazzling loveliness as the road took a turn over the brow of the hill. It was a sight to make a Jewish lad gasp with awe and wonderment. Across the intervening Kedron valley the eye took in the great wall pierced with gates, the crowded buildings rising tier upon tier, and crowning all the snowy marble majesty of the Holy House topped with its roofs of glittering gold. Many more times Jesus would behold this spectacle, but this first occasion must have been indelibly impressed on his memory. How joyfully he raised his voice in unison with the thronging pilgrims, chaunting the age-old psalm:

> I was glad when they said unto me,
> Let us go into the House of the Lord.
> Our feet shall stand within thy gates, Jerusalem.
> Jerusalem is builded as a city compacted together:
> Whither the tribes go up,
> The tribes of the Lord,
> Unto the testimony of Israel,
> To give thanks unto the Name of the Lord....
> Peace be within thy walls,
> And prosperity within thy palaces....

So this was the House of our Father in heaven! Its beauty was no less than Jesus had visioned. Its courts, its cloisters, its service of song and sacrifice, filled the boy with an emotion that was near to tears. His heart was uplifted in ecstasy and adoration reaching up to God on high with the lazy column of smoke from the burning incense that rose until it was lost to view in heaven itself.

Joseph pointed out to his son with pride all the features of the Temple, the cloisters, and especially Solomon's Porch, with its triple colonnade flanked by Corinthian pillars, where meetings were held and the famous Doctors of Jerusalem held converse and discussion. Together they threaded their way through the crowded Court of the Gentiles paved with huge slabs of coloured marble, and paused to read one of the inscriptions, set on the low balustrade which fenced in the Temple proper, forbidding non-Jews to proceed further on pain of death. Mounting the steps they passed into the Women's Court by the Beautiful Gate of burnished brass. There were the women's galleries, the thirteen trumpet-shaped chests for freewill offerings, the chambers at the four comers used for various purposes. Another flight of steps led on through the Nicanor Gate into the further courts, the Court of Israel and the Court of the Priests. In the last stood the immense altar and the brazen laver. On either side were the buildings for priestly uses of all kinds necessary for the service of the Sanctuary. Beyond could be seen the edifices which enshrined the Holy Place and the Holy of Holies; but into those sanctified precincts none might come except those that ministered, pure of flesh and raiment, and into the holiest of all, behind the second veil, only the high priest once a year with the blood of propitiation on the solemn Day of Atonement.

Leaving the Temple, and descending the steps into the Tyropoean valley, there was all the city to see, the royal palaces, the hundreds of little streets with their bazaars devoted to different trades, the old and new fortifications, the strong towers built by Herod, and a bewildering confusion of men and beasts, of strange tongues, and of merchandise garnered from all the comers of the earth.

The brief days of the festival did not allow much time to take in all these things; but they sufficed at least to open the eyes of Jesus to the reality of the kingdoms of this world which lay beyond the Great Sea and the caravan routes, and to give him a glimpse which he had never had before of the races that peopled them. It was amazing how these thousands were drawn as with a magnet to Zion, how indeed God's House was a house of prayer for all nations. The boy's horizon had suddenly widened, but it made him more than ever proud of his spiritual inheritance as a son of Abraham.

A western lad coming out of the country for the first time into the bustle and strangeness of the metropolis would probably have been awkward and gauche; but Jesus, like any eastern lad, moved about with easy self-possession. If he felt any shyness he did not exhibit it, and it is likely enough that he accepted both the city and its medley of peoples with the confident assurance characteristic of his race. He thus was able to enjoy and to absorb the atmosphere of his surroundings in full measure. With youthful friends or relatives he was free to roam wherever he wished without giving his parents more than a momentary concern as to his whereabouts. He was in good company, and could not come to much harm.

Mercifully, there was no fear of a disturbance this Passover. All precautions had been taken by the procurator in collaboration with the Jewish authorities, and a strong body of troops garrisoned the Antonia overlooking the Temple area. There was a good deal of growling and cursing on the part of the hot-heads at this innovation, but for the most part the worshippers were thankful that they could observe the festival in peace.

All too quickly the days passed, and it was with something like dismay that Jesus realized that the hours had been so taken up with the ritual of the feast and with sightseeing that there had been no opportunity to obtain an answer from the sages to his urgent questions. Forgetful of all else he slipped away and set out for the Temple, his heart throbbing painfully with eager anticipation.

In the bustle of preparing the pilgrim caravan for its homeward journey the boy was never missed. He was doubtless somewhere in the company. At the end of the first day's march, however, he had not put in an appearance, and his parents became seriously alarmed. They searched everywhere among their kinsfolk and acquaintances; but no one had seen him. There was nothing to do but to turn back. Deeply anxious now, Joseph and Mary inquired at every likely place in the city without success. At last, on the third day, they came into the Temple, and there among the

Doctors of the Law they found the truant. Serenely unconscious that anything was amiss Jesus was listening greedily to the discourse of the sages, and impulsively putting his questions. For a few moments his parents watched with amazement, and then his mother could contain herself no longer, and hurried forward, overcoming her nervousness as a woman in breaking in upon the deliberations of the disciples of the wise. Where the boy had spent the days, how he had subsisted, were a complete mystery. All that mattered now was that he was safe and sound. Relief gave place to vexation. "Son, why hast thou thus dealt with us? Behold, thy father and I have sought thee sorrowing."

Jesus turned. That his parents should have been at such pains to look for him came to him as a complete surprise. "How is it that ye sought me?" he asked with astonishment. "Did ye not know that I must be in my Father's House?" Why had they not come at once to the Temple? Where else did they expect him to be?

One of the elders, who had been an amused spectator of this little scene, inquired of Mary, "Art thou the mother of this child?" "I am," she said. The teacher hastened to pour oil on the troubled waters. "Blessed art thou," he replied in kindly tones, "for God hath blessed the fruit of thy womb"[18]

It is a revealing glimpse that we are given here of the working of the boy's mind reaching out after a man's knowledge and discernment. We note how absorbed he is in deep things. But despite his quest, he is still so naively and charmingly the child who has never given a thought to the fact that his parents will be worrying over his absence. It is their failure to come to the obvious place that he cannot understand, and which shows us that he is beginning to grow apart, to take the lonely road. He has not apprehended that his mother and father have no inkling of his heart-searchings and wrestlings. We may not strain his words to make them imply any premature conviction of a unique relationship with God. But they do imply a pre-occupation with spiritual problems, and an experience of personal contact with the Father in heaven, which could only be the outcome of constant private prayer.

When Jesus left Jerusalem it was with the realization of a new independence. He had a life of his own to lead: he was a distinct individual, with separate thoughts, actions and aspirations. His alone now was the choice between good and evil. The incident had really shocked him into a first consciousness of the responsibilities of manhood, or, perhaps, this was one of the tilings taught him by the sages, for they held that a boy of his years had attained his majority in the sight of God.

Jesus returned to Nazareth, and was subject to his parents. But his filial obedience, however lovingly and willingly given, was no longer the unreasoning obedience of childhood. He was aware that this was a sacred duty which he was required to perform. He was increasing in wisdom as well as stature, and therefore in favour with God and man.

CHAPTER V

The Son of Man

There is a great gap in our knowledge of the life of Jesus between the ages of twelve and thirty, a period of nearly eighteen years. No single record remains to illuminate one hour of that long hiatus. Boyhood passes into adolescence, and adolescence into early manhood, and all those important changes in body, mind and circumstance involved in the process of growing up are almost a sealed book. The seal is not quite secure, so that with keen penetration supplemented by outside information we can compose a short account of the developments which our curiosity is so anxious to determine. It will have verisimilitude; but no claim to strict accuracy, it will have the support of history and psychology; but no pretensions to be more than a tentative reconstruction. We know something of what went before, we know a great deal of what followed, so that moving from the two positions in the darkness towards a point of junction, like those of old who cut the tunnel of Siloam through the living rock, we may create a channel, even if it be an artificial one, through which the waters of a great personality will flow softly.

It is the West that demands of us this effort; the East is content with silence. Sufficient for the Jew that a man is called of God at a particular moment of his life to perform a divine service; what lies behind that moment is of small consequence. It is indeed most proper in the supreme revealers of the will of God that they should come suddenly out of obscurity. There survives an old comment on the words in the *Song of Songs*: "My beloved is like a roe, or a young hart" - "A roe appears and is hid, appears and is hid again. So our first redeemer (Moses) appeared and was hid, and at length appeared again. So our last redeemer (the Messiah) shall be revealed to them, and shall be hid from them, and shall be revealed again."[19] There is therefore even a sort of prophetic necessity and historical precedent for the darkness that temporarily eclipses a sun of righteousness. But the Greek, who stands for all the rest of inquisitive humanity, is a seeker after knowledge - he is a scientist - and has furnished our language abundantly with words representative of his questing and probing mind. He expects a series of preparatory adventures and encounters which will bring out the qualities of the hero, and we must endeavour to satisfy him.

In contemplating that long period of eighteen years, let us recognize that there are many varieties of time in our experience. There are the hours which seem as a moment in sleep, and there are the interminable minutes of pain. There is also city time and country time. To the city dweller the many sources of excitement, the constant coming and going, the wide range of activities, the succession of a day life by a night life, prolong the tale of years. So rapidly do events follow one another in his crowded scheme of existence that even a few weeks in the past seems so great a while ago that memory hesitates and loses assurance of all but the most recent happenings. It is otherwise with the countryman. Both his opportunities and his activities are restricted. One day is very like its fellow. He counts the four seasons of the year much as the townsman counts the four weeks of a month. So forthright and simple is his life that any unusual circumstance stands out boldly, and is perfectly remembered and discussed long after as if it had happened yesterday.

Jesus was a countryman, and we can therefore greatly abbreviate those eighteen years, being assured that nothing outwardly remarkable took place in all that time to give his neighbours any special impression of him. In the early days of his public career he gave an address in his own synagogue at Nazareth. "And all bare him witness, and wondered at the gracious words which proceeded out of his mouth. And they said, Is not this Joseph's son?" It is clear that nothing in his conduct throughout the years that had gone before had given anyone reason to suspect anything unusual of him. The natives looked at the man with new eyes. Could this really be the son of old Joseph with whom they were so very familiar? It seemed incredible, and produced in the event such an open clash of temperament that Jesus nearly lost his life.

Had Jesus grown up in a big city he must inevitably have been drawn into the vortex of discussion and controversy on politics and religion, which is part of the normal urban youth's leisure occupation if he is at all seriously minded. He could hardly have failed to declare his ideas in a circle however limited, and there would be those who were well aware of his viewpoint and distinctive qualities. Indeed, it is highly probable that he would have manifested himself while yet in his teens, and have assumed some kind of party leadership. His entrance into public life would have held no element of surprise for his intimates.

But in rural Nazareth there was no such compulsion put upon him. On the contrary, the conservatism and single-track mentality of the locals would impose a reticence on anyone with opinions such as might be considered advanced or eccentric. There would be a natural desire, especially in one who was fond of human companionship and happy in his surroundings, to avoid the risk of being misunderstood. In the country, life can be made insupportable for an individual regarded as queer. Mistrust of the unlike in a peasant, when coupled, as in Galilee and elsewhere, with superstition, often develops into violent hatred and unreasoning fear; the erstwhile gossip is shunned as a wizard, or one possessed of a devil. Every consideration would militate against any giving of confidences or premature disclosure of such conceptions as must have been shaping themselves in the mind of Jesus. The secrets of his soul would perforce be hidden even from those nearest and dearest to him, for, as he had to admit later, "a prophet is not without honour, but in his own country, and among his kin, and in his own house." It was his own relatives in the end, who, when the great adventure had begun, "went out to lay hold on him: for they said, 'he is beside himself.'" At that time, and for many months afterwards, the fear of misrepresentation went with him, so that again and again when he had demonstrated his powers of healing he needed straitly to charge the relieved sufferers that they should not make him known.

But there were not only the instinctive justifications for silence. Jesus had a duty to perform as head of his family, which devolved upon him through the early loss of his father. Bound to support his widowed mother and his younger brothers and sisters, his position in the little town would have been altogether untenable if he had allowed himself freedom of speech. Indeed, it ultimately became so as soon as he had declared his message. What business would have come the way of this "mad" carpenter? Who would have entrusted him with their commissions? He would have been made a mock of by every child and hounded out of the community. He did not, in those days, want to leave Nazareth. Every aspect of the lovely countryside about him was conducive to peaceful study and meditation on the manifold problems that vexed him. Out on his beloved hills he could spend long hours in prayer and inward communion, without anyone being the wiser or thinking aught amiss. He was most concerned not to anticipate by some reckless and ill-considered action the step which gradually he understood to be inevitable. He was content to bide his time. If he was in the right, and not, deluding himself, the call would come one day, and he believed that when it came it would be unmistakable. In that day, doubtless, his brethren would be old enough to fend for themselves, his sisters would be settled in life, and he would be relieved of his domestic responsibilities. The lesson which he had to learn for himself he could teach to his people. Do not force the pace. God will manifest Himself at the proper season, and not before. Be ready! Watch!

So it came about that there was very little in the outward bearing of Jesus during the eighteen years of his preparation to indicate to anyone the vital and radical changes which were taking place within him. We have to attempt to penetrate into his inner consciousness if we are to comprehend the trend and evolution of his ideas. This is not as difficult as it might seem, for no one has offered a more complete self-expression. We can know him so well because above all tilings he desired to be known.

It was painful to Jesus to withhold himself. He was not by nature one of those who love to surround themselves with an atmosphere of mystery. He could see no virtue in esotericism. "He that doeth truth," he said, "cometh to the light, that his deeds may be made manifest, that they are wrought in God." He was no advocate of secret councils and dark initiations. "There is nothing covered that shall not be revealed; and hid, that shall not be made known. What I tell you in darkness, that speak ye in light: and what ye hear in the ear, that proclaim ye upon the housetops." His whole life revealed the richness of his capacity and his longing to give without stint of all that was in him. The story is told that one day in the Temple Jesus sat over against the treasury, and beheld how the people cast money into the treasury: and many that were rich cast in much. And there came a certain poor widow, and she threw in two mites, which make a farthing. And he called his disciples, and said unto them, "Truly, I say unto you that this poor widow hath cast more in than all they which have cast into the treasury: for all they did cast in of their abundance; but she of her want did cast in all that she had, even all her living." That widow was a kindred spirit.

Jesus was filled with compassion, with a spring of love that welled up within him and overflowed; and in return he passionately longed for love and understanding. The keynote of his teaching is love, love of friends, love of neighbours, love even of enemies. The harlot is forgiven in her repentance because "she loved much." Such love as this does not demand a response, it is bestowed freely, but it yearns for it, and hopes for it: it cries, "Simon, son of Jonas, lovest thou me?" And yet it knows that its own immensity cannot be equalled. Even so there is regret at the limitation. "If ye loved me, ye would rejoice...." "If ye love me, keep my commandments." The emphasis is all on that little word "if." Such love, also, is infinitely forgiving, not seven times, but seventy times seven times; for understanding is its handmaid. Comprehension of this kind is so rare that, when it manifests itself, it calls forth blessings. "Blessed is he, whosoever shall not be offended in me." How many have really grasped his identity? Jesus wants to know that. It is the proof of understanding. "Whom do men say that I, the Son of Man, am?" Let that pass. "Whom do ye—my friends—say that I am?" And Simon Peter answered and said, "Thou art the Messiah, the Son of the Living God!" And Jesus answered and said unto him, "Blessed art thou, Simon bar Jonah!" Jesus was concerned by every means to break down the obtuseness of his contemporaries. He called every witness to his aid, the witness of God, as revealed in his own mighty works, the witness of Moses, as contained in the lawgiver's writings, the witness of John the Baptist, as given in his verbal testimony. So urgently did he long to be known and believed. No rewards were too great for those who had forsaken all things for his sake.

All these revelations of the heart and mind of Jesus are evidences of the man before his public ministry. The great love of his boyhood and adolescence had been his father. It is probable that Joseph died while Jesus was still in his teens. There had been a strong bond of affection between them, and since the day that the beloved old man had been carried to his grave Jesus had had no human soul in whom he could wholly confide. He had suffered, as all highly sensitive beings do suffer, the agonies of loneliness. The place of the loving father on earth was gradually taken up by the Father in heaven. The youth's adoration was centred on God. It was a mystic and very personal relationship, which Jesus described in the words: "No man knoweth the Son, but the Father; neither knoweth any man the Father, save the Son, and he to whomsoever the Son will reveal Him."

It is somewhat difficult for us in the West, with our different standards, our matter-of-factness, our stunted spirituality, and our restrained emotionalism, to enter into the process which elevated this intense filial piety to its highest plane. If we had not solved the problem of the person of Jesus in our own cold way through a doctrine of his deity, and thus given an unexpected literalness to his assertion of divine sonship, we might have been tempted to regard his claims as a form of religious mania. Many of his own people thought them blasphemous. But for Jesus the relationship was simple and real, unique only in the sense that this Divine adoption was peculiarly proper for the Messiah; but it carried with it no pretensions to deity. There was no suggestion that he was God masquerading as man. He disclaimed all the attributes of the Absolute. When he was addressed as "Good Master," he answered, "Why callest thou me good? There is none good but One, that is God."

How closely does the description of God which Jesus gives conform to the character and activities of his own father! Jesus is the firstborn of his father: he lies in his bosom, and is loved by him. He came forth from his father. He loves and honours his father, and delights to do his will, and all who love him will be loved by his father. The father has a care for his children that none of them should perish, and he knows what their needs are before they ask him. His children are to forgive others, if they expect him to forgive them. The father is a worker, and the son also works. The plants which the father has planted will survive. The father has given all things into the hand of his son, and as the firstborn he eventually receives the inheritance. If we will, by thus substituting the small letter for the initial capital, we can see the lineaments of Joseph in the portrait of the Heavenly Father depicted in this combination of references. If we wish farther to see parenthood through the eyes of Jesus, we have only to read his beautiful parable of the Compassionate Father, which by a reversion of the values we call that of the Prodigal Son. So much did the name of father mean to him that he would not have it applied, out of courtesy, to any reverend senior.

So we may perceive in a measure how God became for Jesus the apotheosis of what fatherhood had meant in his experience. It is a wonderful tribute to the qualities of a man whose influence has received scant recognition, and who represents the Jew in one of his most appealing roles, widely acknowledged even to this day.

When the great blank came in his life, Jesus must have hoped that in their common sorrow a new chapter would open in the relationships between his mother, his brothers and sisters, and himself. He felt deeply for Mary in her widowhood, and for the children bereaved so young. His teaching reveals a great tenderness for the widow, and love for the little ones. When the rime drew near for his own departure from the world poignant memories were stirred. "I will pray the Father," he said, "and he shall give you another comforter, that he may abide with you for ever; even the Spirit of Truth.... I will not leave you orphans."

It had not been easy for him to realize that no true understanding was to be expected from the survivors of his home circle. He did his duty virtuously, as became the head of the house, and his mother looked up to him with pride; but she was psychologically incapable of comprehending him. There is evidence that she developed into one of those rather fussy women with outspoken and strongly critical views on affairs in general uninspired by any real knowledge and frequently based on wrong or ill-digested information. She no doubt worried about every little item in her housekeeping, magnifying essential frugality, and loved to interfere in the domestic management of her neighbours and kinsfolk. Had she not seven children to bring up on little or nothing? Perhaps Jesus even had a personal recollection of his mother in mind when he told the story of the woman who had lost a piece of silver, worth about sixpence, and who lit a lamp, and swept the house through until she found it. Mary's religion was of that unquestioning type which is content with simple conformity with prescribed observances. Most Jewish women were like her: their place was definitely in the home. The enthusiasms and dreams of girlhood had long been forgotten. She had for so many years been the admirable background to Joseph's life, the mother of his children, and the keeper of a Jewishly orthodox house. From this quarter Jesus could receive no help in his spiritual strivings. Martha, a woman friend of later years had very much the same temperament.

Jesus was driven in upon himself. He had to fight his battles alone. And it meant everything to his development that he had to do so. In this sense his being deprived of his father may be regarded as providential. His one human prop was taken from him, and he had to stand squarely on his own feet. All his hopes now were set on high, and only through long hours of lonely study, and prayer, and meditation, did he attain to peace and certainty. It was a gruelling and testing experience, necessitating the leading almost of a dual life, foreign to his whole nature, which clamoured for companionship. Only when his heartbroken cry of "Father, Father!" was answered, and he knew the ecstasy of the supreme communion, did he learn the inner meaning of his existence, and the mission for which he was ordained. The thought of marriage and its sweet solace must often have come to him, but he set it aside, first because his sisters had the prior claim to be provided for, and second because he came to know the singularity of his destiny.

No one realized through what turbulent waters his spirit, outwardly serene and full of charm, had progressed to reach its haven. Still less did anyone realize what his human need had been, and what a blessed relief it was to him, when at length his call came, to be able to gather about himself a group of intimates, his disciples, to whom he was free to bare his whole soul and declare all his counsel. Then the pent-up floods of his being were released, and he related with amazing frankness not only his objective, but his subjective experiences. This was specially true of his conversations with Simon the son of Jonah, and James and John the sons of Zebedee. He lavished his love upon them, and his joy at the company of these three is shown by the fact that they were the only ones to whom he gave nicknames. Simon, was the rugged Rock, James and John were the two Thunderers. They could be the recipients of such confidential revelations as his Transfiguration, and probably also of his Temptation in the Wilderness. They occupied the place which his family had failed to fill. When on one occasion he was told, "Behold, thy mother and thy brethren stand without, desiring to speak with thee," he made answer, "Who is my mother? And who are my brethren?" And he stretched forth his hand towards his disciples, and said, "Behold my mother and my brethren! For whosoever shall do the will of my Father which is in heaven, the same is my brother, and sister, and mother." He says nothing of his earthly father. His father had been a father indeed, and now he had been absorbed into that greater and enduring Fatherhood which was God.

Thus, by a similar process to that by which the nature of the soil through which a river has flowed can be determined by the composition of the deposits at a lower level, we are able to decide with some assurance what was the earlier life of Jesus by its subsequent expression. But we have not yet analysed all the material secured to us by this means. There remains something to be said about his outlook on the external world, and something more about his inward and spiritual development.

At an early stage in his public life Jesus delivered one of the most imemorable speeches ever made by man, which is commonly known as the Sermon on the Mount. His audience consisted in the main of the peasantry and yeomanry of Palestine, people who were gravely concerned about the economic situation and about the outcome of the foreign political domination.

With such an audience as this anything but a message calculated to illumine the immediate and vital problems would fail of its purpose. Against too many pulpit sermons the criticism is often justly levelled that the speaker is out of touch with realities: the sentiments expressed are elevated and beautiful and true; but they do not sink home because the state of mind of the hearers does not predispose them to apprehend what is said. Many people have a picture-book impression of the Christ with two fingers uplifted talking eternal verities over the heads of a number of awe-stricken rustics. How false this picture is! Jesus made no such blunder. Guided by the history of the past, possessed of a keen insight into the lamentable conditions of the present, actuated by the highest patriotic and moral motives, and with an unbounded faith in the promises of God, he gave to his generation his wise and considered advice, the fruit of many years' earnest thought. He addressed himself to matters that were in every mind there present, he dealt with grievances that cried to heaven for redress, with crooked souls and warped spirits that needed to be made straight before they could enter the Kingdom of God.

We shall have an opportunity to judge of the relevance of the message of Jesus in the appropriate place. But we must stress here that his masterly grasp of the political, religious, and economic conditions then prevailing, and his perfect understanding of the psychology of his audience, argues a long and intensive study of his complex subject. The man who could make that speech had a first-hand knowledge of men and affairs, which could only have been gained by habitual and keen observation. The life of his people in work and worship, in house and field, in joy and grief, was to him an open book. His own inward and spiritual life did not shut him off from his fellows, it drove him forth into the highways and byways.

The requirements of the exalted office for which Jesus believed himself to be destined provided at once the incentive to look about him and an acute perception of the implications of what he saw. It was, as he was well aware, a sign of the Messiah that "the Spirit of the Lord should rest upon him, the spirit of wisdom and understanding, the spirit of counsel and might, the spirit of knowledge and of the fear of the Lord; to make him of ready discernment, so that he should not judge after the sight of his eyes, neither reprove after the hearing of his ears, but judge with justice and equity." The years of his preparation enabled him to acquire these spiritual treasures, permitting him more and more to see the world through God's eyes, with God's love and compassion, with God's truth, and righteousness, and holiness.

If Jesus was at all inclined towards asceticism, he deliberately repudiated it as incompatible with the service demanded of him. He came eating and drinking; for how else could he be on terms of intimacy with humanity. He associated with publicans and sinners: he did not shrink from contact with the leper. He rejected the admonition of the elders, and conversed freely and unselfconsciously with women. Even harder for a good Jew and Galilean, he had to overstep the boundaries of racial prejudice, and extend the right hand of fellowship to Syrian and Samaritan, the hereditary foes of his people. We are not now able to count the cost to him mentally and physically in thus transcending the taboos of tradition, and the feelings and habits of a lifetime.

The growth in grace, which finally produced this all-embracing lovingkindness, must needs be slow, and at times painful in the extreme. So long as he remained in his home at Nazareth a certain restraint was imposed upon him. His own circle would inevitably frown on any lapse from orthodox conduct. The presence of the seeds of conflict can be realized from the fact that James, the brother, a year or two younger than Jesus, was almost his exact opposite. He was a strict Nazarite, touching neither wine nor strong drink, and rigidly observant of the minutiae of his religion, so that he earned the encomium of "the Just." It says much for the magnificent self control of Jesus that there was no actual cleavage and dissension in the family, though there must have been not a few passages-at-arms, and that this same James yielded in the end to the influence of his brother's life and teaching, and after his death became the President of the communities of the Nazarenes, as the primitive Christians were called.

If we are impatient at the tale of years which preceded the activities with which we are more or less familiar from the Gospel records, we may be certain that for Jesus they were not a day too long. Only by little and little was he able to submit his whole self to the control of God, and to attain to that repose of spirit reflected in the prophetic title of Prince of Peace. At a time when human relationships were strained to breaking point, when the demon of fear stalked abroad, he was enabled to move about with a calm dignity, completely at ease, exercising the magnetic and healing power which they possess who are accustomed to practise the presence of God. Of all the gifts that were his to bestow, one of the greatest and most acceptable was the gift of his peace.

We draw very near here to the inner secret of the being of Jesus. We have learned to know him, it may be, better than we did before; but there is a mysterious something that still perhaps baffles and eludes us. How came he to the full realization that he was the Messiah? Whence did he obtain that certainty, which ever after through all the vicissitudes of his career never left him? There was in his voice a ring of authority which astonished those who heard him. Men who were accustomed to command were intrigued by it. "By what authority doest thou these things?" he was asked, "and who gave thee this authority?" And Jesus made it clear that he derived his right from on high. There had come a day, since when he no longer thought of himself as Jesus of Nazareth: he thought of and afterwards referred to himself as the Son of Man. He had participated in that mystical experience, known to prophets and saints, when the veil between heaven and earth is drawn aside, and for one brief moment the soul of man enters into the presence of that dazzling light which is the garment of the Great Reality. No words may be formed to tell the uttermost of that vision; but from the inadequate descriptions set down by those who have been thus blessed we are permitted to catch a gleam of that radiance, and to believe.

When and where this first revelation was vouchsafed to Jesus we do not know. Perhaps it was soon after the death of his father, and he had gone out into the night seeking to be alone with his thoughts and his grief. His ready acceptance and comprehension of the phenomena which attended his baptism years later shows that he must already have been familiar with the world of spirit through a prior experience. He that was now called a prophet had in his youth become a seer.

Jesus stood on the crest of a hill, his face upturned towards the velvet vault of heaven spangled with a myriad twinkling pin-points of light, and as he gazed, with a gentle breeze caressing the hair that flowed down upon his shoulders, there came to his mind those lines of the psalmist which have continually renewed their truth to thousands ever since they were written:

> "When I consider the heavens, the work of Thy fingers,
> The moon and the stars, which Thou hast ordained;
> What is Man, that Thou art mindful of him,
> And the Son of Man, that Thou visitest him?
> For Thou hast made him but little lower than the angels, And hast crowned him with glory and honour.
> Thou madest him to have dominion over the works of Thy hands;
> Thou hast put all things under his feet."

Out of the infinite, and yet deep within his being, there came a still small voice to him, "Son of Man! Son of Man!" It was the call of God to his solitary humanity. His soul yearned towards its Maker, and he fell on his face and worshipped.

"Son of Man! Son of Man!" The words persisted like an echo. All their associations flooded in upon him. "I saw as it were the appearance of fire, and it had brightness round about. As the appearance of the bow that is in the cloud in the day of rain.... This was the appearance of the likeness of the glory of the Lord.

... And he said unto me, Son of Man, stand upon thy feet and I will speak unto thee." That had been the experience of the Prophet Ezekiel. Even now he could sense something of that brightness. He was uplifted and exalted. God was very near.

"Son of Man!" Why did those words impress themselves on his brain in letters of fire, as if they had meaning for him alone? "I saw in the night visions, and, behold, one like the Son of Man came with the clouds of heaven, and came to the Ancient of Days, and they brought him near before him. And there was given him dominion, and glory, and a kingdom, that all people, nations, and languages should serve him: his dominion is an everlasting dominion which shall not pass away, and his kingdom that which shall not be destroyed." That was the vision of the Prophet Daniel. Was it then true that he, Jesus the son of Joseph, was the chosen one? His heart throbbed in his breast, and there was a beating upon his brow like the beating of the sea. In a prayer of adoration that made no movement of his lips he repeated: "His throne was like the fiery flame.... Thousand thousands ministered unto him, and ten thousand times ten thousand stood before him."

The awe of a great knowledge possessed him. His spirit soared towards the stars.... He saw himself singled out from all other men, raised up to the throne of God....

The rest must be told in the language of a disciple, who, a century later, sang of this vision of his Master.

> "I rested on the Spirit of the Lord: and the Spirit raised me on high: and made me stand on my feet in the height of the Lord, before His perfection and His glory.... The Spirit brought me forth before the face of the Lord: and although a Son of Man, I was named the Illuminate, the Son of God: while I praised amongst the praising ones, and great was I amongst the mighty ones. For according to the greatness of the Most High, so He made me: and like His own newness He renewed me; and He anointed me from His own perfection: and I became one of his neighbours; and my mouth was opened, like a cloud of dew; and my heart poured out as it were a gushing stream of righteousness, and my access to Him was in peace; and I was established by the spirit of his government."[20]

It was finished. Slowly Jesus returned to a consciousness of his surroundings. The stars still shone out of the still sky. The moon bathed the landscape in its mysterious light. But he himself was a changed man. A new solemnity sat upon him. For a while he remained in silent meditation, pondering and wondering, before he turned his steps towards his home. He had received his consolation. There was much to learn, much still to be explained; but now he was set upon a course which he would pursue steadfastly with simple faith in God's guiding hand. Nothing could ever shake the conviction that had come to him, nothing could obliterate the vision.

On another night, the last in his earthly life, when all his work seemed to have crumbled into dust, still he remained unalterably true to the voice that had called him. He was arraigned before the Court of the Priests, and the high priest cried aloud to him, "I adjure thee by the Living God, that thou tell us, art thou the Messiah, the Son of the Blessed?" And Jesus answered firmly and with sublime assurance, "I am: and hereafter ye shall see the Son of Man sitting on the right hand of Power, and coming in the clouds of heaven."

CHAPTER VI

Come and See

Jesus waited. Israel also waited. The changes that time inevitably brings had passed over the earth. Augustus Caesar had assumed full divinity doubtfully in death. Tiberius had long reigned in his stead. Governor succeeded governor in the rulership of Judea: Coponius was followed by Marcus Andrew son of Jonas, and he by Annius Rufus, Valerius Gratus, and Pontius Pilate. High priests had been deposed and appointed at the will of the governors. Annas the son of Seth replaced Joazar, and was superseded in turn by Ishmael the son of Pheabi, by his own son Eleazar, by Simon the son of Kamith, and by his son-in-law Joseph Caiaphas.

So far there had been no radical interference with the liberties of the people or with their religious customs. And therefore the brooding spirit of unrest was restrained from manifesting itself through the deeds of violent men. But with the coming of Pilate there was good reason to fear that this state of at least surface tranquillity would not long continue. The new procurator was insolent, overbearing, rapacious and quick-tempered, the most undesirable type of official that could have been selected to govern a people so sensitive as the Jews. He was determined to stand no nonsense from anyone, and most unfortunately his arrival coincided with the beginning of a Sabbatical Year, when the cessation of agricultural activities gave the population more leisure to concern themselves about other matters, and when their thoughts were directed to the subject of freedom. That Sabbatical Year, heralded by the trumpets of Jewish New Year's Day in September A. D. 26, was to receive a significance unique in the history of Israel.

Acting on his own initiative, or on information of impending trouble, Pilate's first major act was to move up his troops from Caesarea to Jerusalem, there to go into winter quarters. The entrance into the capital took place at night, and, against all precedent in Judea, the legionaries were allowed to carry their standards with the medallions bearing the portrait of the Emperor, and to plant them in the Holy City. When it was seen the next morning that Pilate had deliberately violated the Jewish law relating to images, there was uproar. Crowds flocked to Caesarea both from Jerusalem and the country round about, and besought the governor to remove the standards; but he was adamant: he would let these people know that Rome was master, and that the honour of Caesar was more important than their silly superstitions.

The people would not go away, however, and besieged him with their plaints and entreaties day after day. There was no peace from their clamour. Angrily on the fifth day he told the leaders to gather their following before his judgment-seat on the morrow in the open place of the town. He was determined to put an end to the intolerable nuisance, and gave orders for his soldiers to be posted in concealment all round the square. Morning came, and the governor stalked grimly through a lane opened up through a sea of humanity that surged about him. When he was seated, the leaders again preferred their request. "Show us some proof," they urged, "that Caesar desires the destruction of our laws!" Pilate's answer was to raise his hand in a signal, and from every side his men closed in on the unarmed multitude. "Now," he threatened, "you will either leave off this disturbance, and disperse quietly, or take the consequences." The response took him by surprise. As if moved by a common impulse the people threw themselves on the ground and bared their necks, crying that they would rather die than transgress their laws. Blustering Pilate was out-manoeuvred: he dared not proceed to extremes. With an ill grace, he gave way, and commanded the standards to be carried back to Caesarea. It was a great moral victory for the Jews, success for a policy of non-violence. But the governor was determined not to forget this affront to his authority. He had a score to settle with these Jews, and he meant to pay it.[21]

Such was the ominous opening of that eventful Year of Release. It sent a wave of excitement rippling over all the land of Israel. It provided matter for eager discussion throughout the winter. The ripples reached even to the wilderness, and there they stayed. That strange man who had so moved the people in the days of the taxing stirred in his retreat. "The word of God came unto John the son of Zacharias in the wilderness. And he came into all the country about Jordan, preaching the baptism of repentance for the D remission of sins; and saying, Repent ye: for the Kingdom of Heaven is at hand!"

Almost in a moment the country was awake from end to end. The seductive voice of love called soflty,

> "Rise up, my fair one, and come away.
> For, lo, the winter is past;
> The rain is over and gone;
> The flowers appear on the earth;
> The time of the singing of birds is come."

But high above the voice of nature, of man and maid, rose the strident tones of the prophet. "Repent ye: for the Kingdom of Heaven is at hand!"

From all parts the people flocked to hear him, and to be baptized. It was the Sabbatical Year, the sacred seventh year. Would it also be the Messianic Year, the year of deliverance?

Galilee sent its thrilled contingents, labourers, artisans, fishermen from the lake. All kinds and classes made their way to the banks of Jordan, Pharisees, Sadducees, Zealots, priests and Levites, soldiers and publicans. Who could stay away? Simon and Andrew, Philip and Nathanael, were gone from Bethsaida. Mary and her children were anxious to go from Nazareth. Only Jesus was reluctant. This might be the call for which he waited; but no sign had come to him: he could not be sure. And how could he doubt when the summons really came?

Impatiently the family gathered about him. "John the Baptist baptizeth for the remission of sins: let us go and be baptized by him." But Jesus put them off. "Wherein have I sinned that I should go and be baptized by him?" And then, as they stared at him, he added hastily, "Unless this very thing that I have said is a sin of ignorance."[22]

They were going, anyway. He could come if he liked. He let them go.

Jesus was racked with indecision. He prayed earnestly for light. And light was given to him. Years after, he was discussing the baptism of John with the Jewish authorities in Jerusalem, and his memory went back to this time. He told a story.

A certain man had two sons; and he came to the first, and said, "Son, go work to-day in my vineyard." He answered and said, "I will not"; but afterward he repented, and went. And he came to the second, and said likewise. And he answered and said, "I go, sir"; and went not. Whether of them twain did the will of his father?

And his hearers could not help but answer that the son who did his father's will was he that said, "I will not go"; but afterward repented, and went.

Thus Jesus set out alone, and at last found himself among the throng that lined the banks of the Jordan. Inevitably, as the people were baptized, he found himself pushed nearer and nearer to the front, until at last he came within sight as well as sound of the speaker. He had never seen John before, or heard his voice; and he could not fail to be intrigued by his extraordinary personality.

The scene was one to affect a much less impressionable being than Jesus. Women were weeping, and strong men were crying aloud under the stress of their emotion. Some were beating their breasts in deep contrition, others had fallen to the ground, and were in danger of being trampled on in the press. Here and there a mocking visage showed; but the burning words of the prophet quickly wiped the grin from such profane lips. "O generation of vipers," he hailed them, "who hath warned you to flee from the wrath to come? Bring forth therefore fruits worthy of repentance, and begin not to say within yourselves, We have Abraham for our father: for I say unto you, that God is able of these stones (*abanim*) to raise up children (*banim*) unto Abraham. And now also the axe is laid unto the root of the trees: every tree therefore which bringeth not forth good fruit is hewn down, and cast into the fire." Membership of the House of Israel was no guarantee of salvation. Like the proselyte, the natural son of Abraham must seek re-admission into the Kingdom of God by baptism and confession of sin, as if he were an alien.

They shouted questions at him. For each he had a ready answer; for the tax collectors, "Exact no more than your due;" for the soldiers, "Terrorize no man, neither accuse any falsely; and be content with your wages;" for all, "He that hath two coats, let him impart to him that hath none; and he that hath meat, let him do likewise."

Could this indeed be the Messiah? As if he had read their inmost thoughts, John thundered, "I indeed baptize you with water; but one mightier than I cometh, the lace of whose sandals I am not worthy to unloose: he shall baptize you with the fire of the Holy Spirit: whose fan is in his hand, and he will thoroughly purge his floor, and will gather the wheat into his garner; but the chaff he will burn with fire unquenchable."

The pregnant words smote on the ears of Jesus. Surely this man spoke with the voice of God. The general enthusiasm was contagious: he was caught up in it, whirled about in the eddies of the swift current. Something within his soul cried out. He stepped forward, into the water. The chill stream was over his feet, sending the blood coursing back to his fast beating heart. The hairy hand of John was upon him, sending him down, down, into the depths. Jesus prayed.

Slowly he rose up out of the water. A great roaring sound was in his ears, crashing and reverberating. The world seemed to rock on its foundations. What had happened? He did not know whether he was in the flesh or in the spirit. He opened his eyes, and as he did so the heavens were rent and a jagged streak of lightning flashed down and lit up the scene with an eerie glare. Again the thunder pealed, and the people gave back terror-stricken. A dove fluttered on to the shoulder of Jesus, stayed a moment, and was gone. Some could have sworn that it entered into him.

John was startled at the strange portent. Shaken by the earthquake, half blinded by the lightning, he peered at the man beside him, and his dry lips framed the words, "Who art thou, lord?" But there came no answer. Jesus was oblivious of his surroundings. Out of the thunder a voice had spoken to him, a *Bath Qol*, an echo, and it had said: "Thou art my Son; this day have I begotten thee." The Spirit of God had descended upon him in the likeness of a dove, and had sung to him this song:

"In the prophets I sought thee,

In thee to rest me.

Thou art my sure rest:

Thou art my eldest,

Reigning for ever."[23]

A mighty joy and a great awe possessed him. His call had come! John again intervened, falling to his knees, and crying out, "I beseech thee, lord, baptize thou me!" Brought back thus forcibly to a consciousness of his surroundings, Jesus turned a bemused glance on the kneeling Baptist. He half lifted a protesting hand. "Let be!" he said, "for so it is fitting that all things should be fulfilled."

He moved away up the bank, out of the press. Night was coming on: he wanted to be alone. On and on he went into the wilderness, walking automatically, neither knowing nor caring whither his footsteps strayed. At last, in utter weariness, he sank down in the shelter of some rocks, and fell asleep.

When he awoke it was still night. Utter silence reigned, broken only by the occasional bark of a jackal. He was cold and hungry. Well, it had come, the day for which he had so long waited; it had come, and it had gone. Nothing had really changed, or had everything changed? Was he the same man, or was there a new power in him, the power of the Spirit of God. He could still feel acutely the chill air, and the gnawing of an empty stomach. The excitement had died out of his blood, leaving him depressed and almost miserable. His brain was the most living thing in him: it wanted to race ahead visioning all sorts of possible and impossible situations. What was he to do? How was he to begin his work? Would they expect him to perform miracles, like Moses in the wilderness? He was in the wilderness. He regarded a flat stone: it looked very much like a barley cake. Supposing....

"If thou be the Son of God," urged a voice within him, "command this stone that it be made bread."

He shivered. This was not the way of faith, but of unbelief. Forty years Israel had had to wander in the wilderness—to learn what? "That man doth not live by bread alone, but by every word that proceedeth out of the mouth of God."

Beyond the wilderness was the Land of Promise. Mighty nations were to become subject to the Children of Israel. Was not the Messiah to reign on Mount Zion, and would not all people serve him? Suddenly it was as if he were transported to the summit of an exceeding high mountain, and in one vast sweep the kingdoms of the world lay about him. He saw great cities, with their vast buildings and busy streets, like those he had seen in Jerusalem. He saw the sea covered with vessels, like the fishing fleet of his homeland lake magnified tenfold. He saw the long caravans of the merchants stretching away like an army of ants into the limitless desert. Said the voice: "All this power will I give thee, and the glory of them: for that is delivered unto me; and to whomsoever I will I give it. If thou therefore wilt worship me, all shall be thine."

A cold wind blew, and the picture dissolved swiftly into nothingness. Only the tricky rock beside Jesus seemed to shape itself into a great image robed and wreathed, half Baal, half Caesar. Had not Moses bade Israel beware lest, in the luxury of their possessions, they forget the Lord who brought them out of the Land of Egypt? Away with the cursed thing! "Thou shalt worship the Lord thy God, and Him only shalt thou serve."

But the word of the Lord would go forth from Jerusalem. All nations would come to Zion to learn the Law and to worship. He could see them, standing on a pinnacle of the Temple; he could see them flowing into the Court of the Gentiles. Here there was no danger of forsaking God. He beheld the priests at their ministry, and the smoke of the sacrifices rose up into his nostrils. What would they say if now he descended in their midst wafted gently down on the billowing clouds that rolled beneath? How was it written? "He shall give His angels charge over thee, to keep thee; and in their hands they shall bear thee up, lest at any time thou dash thy foot against a stone." Signs and wonders! Israel had always demanded signs and wonders. Was it not also written "Thou shalt not tempt the Lord thy God, as ye tempted Him in Massah"?

So the night wore on, while the fantasies of his mind wove strange patterns, wandering and turning about like the people in the wilderness. For every year of their pilgrimage Jesus seemed to have lived a day, being tempted and resisting temptation, coming back always to the one clear issue, that, whatever lay before him, he must hold fast to God, his refuge and his strength.

At length towards dawn Jesus propped his head on a pillow of stones like Jacob, surnamed Israel, and by a twist of the patriarch's dream he saw himself as a ladder reaching from earth to heaven, with angels ascending and descending on his body, and at his head the voice of God proclaimed, "Behold, I am with thee, and will keep thee in all places whither thou goest." And so, comforted, he slumbered peacefully until the sun was high in the heavens....

He was discovered by some wanderers in these unfrequented parts, who gave him food and drink, and asked no questions. Gratefully he received their ministrations and, much refreshed, he went his way. The darkness had fled from his soul as well as from the sky above, but it had left its traces in a dignity that was almost a melancholy which appeared in his features.

The feet of Jesus led him back irresistibly to the river, to Bethabara where John was baptizing. It may have been curiosity that made him determine to revisit the scene, but it is more probable that he felt that there, where the great moment of his life had come, the next step would be made known to him.

It was evening when Jesus arrived at the Jordan, and few were left of the crowds that had stood there throughout the day. Jesus made no attempt to speak to John, and John when he noticed him made no move to approach him. Both felt a certain diffidence. But looking on the man of mystery as he walked with that strange sad air, the Baptist was heard by his nearest disciples to mutter, "Behold the Lamb of God: he is bearing away the sin of the world." And so it befell the next day.

This time two of John's followers detached themselves from their master and shadowed the pacing figure. Jesus turned, and saw them following, and inquired, "What seek ye?" They said to him, "Rabbi, where lodgest thou?" He answered mildly, "Come and see."

Without another word he continued his way, and the two respectfully fell in behind him. None of the trio could trust himself to speak. Each heart was throbbing painfully with an intensity of expectation. Their forms, in the waning light, cast long shadows upon the ground, shadows that moulded themselves to the rocks and entangled themselves in the scrub, intensifying the mystery of this slow march towards the unknown. The man in front moved forward with deliberate steps, seemingly heedless of his silent escort, yet all the time his brain was busy with questions. Were these to be the first of his following? The two who came after were no less occupied with wondering conjecture. Who was the nameless one who went before them, his hair and dress gilded with the dying glory of the sun?

They reached the temporary tent where Jesus had found a lodging, and stayed with him that night. What things were spoken there by the fitful gleam of the oil lamp, we do not know. But this we do know, that Jesus triumphed and conquered. His audience was receptive, willing and eager to be convinced. A bond of communion already subsisted between them. Doubtless he began guardedly, feeling his way cautiously into their minds. And what he found encouraged him to continue. He talked more freely, fervently, pouring out his soul, giving to these strangers the confidence which he had withheld in all the years from his family and friends. What a relief it was to be able at last to let himself go, to bare the secrets of his bosom. There was magic in his voice: he was exalted, radiant. The words cascaded from his lips in a glittering torrent, while the puny flame of the lamp rose and fell uncertainly as the oil was exhausted, binding the spell tighter. Andrew and the nameless other sat on entranced. The hours slipped swiftly away, and no one heeded their going. A new day dawned....

Two men stumbled out of the tent, shielded their eyes a while from the sudden glare, and then departed swiftly, like messengers whose fateful tidings must be quickly told. They sought out Simon, the brother of Andrew, and gasped out, "We have found the Messiah!" "Where?" came the startled question. "Come and see!

Jesus, a happier Jesus, flushed with his initial success, awaited the return of his disciples. They brought a doubting and hoping Simon with them. Jesus gazed for the first time upon the rugged weather-beaten features of the fisherman whose simplicity of faith and unswerving loyalty would prove to be such a solid comfort in the months that lay ahead. With a keen insight into character, and an instinctive premonition, he addressed him: "Thou art Simon bar Jonah: thou shalt be called Kepha (Rock)." And with those few words he won him for ever.

The day following Jesus would return to Galilee; but first he would see another of the Galilean fishermen, of whom they told him, Philip of Bethsaida. He also was persuaded by the word of Jesus and the burning conviction of his own friends. Philip went in quest of Nathanael, and declared, "We have found him of whom Moses in the Law, and the Prophets, did write, Jesus of Nazareth the son of Joseph." "Nazareth!" retorted Nathanael incredulously. "Can good come out of Nazareth?" Again the all-sufficient formula was used. "Come and see!"

Nathanael was a different proposition from Simon, a man equally simple and honest at heart, but who loved to pose as a canny and cautious person. Jesus had him unmasked in a moment when he greeted him obliquely: "Behold a genuine son of Israel, in whom is no guile." Nathanael could not restrain his astonishment. "Whence knowest thou me?" Jesus was in high good humour: "Before that Philip called thee, when thou wast under the fig tree, I saw thee." Those keen powers of observation, which only yesterday had caught the son of Tolmai unawares at his private devotions, now played their part. Nathanael burst forth, "Rabbi, thou art the Son of God; thou art the King of Israel." Amused at the man's involuntary disclosure of his real self, but none the less pleased with his avowal, Jesus said banteringly, "Because I said unto thee, I saw thee under the fig tree, believest thou? Thou shalt see greater tilings than these."

On the instant, however, he grew serious. The strange unearthly look came into his eyes, which his disciples would learn to know so well but could never fathom, and he spoke in that oracular fashion which aroused their awe while it passed their comprehension. "Truly, truly, I say unto you all, hereafter ye shall see heaven open, and the angels of God ascending and descending upon the Son of Man."

It was those occasions, when Jesus was rapt away to mystical heights which they were not equipped to scale, which continually reinforced their faith in him. They marked him out as a man apart, even when he was engaged in some normal occupation, or mixing on terms of equality with his fellows. No less did they condemn him to a keenly felt loneliness, which sometimes found utterance in speech, and which only his own faith made endurable. The solace of true intimacy on earth was ever to be denied him, longingly as his human need sought it in the innermost circle of his friends. The path to the Kingdom was so narrow that but one at a time might tread it, and he must lead the way, while beside yawned the horrid abyss of Abaddon.

Mercifully the lights and the shadows of the future were to-day but dimly perceived. There was much over which to rejoice, and for which to praise the Heavenly Father. The work had begun, and the road back to Galilee was full of promise. Where one man had come uncertainly from Nazareth to Jordan, five or perhaps six were now returning, and the face of one of them was like the Son of God.

CHAPTER VII

The Year of Conciliation

A Rumour had preceded Jesus into Galilee, tidings of strange events, of which no man knew the truth, which had happened at the Jordan where John was baptizing. Men and women, who had cast their sins into the swift flowing river, had come back to their homes in the hills and along the shores of the lake in a state of religious fervour and excitement. It was they who originated the reports which circulated rapidly among the towns and villages. A great Prophet has arisen in Galilee. John himself has testified to him. The Prophet came to the Jordan, and no sooner had his feet touched the water than a fire was kindled,[24] and the heavens were rent by a thunderclap. Who was the Prophet? No one knew; but he was a Galilean, one of their own. Repent! Repent! for the reign of God is at hand!

There was a strong predisposition to credit such news, which would not yield to any considerations of reason. Those who had ambition to profit by the pitiful credulity of the masses found no difficulty in doing so in those days. But there was no real need to promise miracles, still less to perform them; for if once an outstanding personality had gained the ear of the people the miracles made and multiplied themselves in minds that would not be deprived of such outward and evident tokens of God's intervention in their sorry lives. And sometimes the miracles actually took place, worked in part by the confident words and spiritual strength of the Master, whoever he was, but far more by the eager and responsive faith of the disciple.

Hard on the heels of the rumour came Jesus himself, returning to his native city: "and there went out a fame of him through all the region round about. And he taught in their synagogues, being glorified of all."

It is a curious ground for rejecting the claims of Jesus that his miracles are found to be incredible. For if ever man refused to follow the way of the wonder-worker, he is that man. In the

fevered night which followed his baptism he had set his face steadfastly against the immorality of tempting God by demanding demonstrations of the Divine power in his favour. When sign-seekers came to him, he groaned deeply in his spirit, and said, "Why doth this generation seek after a sign? Truly I say unto you, there shall no sign be given unto this generation." And he left them. Again, when a certain nobleman besought him to heal his sick son, Jesus protested to him, "Except ye see signs and wonders, ye will not believe."

It was Jesus's misfortune that at that day and time there was no escape from the embarrassing reputation of a miracle-man. So far he could be true to his principles, to avoid any direct appeal to God for His interposition, even in his own direst extremity. When, in his last hours, the officers came to arrest him, and Peter would do battle on his behalf, Jesus rebuked him with the question, "Thinkest thou that I cannot now pray to my Father, and He shall presently give me more than twelve legions of angels?" But the prayer was never spoken. Only to the extent that his tender heart found it difficult to resist the clamour of the sufferers who thronged about him for healing did Jesus allow his compassion to overcome his repugnance for anything savouring of the miraculous, and he gave of his own mental and spiritual powers to his utter exhaustion to aid the faith of his petitioners. Whenever possible he urged those who were relieved to tell no one; but his plea was useless, for invariably the joyful individual published the matter abroad. These genuine deeds of mercy, or "works"—for Jesus would give them no higher name—were magnified out of all proportion, as it was, and lent colour to the much more fantastic performances with which he was credited. Jesus adduced the witness of his works only when every other argument had failed to impress. The words were absolutely wrung from his lips. "If I do not the works of my Father, believe me not. But if I do, though ye believe not me, believe the works."

Jesus had yielded to the solicitations of his new friends to accompany them to Bethsaida, their home town, and to speak in the synagogue; but he was anxious to reach Nazareth, and he had promised to attend on the way a wedding at Cana of Galilee. The bridegroom was a connection of his mother's family, and she herself was there thoroughly enjoying the break in the monotony of her

existence and revelling in the opportunity to exert herself in the supervision of the elaborate preparations.

Whether through inadequate provision, or the presence
of an unexpectedly large gathering which strained the resources, the supply of wine ran short. The circumstance
was deeply distressing. Mary sought out her son, and informed him vexedly, "They have no wine." What she expected him to do about it is by no means clear; but her
tone indicated a request rather than a statement of fact.

Jesus, being very sensitive of his position, had kept as
much as possible in the background. He was therefore
far from welcoming an appeal which he understood as
implying that he had power to make good the deficit by
some surprising performance. This was not the Messianic banquet, when he, the Bridegroom of Zion, would
be expected to furnish wine for all the righteous. "What
concern is this of ours?" he protested. "My hour is not
yet come." Nevertheless, being his mother, Mary advised
the servants, "Whatsoever he saith unto you, do it."

Presently there was borne to the ruler of the feast an un-
limited quantity of fresh liquor. He tasted it. It was excellent. Jocularly he hailed the bridegroom: "Every man
at the beginning doth set forth good wine; and when
men have well drunk, then that which is worse: thou hast
kept the good wine until now."

According to the only account of the incident the wine
had come from six clay amphorae containing water for

ablutionary purposes, and Jesus had instructed the servants to obtain it from this source. Authentic as is the setting of the story, legend has obviously been at work desiring to enhance the reputation of the Master. The legend may well have been contemporary, for the disciples had as yet come little under their leader's personal influence, and they were at all times superstitiously credulous. Neither, quite literally, was the occasion one for sober thinking.

From Jesus's point of view it would have been a most damaging tale that he had turned water into wine. If it had actually been spread abroad, and he had heard it, it may have decided him to dismiss his enthusiastic followers to their homes until he should require them again. His progress had already been marked far too frequently by the kind of demonstrations he was most anxious to avoid. He had moved in a blaze of publicity inspired in large measure by his ardent attendants. His soul revolted at the prospect of appearing in Nazareth, where he was so well known, in the guise of a thaumaturgist. He shrank from the jeers and the laughter which must greet the carpenter turned wonder-worker. He wanted to win his own people by the simple power of his message.

Besides all this his homecoming would reveal to him his future course of action. He had formulated no plans: he had no fixed programme. He recognized that he would find everything the same, and yet not the same. He had no foolish impulse to play the great man before his fellow townsfolk. He hoped profoundly that they had not been influenced against him by the wild reports that had been disseminated. For every reason, therefore, he desired to return as naturally and unobtrusively as the situation would permit.

The crucial test would take place on the impending Sabbath. At Cana he had been invited by the minister of the Nazareth synagogue to read the portion from the Prophets and to give the address. When his name was called he walked quietly to the dais, and received the scroll of the Prophet Isaiah. Among the crowded congregation heads were craned forward: there was a rustling and a shuffling and a subdued coughing. Jesus turned to the passage which we know as the sixty-first chapter of Isaiah, and began to read.

When he had finished he raised his head, and in a steady voice he repeated the opening words in the vernacular Aramaic. "The Spirit of the Lord is upon me, because he hath anointed me to proclaim good tidings to the poor; he hath sent me to heal the brokenhearted, to proclaim deliverance to the captives, and recovering of sight to the blind, to set at liberty them that are bruised, to proclaim the Lord's Year of Conciliation."

And he rolled up the scroll, and gave it again to the minister, and sat down. And the eyes of all them that were in the synagogue were fastened on him.

"This day is this scripture fulfilled in your ears." Coming directly in ringing tones, without preamble, the startling assertion electrified the audience, and all wondered at the gracious words which proceeded out of his mouth. It was the Sabbatic Year, the Lord's Year of Conciliation, when there was neither planting nor sowing, when slaves were freed, and debts were forgiven. Was the speaker also giving them to understand that this was the Year of Redemption, the Messianic year? And was he inferring that he had been chosen of God as the bearer of these tidings?

Among the well-to-do members of the synagogue neighbours nudged one another. "Is not this Joseph's son, the carpenter? Is not his mother called Mary, and his brethren, James and Joses and Simon and Judas? And his sisters, are they not all with us? Whence then hath this fellow all these things?" What audacity! They had heard tales, of course, impossible tales told by stupid people whom he had impressed. But he need not think that he could try that sort of thing here where they knew all about him. Why, it was almost blasphemous! How ever had the minister been so weak as to ask him to speak? There would be a meeting, and the clerk of the congregation would be severely censured.

So what he feared had indeed happened. Jesus could not fail to mark the sneers and the grimaces of annoyance of the rulers of the synagogue as they sat before him in the chief seats. His mind readily grasped the purport of the lifted eyebrows, the whispering and the muttering, and he was filled with indignation. In a moment the animated features hardened and set, and the mild eyes glittered dangerously. He bent his gaze full on the cav-illers, and spoke with a cold emphasis that was not without sarcasm.

"Ye will surely say unto me this proverb, 'Physician, heal thyself.' Whatsoever we have heard done in Kefar-Naum, do also here in thine own country. Truly I say unto you, no prophet is accepted in his own country. But I tell you of a truth, many widows were in Israel in the days of Elijah, when the heaven was shut up three years and six months, when great famine was throughout the land: but unto none of them was Elijah sent, save unto Sarepta, a city of Sidon, unto a woman that was a *heathen*. And many lepers were in Israel in the time of Elisha the prophet; and none of them was cleansed, saving Naaman the *Syrian*."

The expressions changed, as he delivered himself of these biting words, from mockery to surprise, and from surprise to rage, a rage that was shared by those seated behind, who had no suspicion of the provocation that had called forth the outburst. All that the excited villagers were aware of was the magnitude of the insult which held up heathen and Syrians as worthier than themselves. In a moment there was uproar, and a fanatical and hostile mob was surging towards the dais. Young hotheads threw up their hands and yelled anathemas, which might endure reporting as "Traitor!" "Go back to Rome!" "Who's paying you?" if this had been the twenti-eth century.

The anger of Jesus had evaporated as quickly as he had uttered his thoughtless speech. He was wretched and miserable at his lack of self-control. Now he had lost, perhaps for ever, the prospect of winning the people of Nazareth.

Depressed at his own failure, Jesus suffered himself to be hustled and jostled out of the synagogue, and out of the town, without protest. The conscience that convicted him of readiness to take offence made him heedless of the threats and the clamour going on about him. Only when they reached the brow of the hill above the clustering houses did he awaken fully to the intention of those who were hounding him out of his home. They were bent on his "accidental" death. In a few moments he would fall, through no one's individual act, over the edge of the cliff, to be dashed in pieces. He would not say that he did not deserve such an end. But the affair had gone far enough: he would not have them guilty of his blood. He roused himself by an effort, and turned on those nearest to him, men whom he had known since they were children together, a look of such penetrating pathos that shamefacedly they drew away and let him go.

For a while contemptuous voices followed him as he stumbled along the road; but he neither responded nor once looked back.

The sense of loss at first was so great, mingled as it was with the misery of humiliation and self-accusation, that for a time he could do no more than revolve the facts ceaselessly, dwelling on every detail of the past hour, conjuring up the faces one by one as out of a nightmare memory, examining the emotions limned on every visage, while his waking brain weighed and assessed the minds behind the faces. He heard himself again speaking, the confident fresh voice: he regarded his bearing, the nature of his message, and he. measured the man he claimed to be against the man his townsfolk thought they knew. Had they not a right to reject him? Must he not have appeared ridiculous in their eyes, with pretensions that at present were outwardly nothing more than grotesque? Had he not been foolish, untested and unproved, to come back to Nazareth so soon, and to invite the inevitable consequence? But he had not seen that the consequence was inevitable. While disowning blatant miracles, he had himself expected a subtle miracle. He magnified the folly of his pride until it overwhelmed his sensitive soul. He cast himself upon the ground and prayed with tear- blinded eyes. His body pressed upon the scarlet anemones, bruising and crushing the tiny flowers as his own heart was bruised and crushed. How lamentable, nay criminal, had been his reckless language, grieving his own brethren! In after time he told his disciples that he is the worst of criminals that grieves the spirit of his brother.[25] His anger had been justly met by a greater anger.

Presently he grew calmer, and, as if in answer to his prayer, the words of the psalmist came to him and moved upon his lips.

"Bless the Lord, O my soul:

And all that is within me, bless his holy name.
Bless the Lord, O my soul,
And forget not all his benefits:
Who forgiveth all thine iniquities;
Who healeth all thy diseases;
Who redeemeth thy life from destruction;
Who crowneth thee with lovingkindness and tender
mercies....
The Lord is merciful and gracious,
Slow to anger, and plenteous in mercy.
He will not always chide;
Neither will he keep his anger for ever.
He hath not dealt with us after our sins;
Nor rewarded us according to our iniquities....
Like as a father pitieth his children,
So the Lord pitieth them that fear him.
For he knoweth our frame;
He remembcreth that we are dust...."

"Slow to anger, and plenteous in mercy"—that must be his watchword henceforth. It was one thing to announce "The Spirit of the Lord is upon me." It was another to exhibit the presence of that Spirit. The lesson had been valuable, and he could now thank God for it. It was better to have begun by making a mistake than to live in a fool's paradise. It was good that he had gone up to Nazareth, good to have been made so keenly aware of the dangers of arrogance. He had come near to falling into a deeper gulf than that into which his people would have cast him; and by great mercy he had been delivered.

And so, as Jesus resumed his journey, his depression lifted, and the darkness fled from his soul. The man had shown his worth by refusing to delude himself, and Nazareth became a symbol not of defeat, but of victory.

And he came down to the busy mart of Kefar-Naum, to the ancient tribal border of Zebulon and Naphtali; and because the light was in him "the people which sat in darkness saw great light," even as the Prophet Isaiah had foretold.

CHAPTER VIII

Follow Me!

The man who stood on the shores of the Sea of Galilee and gazed across its azure waters to the hard outlines of the Gaulan had undergone a subtle transformation. There was determination in his bearing, a masterfulness not previously apparent either in his voice or in his utterances. He wanted but little to be the associate of Judas of the neighbouring mountains, Judas the Zealot. Only the melancholy that mingled with the sternness of his visage and the kindness of his eyes distinguished him from the sons of violence. The experience at Nazareth, rather than cowing the eager spirit, tad removed from his composition every trace of timidity. Where before there had been hesitation to thrust himself forward before his critics, there was now complete abandonment to his calling. Essentially he was as much an outlaw as any of those desperate characters whose watchword was "No king but God!" As such he could know no fear. They only are afraid who have something to lose. He had been deprived of everything that sentiment could cherish.

He had gone up to Nazareth still with the dew of morning upon him, the youthful prophet whose lips were touched with grace, ready to receive the world in enfolding arms of love, and to be received by it. But the world, his world, had bade him with its mocking laughter become aware of realities. His love was an impertinence: his pretensions an insult to intelligence. There could be nothing but scorn for the suitor with ambitions so far above his station. The disdainful beauty of his native hills had rejected him. He had been suffered to slink forth like a cur turned away with kicks and curses. The door had closed behind him. He was Jesus of Nazareth— of Nazareth now in name only. Nazareth would have none of him, nor would he see her more until....

To-day he was Jesus of no-city, Jesus the wanderer. He bore no grudge against those who had done this thing to him. They had made him into a man. In spite of his thirty years, there had remained something very boyish about him. Now childhood, except for the sense of wonder and an odd spark of fun, was past. But the promise of home life, all that gives a man a claim to peace and happiness and rest in one spot, which makes all geography beside the stuff of dreams, even that he recognized was gone. He had been painfully, and he believed purposefully, released from every human tie, wrenched loose from his moorings, and turned adrift, the better to carry out the will of God, upon whose guiding hand he must depend alone henceforth. His life must be in his mission, and of his mission he must make a home.

Since the first intimation of his future had come to him he had known the spiritual gain of his election, and speculated mystically on its temporal triumphs. He had insufficiently contemplated what he might have to lose. The awakening had been rude, but salutary. There had

been no opportunity for family farewells, for tender part-
ings. Perhaps in the little house on the hill they were
mourning for him as for one who was dead. Alas, they
must grieve on until time assuaged their tears; for there
could be no resurrection into that life. The service of the
Kingdom was a jealous service: it demanded both soul
and body. On more than one occasion he had hard things
to say to enthusiasts who offered too readily to join him.
He would allow them to have no illusions about the
nature of their undertaking, and the hardest thing he
could say he had said already to himself.

"Sir," said one, "suffer me first to go and bury my father."
Jesus answered, "Let the dead bury their dead: but go
thou and proclaim the Kingdom of God."

And another said, "Sir, I will follow thee; but let me first
go bid them farewell, which are at home in my house."
And Jesus said to him, "No man, having put his hand to
the plough, and looking back, is fit for the Kingdom of
God."

Here spoke unforgettable experience.

Men strove with self-effacing devotion for lesser causes
and for lower ideals; how much more the servant of the
Highest? Those whom he would choose to share his enterprise would be no less consecrated and sincere. They
would be a small but faithful band, bold but not reckless,
outspoken but not argumentative, zealous but not belli-
cose, constantly waiting on God in prayer, and instantly

obedient to the impulse of His Holy Spirit. They would be a mobile force operating throughout the Land of Israel, urgently testifying to the near approach of the rule of Righteousness and Truth.

Where better could recruits be found to form this spearhead of the Kingdom than among the hardy, the pious, and loyal fishermen of Galilee? He thought of Simon the Rock, of Andrew his brother, of Philip and Bartholomew. These men had recognized him as Messiah by a God-given instinct. They only needed to be trained and taught. Others would be added to them in due course. Here by the Sea of Galilee he would lay the foundations of his work, among the unsophisticated liberty-loving people, sheep without a shepherd, sufferers without a physician, toiling and struggling, and ever waiting for the day of fulfilment of the promise made to the fathers, but reserved for their needy children, the day of Redemption.

The work must be begun at once and, having been begun, God prospering it, must be pressed forward tirelessly until the glorious consummation.

For a few moments longer Jesus looked out over the lake to the land whose marred visage seemed to reflect his own as in a mirror. He stood solemn and silent. Then with quick decision he turned about, and raising his arms towards all who passed along the waterfront he cried in ringing tones, "The time is fulfilled, and the Kingdom of God is at hand!"

There were no mocking faces among the crowd that gathered quickly at the call. It was as if a trumpet had sounded, and its brazen notes had penetrated deeply into each shuddering soul, or a tempest had risen and flung itself suddenly through the gorges causing the still lake to rear in agitated waves. "Who cries?" "What is amiss?" There was surprise and almost consternation on the faces of the startled throng. Never had the lakeside echoed with such a resounding personal challenge. Even the pigeons were roused from their torpor and wheeled in dismayed flight. Was this one of the Baptists? Was John coming into Galilee?

But Jesus offered to baptize none of his audience, neither did he seek to hold them with a burning discourse. He urged them to repent, and abruptly turned to depart. But not thus would they let him go. They would know more of this preacher who had so strangely appeared in their midst. Jesus found himself heading a procession that trailed raggedly at his heels, stopping when he stopped, and again moving on. Others joined in out of curiosity, padding the basalt boulder-strewn beach towards Bethsaida. Big- eyed children tumbled about the stranger's feet, and stared up cheekily at eyes that were busy scanning the boats on the lake. They drew his gaze, brought a smile to his lips, and a hand was laid gently on a small head in blessing. The tension was broken. Everyone could smile now. There was humanity in this teacher, despite his stem warnings. Tongues were loosed, and it was a thoroughly good-humoured company that kept pace with the visitor at a respectful distance, and speculated on his errand.

At last the questing vision of Jesus found what it sought, a particular fisherman's boat standing off the shore. The oarsmen were at rest, following closely the operations of the man who was skilfully casting a hand-net on the far side, while another beside him peered fixedly into the water watching for the shoals of fish. All the occupants were so intent on their business that they did not notice the approaching crowd, until a voice hailed them, "Peace be with you, sons of Jonas!" The voice awakened swift memory. He that observed started up, and he that cast his net drew it in swiftly. Both turned towards the shore, and Simon cried to his brother Andrew, "It is the Master!" Again the voice of Jesus rang out across the still water, "Follow me, and I will make you fishers of men!" The people around laughed gleefully at the joke.

At once the boat was put in. Hardly waiting for it to ground, the two brothers raised their skirts and were over the side wading to the land. Jesus welcomed them warmly. It cheered his heart to find them so ready. This was how he had hoped it would be. The neglected crowd thinned and dispersed. Evidently, for the present, the show was over.

Although Simon and Andrew had responded with alacrity to the call of Jesus, and were eager to follow him without hesitation or reserve, they could not fail to speculate on what might be their leader's immediate objective. Indeed, they had already given much thought to the matter. To them it seemed obvious that the first essential was to create a small band of trusted lieutenants, at once a council and a bodyguard, and then to rouse the countryside. They were too much in awe of Jesus the Messiah, though not of Jesus the man, to put their views directly to him; but with a deferential boldness Simon managed to convey—he hoped that he would be forgiven—that he had disclosed the joyful news—in strict secrecy, of course —to his partners in the fishery James and John, the sons of Zebedee, men, he would take his oath, as zealous and loyal as himself. Would not the Master invite them to join him? Jesus smilingly agreed. It was a novelty to have the aid and initiative of friends, to release for a moment his grasp of the tiller, and to enjoy the sweets of delegated responsibility. Relieved and gratified, Simon indicated that his colleagues were in their ship nearby.

James and John were mending their nets when Jesus called them, and immediately they left their father Zebedee in the ship with the hired servants, and came ashore. The new recruits, Jesus perceived, were powerful men, honest and dependable, but with the pugnacity so frequent in seamen. He nicknamed them later Boaneragsha, the sons of riot.

The messianic force, when joined shortly after by Philip and Bartholomew, if by no means imposing, was at least formidable enough to preserve the Master from molestation, and could give a good account of itself even against greatly superior numbers. While Jesus had no intention of engaging in a fray, and felt the sufficiency of the Divine protection, he could not fail to derive a certain comfort from the proximity of his henchmen.

On the next Sabbath they attended the synagogue at Kefar- Naum, and Jesus addressed the worshippers. Once again there was a disturbance; but not this time as in the synagogue at Nazareth. One of the congregation, excited by the burning words of the speaker, was seized with a frenzy, and suddenly screamed out, "Ay-o! What have we to do with thee, Jesus of Nazareth? Art thou come to destroy us? I know thee who thou art, the Holy One of God!"

There was sensation, and some rushed to restrain the man. But Jesus was master of the situation, and in a penetrating voice that echoed from the pillars of the building he cried, "Silence! Come out of him!" There came an answering cry, followed by a convulsive struggle, the muscles of the poor creature gradually relaxed, and in a few moments the fit was over, and the dazed epileptic was able to be helped out by his friends.

The cause of the commotion, anxious to avoid any exaggeration of the circumstances, left the synagogue immediately. Nevertheless an excited babble broke out behind him. "What is this?" "New teaching, and with authority!" "He commands the foul spirits, and they obey him!" Amazement was written on every face, and the news travelled swiftly as it was repeated from mouth to mouth.

The incident had a powerful and unlooked-for effect in bringing the people flocking about Jesus. What a God-sent opportunity was here in the presence of this wonderworking rabbi to secure the well-being of suffering

loved ones! Quick minds leapt to the practical possibilities which must be exploited at all cost. Filled with the
impatience of a new-found hope family on family could
scarce wait for the hours of Sabbath rest to run their
course. If Jesus the son of Nun had once prayed that the
sun might stand still in the heavens, how much more did
these who sought Jesus the son of Joseph pray that the
great luminary would hasten his descent. No sooner, indeed, had the first star put forth its faint and flickering
light in the darkening firmament than from all quarters
they gathered, old and young, carrying the sick, aiding
the steps of the feeble, thronging in an agony of eager
anticipation to the already marked door of Simon's
house. The only question was, would they be in time?
Would the rabbi have already conveyed himself away?

Jesus was still there, surrounded by his disciples, whose
awe of him was intensified. But blending strangely with
their reverence was an element of showmanship. They
had accompanied him from the synagogue wondering
and triumphant, basking in the reflected glory, savouring
to the full the sense of their special relationship to the
Master, and exhibiting an incipient tendency to propriet-
orship. Already they were beginning to look upon his
evident powers as a joint stock-in-trade, and to assume
that they had a managerial right to permit or forbid access to him. This tendency, as it developed, was only defeated by the sturdy independence of Jesus himself. He
discovered that he dared not indulge in the pleasure of
yielding up his authority, even temporarily. He had to
make it clear that he would not be managed, or controlled, either in his movements or in his contacts, and

he demanded implicit obedience, while he retained his full freedom of action. "Ye call me Master and Lord," he told his wayward disciples, "and ye say well; for so I am." Almost to the end he insisted on this basis of their association, and when finally at the near prospect of death he exchanged the term "servants" for the more intimate one of "friends" he still reminded them: "Ye have not chosen me, but I have chosen you." At the same time he gave to lordship a new interpretation: for him it meant not despotism, but devotion. The messianic rule was not as that of Caesar and the kings of the earth. Service was the true test of sovereignty. "The kings of the Gentiles exercise lordship over them; and they that exercise authority upon them are called Benefactors. But ye shall not be so: but he that is greatest among you, let him be as the younger; and he that is chief, as he that doth serve. For whether is greater, he that sitteth at meat, or he that serveth? Is not he that sitteth at meat? But I am among you as he that doth serve."

In the inner room of Simon's house his mother-in-law lay sick of a fever. To her was brought the tidings that the Master could make her well, and she believed. Presently they told Jesus of her, and he came and took the hot hand stretched out to him in his own cool one. And immediately the fever left her, and she was able to get up and minister to them.

"And at even, when the sun did set, they brought unto him all that were diseased, and them that were possessed with devils. And all the city was gathered together at the door. And he healed many that were sick of divers diseases, and cast out many devils; and suffered not the devils to say that they knew him."

It was difficult to resist the importunity of these crowds of sufferers, so certain of their cure. Jesus was moved with deep compassion. He felt welling up within him a fountain of life that must pour itself forth in response to the pleading eyes and the eager hands. The pleas and the thanks were all about him as he stood at the door framed in the radiance of the soft lamplight. The magnification of God he could approve, the fulsome praises of himself he could discount, but mingling with them were dangerous titles, which he could not accept without rebuke. For the present he must be, like John the Baptist, no more than a Voice proclaiming the near approach of the Reign of God.

At last the narrow space before the house was clear. The last visitor had vanished into the night. The closing door sharply separated light from darkness, just as the Lord of the Universe had made a distinction between holy and profane, between the seventh day and the six working days, between Israel and the nations. *Habdalah!*

The mantle of sleep descended on the household; but for Jesus there was no rest. His brain was burning; every nerve in his body tingled. Before his inward vision the history of the hours passed in review. Again the problem faced him, presented with the pitiful intensity of human need, how to subordinate his ministrations to his message. Poor Israel, so acutely aware of physical sickness, so unconscious of the sickness of the soul! Would his people at length realize that the power that was present to heal the body was the same power that could give victory over sin? Questions pressed upon him with the same importunity as the beseeching throng, clamouring for an answer: he could not fend them off....

Long before the Gergesene plateau had become silhouetted against the rosy luminosity of the dawn, and while the lake lay in grey and glassy placidity, Jesus rose up, and passed silently out of the house. The cool air laved his heated brow, and he was soothed by the still mystery of the night. His feet ascended into the quiet hills beyond the last dwelling of man, and finding a retired spot he threw himself upon the ground and lifted up his heart in prayer. Perhaps, among the words that fell from his lips were those of the beautiful morning meditation, praising the heavenly Father that "with great love Thou hast loved us; and with great and overflowing pity hast Thou pitied us.... Enlighten our eyes in Thy Law, and let our hearts cleave unto Thy commandments, and unite our hearts to love and revere Thy Name, that we may never be put to confusion...

There he remained in repose and peace, while the sun leaped anew into the heavens and the cocks of Kefar-Naum shrilled a welcome to another day. There Simon and the rest found him after an anxious search, arriving hot and expostulating with the greeting, "All men seek for thee!"

Jesus answered them gently but firmly, "Let us go elsewhere to the neighbouring towns, that I may preach there also; for that is the purpose with which I set out."

The disciples found the initiative taken from them, and they had lost it for ever. Willingly would they have tarried, organizing an orgy of exorcism, indulging an appetite for the crude phenomena of revivalism already whetted by their recent experiences. Jesus recalled them to sense and to sanity, to the real business in hand. He would listen to no protest, and dominated by the strength of his personality they submitted. "Follow me!" he had said; and they followed him.

CHAPTER IX

The Speech on the Mount

The fame of Jesus spread far and wide, fame of the great preacher who could cure all mortal ills, fame that was thrust upon him by the enthusiastic and painfully credulous populace, fame that he neither courted nor desired. But what could he do? Struggling masses of misery overwhelmed him at every place that he visited. They caught at his garments, threw themselves at his feet. Faith and hope contended about him, cried at him, prayed to him. It seemed as if the suffering of the whole house of Israel was heaped together, gathered up, and loaded upon him. They tortured his brain, and they tore at his heart strings. The aching pity that was in him could not deny them. He laid hands upon them, and spoke words of cheer. Truly the word of Isaiah the prophet was being fulfilled, "Himself took our infirmities, and bare our sicknesses." Loud rang the hallelujahs of the relieved, speeding away with tidings that sent twelve to replace every one that departed. It became almost impossible to proclaim the message of the Kingdom of God under these conditions. Jesus was unable to go into the synagogues: he could not even enter the towns because of the press. Forced to remain in the open country, still they came to him from every quarter. The strain was terrific. Only in brief intervals at night was there any opportunity for rest, and even the hours of darkness were sometimes disturbed.

Under the cover of night, and wrapped yet more closely in his robe from prying eyes, there came a man of note, a member of the Sanhedrin, Nicodemus the Pharisee, concerned and curious. Jesus was reclining exhausted and apathetic. He made no move to greet his distinguished visitor. Nicodemus was forced to begin the conversation: his tone was flattering and conciliatory.

"Rabbi, we know that thou art come as a teacher from God: for no one can perform such signs as thou doest, unless God be with him."

"Truly," replied Jesus with Oriental obliquity, "no one can perceive the Kingdom of God at all, unless he is re-born."

Nicodemus smiled wryly. "Can a man be born when he is old?" he asked. "Can he enter a second time into his mother's womb, and be born?"

"Truly, he cannot enter into the Kingdom of God," persisted Jesus with more animation, "unless he is born both of his mother's water and of the Spirit. That which is born of the flesh is flesh; and that which is born of the Spirit is spirit. There is nothing surprising in my saying to you, ye must be reborn. The breeze bloweth where it wills, and thou hearest the sound thereof, but canst not tell whence it cometh or whither it goeth: so it is with every one that is born of the Spirit."

"How can that be?" inquired Nicodemus, puzzled.

Jesus was incredulous. "Thou art a teacher in Israel, and knowest not these things! Truly when we discuss it is about what we know, and when we testify it is to our own experiences; and that is the testimony that ye are not prepared to receive. If I have told you terrestrial things, and ye believe not, how shall ye believe if I tell you celestial things?"

He relapsed into silence. The interview was at an end. Nicodemus, disturbed and wondering, rose and took his departure. A strange and remarkable man, he thought, evidently a mystic, but certainly no fool. Probably, through ignorance of the circumstances, he had missed altogether Jesus's allusion to his own spiritual rebirth at the Jordan.

The coming of the Sanhedrist was the first intimation that the popular religious leaders had taken cognizance of the new teacher's activities. Soon the critical pack would be in full cry, and there was a premonition of the impending conflict in Jesus's use of the plural during the interview when asserting his attitude towards fundamentals. It was the hunted who issued the challenge to the hunters, and already they were distinguished, *we* (Jesus and his disciples) from *you* (the acknowledged exponents of doctrine).

The civil authorities had made no move as yet. The very character of the crowds who attended Jesus, the ailing and infirm, was sufficient to discount the suspicion that his actions constituted in any way a menace to the State. No insurrection was to be feared from an unarmed mob of cripples and paralytics. To this extent, the throng of sufferers arriving from all parts of the country were a blessing to the cause, affording Jesus rare but valuable opportunities to proclaim the principles of the Kingdom of God, seditious as some might construe them, before the tetrarch of Galilee or the procurator of Judea became alive to the perilous influence of his preaching.

For, however devoid Jesus was of any intention to head a revolt, he was handling highly inflammable material. A very small spark, an ill-advised word or expression carelessly dropped, would have created a blaze that only rivers of blood could have extinguished. And he knew it. These people pressing upon him were largely the victims of years of misrule, of social disintegration and economic catastrophe. Lives were embittered, hearts were filled with hatred, minds were warped and obsessed with revengeful thoughts. Some were actually demented: nearly all were highly strung. Fervent religiosity mingled with cruel taciturnity. The prevailing superstition, increased an hundredfold by the ecstasies of those who found themselves miraculously restored to health, expectant of a divinely appointed redeemer, would willingly have seized on the figure in the midst, and hailed him as King Messiah. It required the greatest self-mastery on the part of Jesus at this time, and still more later, not to make public the announcement that he was indeed the fulfilment of their longing, being in his own soul convinced that he truly was that man. Thousands would have rallied to his standard. The Zealots in his audience would have borne the news on winged feet into the mountain fastnesses, and presently the armed bands would have gathered swiftly at the joyous summons.

But Jesus had already fought his fight, alone in the wilderness. Not by might, not by force, but by God's Spirit, would his reign be established. Yet he recognized that the situation was becoming dangerous. Somehow he had to contrive to get out of the press, to take his station somewhere where he could be both seen and heard, so that he might be free to speak words of calm reason and sound sense, to give wise counsel and spiritual instruction, to set forth the standards of conduct for which he stood, and for which the nation must also stand.

Having determined to make the supreme effort to enunciate his policy, Jesus gathered his disciples about him and led them one evening up the western slopes of the saddle-backed mountain since known as the Horns of Hattin. Protected on the east by a precipitous descent into the Vale of Arbel, this vantage ground lent itself admirably for his purpose. He could have the people in front of him in full view, while an elevated level space afforded an excellent platform.

That night he spent alone on the mountain in prayer and deep thought. He fully comprehended both the significance and the responsibility of the occasion. Before him on the morrow would be assembled representatives of every part of the land of Israel, who would carry away his words and upon whose allegiance and understanding his ultimate success would depend. He was aware that in their present state of mind they were equally capable of a too violent partisanship and a no less violent repudiation. The speech which he had to deliver must be direct and outspoken, but not provocative; it must denounce abuses, but provide a remedy; it must be messianic, but not revolutionary.

When the new day dawned he was ready. Coming down to his knot of disciples he stretched out his hand towards the distant summit where the white walls of Zefat glistened in the morning sun. "Ye also are the light of the world," he said. "A city that is set on an hill cannot be hid."

Presently the multitudes came together from the neighbouring villages with those who had journeyed from distant regions because of the fame of him that had spread abroad. They found Jesus seated on his chosen eminence with his followers ranged at a short distance below him. It was evident that to-day would not be as other days, and the people halted in a dense semi-circle expectant and subdued.

They had not long to wait. Slowly and without effort Jesus launched forth into that magnificent oration which has become known as the Sermon on the Mount.

We cannot be absolutely sure of the text of the speech, for one form of it has been expanded to an inordinate length by the combination with it of things spoken at other times. But this in itself is a recognition of the importance of the basic discourse. It is possible, however, by comparing the traditional records and excluding passages that are found in more appropriate contexts, to arrive at a fairly reliable version of its contents and phraseology.

"Ashre!" Jesus began, using the time-honoured formula of benediction. "Happy are ye!"

"Happy are ye poor! for yours is the Kingdom of Heaven.
Happy are ye that hunger now! for ye shall be filled.
Happy are ye that weep now! for ye shall laugh.
Happy are ye, when men shall revile you, and persecute you, and shall say all manner of evil against you falsely!
Rejoice and be glad for great is your reward in heaven: for so did their fathers unto the prophets.

"But woe unto you that are rich! for ye have received your consolation.
Woe unto you that are full now! for ye shall hunger.
Woe unto you that laugh now! for ye shall mourn and weep.
Woe unto you, when all men shall speak well of you! for so did their fathers of the false prophets."

At once Jesus had attracted and attached the interest of his audience, the poor, the hungry, the mourning, and the despised. He called them blissful, not in their present wretched state, but because a period is to be put to their unhappiness. The Redemption is at hand.

How the pulse of the crowd must have quickened at the gracious words! How the people must have pressed closer, spellbound, to hear what would follow the propitious opening! This much they would gather, that the Messiah was coming to lift the iron heel of Rome and her minions from off their necks, and to punish the sinners in high places. They would also understand that there would be persecution before the ultimate triumph: the tale of bricks would be more difficult to deliver before the second Moses could save his people. Can it be doubted that the first sentences of the speech are messianic? They reflect the comfortable visions of the ancient prophets and of their successors the apocalyptists. Each expression was a drop of balm on the wounded soul of Israel.

In the catalogue of woes, the rich and well fed would almost certainly be understood to represent the Herodian princes and their court, the priestly aristocracy, and the wealthy landowners - breakers of God's yoke. Upon such the Divine wrath would be poured out at the inauguration of the Messiah's reign. The closing chapters of the nearly contemporary Book of Enoch are full of similar fulminations against the mammon-serving transgressors.[26]

Jesus was careful to name neither party nor person; but, even so, he was crying from the house tops—or more exactly the mountain top—what the people out of fear of the consequences had been accustomed to whisper in private. He spoke boldly, scorning the pseudonymity of the reformers among the scribes and Pharisees, who concealed their identity beneath the names of Israel's ancient worthies.

The story is told that Herod slew the Pharisee members of the Sanhedrin, except only Baba ben Buta whom he blinded, because they refused to acknowledge him as king on account of his Edomite origin. One day Herod, unannounced, sidled up to the blind rabbi, and remarked feelingly, "What fearful crimes are being perpetrated by that base-born slave!" "How can I help it?" said the rabbi. "Why dost thou not curse him?" asked Herod. "It is written, 'Curse not the king; no, not even in thought,'" came the answer. "But he is not a king," protested Herod. "Ah!" replied the son of Buta, "Even if he were only a rich man, it is said, 'And curse not the rich in thy bed-chamber.' Or even if he were simply a ruler, it is also said, 'Curse not the ruler of thy people.'" "Surely," suggested Herod, "that means only if he does the work of thy people." Thus pressed, the rabbi admitted, "I am afraid of him." "There is no one here to inform against you," Herod insinuated. But the rabbi was not to be drawn. "It is written," he said, "'For a bird of the air shall carry the voice, and that which hath wings shall tell the matter.'" The king was astonished at his circumspection, and making himself known, he said, "If I had been aware that the rabbis were so cautious, I would not have put them to death."[27]

By comparison, Jesus had thrown caution to the winds. Yet there was nothing in his words that could be used against him. He now continued:

> "Think not that I am come to annul the Law or the Prophets: I am not come to annul, but to fulfil. Truly, I say unto you, till heaven and earth shall pass away, one *yod* or one flourish shall in no wise pass away from the Law, till all be fulfilled. And whosoever shall annul one of the least of these commandments, and shall teach men so, shall be called least in the Kingdom of Heaven. And I say unto you, unless your righteousness shall exceed the righteousness of the Pharisees and scribes, ye shall not enter into the Kingdom of Heaven."

Such a declaration was in the nature of the oath taken by a sovereign that he will uphold the laws of the realm. At this very time in the popular expositions of the prophetic writings Isaiah ix. 6-7 had been applied messianically, and the phrase "the government shall be upon his shoulder" had been rendered "he has taken the Law upon himself to keep it."[28]

In order to understand why such a statement about the Law was necessary on the part of Jesus—why he had to put it in the very forefront of his address—it must be emphasized that he was speaking mainly to the Commons of the nation. Since the heroic days of the Maccabees the Law had become the people's possession. They had died for it. They had realized in opposing the forces of Syrohellenism how vital it was to their national existence. The Law was no longer solely in the hands of the scribes and pious priests; Seleucid tyranny and the multiplication of synagogues throughout the land had put an end to that. The peasantry were largely with the Pharisees "parted" from the ungodliness of the ruling classes. The Law to them was the light "yoke of God's sovereignty." They were ready at all times, as had been shown in the incident of Pilate and the standards, to risk their lives for the integrity of their faith and customs. For a Jewish leader of those days to have the support of the masses, loyalty to the Law was the first essential.

Jesus was striking a responsive chord in the hearts of his hearers in appealing for a more spiritual, single-minded devotion to the Law, without which entrance into the Kingdom of God was impossible.

He proceeded further to explain his views by reference to the three commandments which the religious leaders in the stress of the times had laid down as finally obligatory. These concerned Murder, Adultery and Oaths, although Oaths is broadened to Idolatry. They stated: "Any sin denounced by the Law may be committed by a man if his life is threatened except the sins of idolatry, adultery and murder."[29]

> "Ye have heard what was said to the ancients, Thou shalt not murder; and whoso committeth murder shall be condemned to the judgment. But I say unto you, that whosoever shall be enraged against his brother shall be condemned to the judgment. And whosoever saith unto his brother *Raca!* (good-for-nothing) shall be condemned to the council of the synagogue. And whosoever saith unto him *Moreh!* (rebel) shall be condemned to the fire of Gehenna....
>
> "Ye have heard that it was said to the ancients, Thou shalt not commit adultery. But I say unto you, that whosoever seeth a woman and lusteth for her hath already committed adultery with her in his heart....
>
> "Again, ye have heard that it was said to the ancients, Thou shalt not forswear thyself, but shalt pay unto the Lord thy vow. But I say unto you, ye shall not swear by a confirming word; neither by heaven, for it is God's throne; nor by the earth, for it is the footstool of His feet; neither by Jerusalem, for it is the city of the great king. Neither shalt thou swear by thy head, in that thou hast no power to whiten one hair or to turn it black again...

The crime of murder was very prevalent in Palestine. Apart from the Zealot raiders, there were numerous bands of brigands and individual highwaymen, who took advantage of the disturbed state of the country to indulge in orgies of robbery with violence. In these circumstances the Supreme Court easily submitted, if it did not actually petition, to be deprived of its power to pass a death sentence. The Court moved its place of session from the sacred precincts of the Temple to a place just outside, and it is an ancient suggestion that this removal was to avoid profaning the Sanctuary by condoning bloodguiltiness arising from the increase of murderers. Life was held very cheaply, human relationships were strained to breaking point—the natural outcome of nervous tension due to the distressful state of public affairs. Jesus, like many of his thoughtful contemporaries, saw that the utterance of an angry or slanderous word was often followed by tragedy. The betrayal of a murderous spirit was tantamount to the actual commission of the capital crime. The Court might abandon its place in the Temple, but God's House was still being profaned by men who went there to offer their gifts while harbouring thoughts of evil against their brethren.

Jesus turned from anger to the subject of impurity. The moral situation was heartbreaking. Territorial barriers had failed to stem the rising tide of corruption which was already engulfing the heathen world. The lewd speech and practices of the citizens of Jerusalem had become proverbial. It was only a few years later that Rabbi Jochanan ben Zaccai ordered the cessation of the ordeal by bitter waters (Numbers v. 11-31), basing his action on Hosea iv. 14, "I will not punish your daughters when they commit whoredom, nor your spouses when they commit adultery." Contemporary writers spare neither priests nor people in their outspoken denunciations of national depravity. That generation was like the generation of the Flood and like the inhabitants of Sodom and Gomorrah. A righteous God would mete out a similar judgment. The chief priests are depicted as "joining themselves with harlots, puffed up because of their priesthood, lifting themselves up against the commandments of God and men, contemning the holy things with jests and laughter."[30] The monied classes are described as "committing adultery with their neighbours' wives, treading God's Sanctuary in all their pollutions, leaving no sin which they did not commit, even worse than the Gentiles."[31] Making every allowance for puritanical and political exaggeration it is still evident that sexual morality was at a low ebb.

Jesus again went to the root of the matter. It was the defiling and lustful spirit which had to be cast out before an entrance could be effected into the Kingdom of God.

Last of the three cardinal sins, Jesus dealt with swearing, a fruitful cause of idolatry. With heathendom at the very gates it had become increasingly necessary to preserve the Name of God from profanation. The people, constantly hearing their Gentile neighbours swearing by their divinities, might easily be led to use the Name of God as lightly. Jesus the son of Sirach had already issued a warning:

> "Accustom not thy mouth to an oath;
> And be not accustomed to the naming of the Holy One.
> For as a servant that is continually scourged shall not lack a bruise,
> So he also that sweareth and nameth God continually shall not be cleansed from sin....

> There is a manner of speech that is clothed about with death:
> Let it not be found in the heritage of Jacob."[32]

Pronunciation of the sacred Tetragrammaton was restricted to the Temple, where the priests, and at length only the high priest, might make mention of the Name with becoming reverence. Outside the Holy House the title *Adonai* (the Lord) was substituted, and then only in worship. In private intercourse even *Adonai* was forbidden, and God was to be referred to as "Heaven," "the Name," "the Place," or "Power." But even when a metonym for the Godhead was employed as an oath, the vow was binding, and its breach constituted a profanation of God's Name. This applied equally when a man vowed by anything dedicated to God such as the sacrifices on the altar, or the gold in the Temple. In deference to popular weakness the religious leaders allowed oaths to which no guilt of profanation attached. Among these they mention "By Jerusalem!" "By the Temple!" "By the life of my head!" Some held that there was no guilt in swearing by heaven or earth.

Jesus, and many with him, felt that this was mere subterfuge. "Whether is greater," he asked, "the gold, or the Temple that sanctifieth the gold? Whether is greater, the offering, or the altar that sanctifieth the offering?" For all sincere persons, simple asservations such as "yes" or "no" have the force of an oath.[33]

The perils of laxity in swearing made it necessary to forbid a Jew to enter into partnership with a heathen, lest

the latter should impose an oath on him, and he be obliged to swear by the pagan's idol; for the Law says:
"Make no mention of the name of other gods, neither let
it be heard out of thy mouth." Jesus condemned swearing, therefore, not only on the ground of its impropriety,
but because it was indirectly countenancing idolatry, and
consequently incompatible with a living faith in the sovereignty of God.[34]

CHAPTER X

As One Having Authority

From enunciating the principles of righteousness which must govern the people if they were to be found worthy to be redeemed, Jesus went on to dissuade them from attempting to anticipate that Redemption by any ill-advised act of retaliation. He had reached the most difficult part of his speech; but he did not falter. Clearly the words were heard:

"Ye have heard what was said, An eye for an eye, a tooth for a tooth. But I say unto you, that ye withstand not evil: but if one would smite thee on the right cheek, turn unto him the other also. And him that taketh from thee thy coat, let him have thy cloak also. And him that impresseth thee for one mile, go with him even twain. And whoso asketh of thee give to him, and of him that taketh away thy goods ask them not again.

"Ye have heard that it was said, Thou shalt love thy neighbour, and hate thine enemy. But I say unto you, love your enemies, do good to them that hate you, and pray for them that persecute you and despitefully use you; that ye may become the children of your Father which is in heaven, who maketh his sun to rise on the good and on the evil, and sendeth rain on the righteous and on the wicked. For if ye love only them which love you, what reward have ye? Do not even transgressors do this? And if ye ask after the peace of your brethren only, what do ye exceed? Do not even the Gentiles likewise? Be ye therefore perfect, like your Father which is in heaven, who is perfect."

The implication of these far-reaching statements has been the subject of the keenest controversy. Was Jesus advocating passive resistance to any kind of ill-usage? Did he favour neutrality in the presence of brutality? A common interpretation would make Messianism synonymous with cowardice. It is needful to emphasize that he had in view the conditions which affected the bulk of his immediate audience. They understood him clearly. When he spoke of enemies they knew that he meant national enemies, those who were neither relatives, friends, nor fellow Jews. There might have been some doubt as to who was intended if the term had been "neighbour"; but "enemy" unquestionably stood for Rome and her Syro-Greek allies. Caesarea, the Roman procurator's headquarters, was opposed to Jerusalem, the city of the great king. "If any one should tell thee that both cities are destroyed, believe him not: if he say both are peopled, again believe him not. If he say, Caesarea is destroyed and Jerusalem is peopled, or Jerusalem is destroyed and Caesarea is peopled, then believe him."[35] So ran the Jewish proverb.

Jesus declared himself in opposition to the methods of the Zealots, who would take the Kingdom of Heaven by violence. He realized that all attempts to hasten the Redemption must inevitably fail, and through their failure they would only increase the misery of the people. He believed that God would directly intervene when the time was ripe. His own policy of non-violence was governed by and had special relation to that conviction. It was his own class, the peasantry, which suffered most, and which consequently was most disposed to retaliate. Many of them had already taken to the mountains and were waging a guerrilla warfare on their enemies. They had lost everything and were utterly reckless and desperate.

It was a hard thing to advocate, this policy of No Reprisals. The wretched people were at the mercy of the legionaries, many of them mercenaries—Syro-Greeks—whose hatred of the Jews was traditional, and who terrorized the populace and subjected them to every petty annoyance which they could devise. Jesus mentions specifically several of these acts of terrorism, and when his allusions are understood, it will be appreciated that it would indeed be "perfection" in any people to remain quiescent under such provocation.

Imagine the plight of the Jewish peasant as pictured by Jesus! At any time rude legionaries may burst into his hovel to plunder his few possessions, brutally striking him if he resist. If he has nothing else worth taking they will strip him of his one coat, leaving him only his outer robe to cover his nakedness. As he proceeds along the road with his donkey he may fall in with a company of Roman soldiers, and be compelled to carry their baggage for miles in the opposite direction to which he is going. The very word for this forced service passed into the language, hebraised from the Greek, so that the *angaria* (impressment) was spoken of with sullen hatred. Requests for money, and borrowing with no intention to repay, was another of the afflictions which the poor peasant had to endure: his little savings must all go to satisfy the rapacity of the avaricious mercenaries.

It is noteworthy that Jewish tradition attributes the destruction of Jerusalem to just such acts of retaliation as Jesus would fain prevent. It is said that the inhabitants of a certain place had a custom to carry a cock and a hen before a bridal procession as symbols of procreation and fecundity. One day some Roman soldiers took away the cock and the hen and, being assaulted by the outraged members of the party, accused the Jews of rebellion against Caesar, with the result that troops were sent to quell the supposed rising. There was a custom in another place to plant a cedar-tree at the birth of a boy, and a pine-tree at the birth of a girl. When a marriage took place the memorial trees of the bride and bridegroom were felled, and the wood used to construct their wedding canopy. One day the daughter of a Roman official (the original says the Emperor) was travelling that way when the axle- tree of her carriage broke. Her attendants went and cut down what unfortunately happened to be one of these memorial trees in order to repair the damage. The Jews attacked them, and on this account were accused of rebellion and summarily dealt with.[36]

The counsel which Jesus gave arose from his deep concern for his people's welfare. He could see that reprisals would only aggravate their unhappy lot: but how to get them to see things the same way? He decided to challenge them to combat their natural impulses, to make a bid for "perfection." Where was the virtue in doing what even, they would agree, was done no less by Gentiles and transgressors? If they would be children of God indeed, let them become like the Heavenly Father, who dispensed His favours impartially. That "excess" of love and benevolence would assuredly make them mete for deliverance.

But Jesus hastened to explain, lest his words be misunderstood, that by "doing more than others" he did not mean a public parade of piety: such behaviour would negative the heavenly reward. There were far too many of the type which "do all their works to be seen of men." They had their reward already in public adulation. Just as in the earlier part of his speech he had grouped his remarks concerning the Law around the fundamental commandments dealing with murder, adultery and idolatry, so now Jesus spoke of piety under the three forms in which Judaism enjoined its practice—alms-giving, prayer, and penitence (fasting). "Three things cancel the harsh decree of Heaven," said Rabbi Eliezer, "prayer, alms-giving and penitence."[37] The equation of fasting with penitence was a very ancient one. Fasting was the outward expression of inward contrition. We have the phrase "fasting for sins," but it was always emphasized that fasting unaccompanied by change of heart was valueless.

Jesus said: "See that ye bestow not your alms before men, so that they may see you; for then ye have no reward of your Father which is in heaven. Therefore when thou bestowest alms, blow not a trumpet before thee like the hypocrites do in the synagogues and in the streets, in order that men may honour them. Truly, I say unto you, already they have their reward. But, when thou dispensest alms, thy left hand shall not know what thy right hand doeth: that thine alms may be in secret, and thy Father which seeth in secret shall Himself recompense thee in public.

"And be not like the hypocrites when thou prayest; for they delight to stand in the assemblies and at the comers of the streets to pray, that men may see them. Truly, I say unto you, already they have received their reward. But do thou, when thou prayest, enter into thine apartment, and shut thy door, and pray to thy Father which is in secret; and thy Father which seeth in secret shall recompense thee in public....

"And ye, when ye fast, be not like the hypocrites; for they begrime and disfigure their faces, that they may appear in the sight of men to fast. Truly, I say unto you, already they have received their reward. But thou, when thou fastest, anoint thine head, and wash thy face, that thou appear not unto men to fast, but unto thy Father which is in secret, who shall recompense thee in public."

It was a well-known rabbinical saying: "He who giveth alms in secret is greater than Moses our master."[38] But Jesus reminded his audience specifically of the procedure at a time of public calamity, so familiar both to him and to them, when the trumpet was solemnly sounded, and prayer in the street or market-place was offered, accompanied by fasting and alms-giving. Men of believed piety were elected to lead the devotions of the people on these occasions. One can readily understand that there were many devout souls who gave themselves to prayer, fasting and charity that God might avert the threatened peril. These would have been ashamed to confess their vicarious atonement. One can as readily appreciate the temptation of less single-minded persons to let it be seen that they were interceding for the nation. The poor people in their desperate plight would follow such with their blessings, assured that there must be a response from heaven to the pleas of these presumed saints.

The mind of Jesus moved on from those who paraded their piety to those who went about looking for small faults in others. He warned his hearers against three types of persons—he had the Oriental fondness for numerical groupings—the ostentatious pietist, the fault finder, and the false prophet. The tragedy was that behind each type there was the insistent anxiety for deliverance, a continuous longing for the presence of God. From the prayer of Moses, "If Thy Presence go not with us, take us not up hence, onwards, Jewish literature is full of such spiritual solicitude, and never more so than in the dark days which preceded and followed the destruction of the second Temple. Again and again there is mention of those whose pure lives made them worthy that the Divine Presence should rest upon them, and of those whose unworthy actions caused that Presence to depart in grief. Salvation itself depended on the measure in which God was with His people. He was their final refuge. All other help had failed.

> "Judge not, and ye shall not be judged," said Jesus.
> "Condemn not, and ye shall not be condemned.
> "For with what judgment ye judge, ye shall be judged;
> "And with what measure ye mete, it shall be measured to you again.[39]
> "And how seest thou the splinter in thy brother's eye, but seest not the beam that is in thine own eye? And how sayest thou to thy brother, 'Suffer it now, brother, that I may pull out the splinter out of thine eye,' and, behold, a beam is in thine own eye? Thou hypocrite, first pull out the beam that is in thine own eye, and then shalt thou be able to see clearly to pull out the splinter out of thy brother's eye. Therefore, whatsoever ye would that men should do to you, do ye even so to them: for this is the Law and the Prophets.
> "Be warned of false prophets, which come to you in sheep's clothing, but beneath their clothing they are as full of guile as ravening wolves. But by their fruits ye shall recognize them. Are grape clusters gathered from thorns, or figs from thistles?"

Brother was looking on brother with a jaundiced eye, and with some individuals the search for error in others amounted almost to a mania. The motive was well enough, but the state of mind was decidedly unhealthy. It was "a generation that judged its judges,"[40] tradition records, and quotes the same proverb about the splinter and the beam.

In this part of his speech Jesus made considerable use of proverbs. It was his common-sense way of dealing with the mental tension and nerviness. He deliberately lowered his tone to the colloquial, and appealed to the homely humour and wisdom of the marketplace. In this way he tried to draw the sting of the *unco' guid*, from whose activities he himself was to suffer continually. Such men made mountains out of mole-hills, tremendous issues out of trivialities. They created schisms and factions.

The old and meek Rabbi Hillel had once told a would-be proselyte, "What is hateful to thee, do not unto others. This is the Law: the rest is commentary." "The rest is commentary," Jesus agreed, and turned the saying round to a positive commandment. If the people would spend themselves in doing good to others, they would have no time for fault-finding and heresy- hunting.

Nevertheless the groups and the parties were there, the petty chiefs who had their hour, and the religious enthusiasts who preached messages of hope, but did little to realize the hopes they raised. On the other hand there were the wolves in sheep's clothing, battening on the people's misery. Jesus had been speaking of the fault-finders, one disruptive element which tended to promote divisions instead of unity. Now he warned against a definitely destructive element, those ghouls who, taking advantage of the distraught and helpless, promised to a longing and expectant nation, believers in the miraculous, signs and wonders which were to presage the Redemption. No miracle was too remarkable for the wretched and credulous multitudes to swallow, with the natural result that they became an easy prey of a host of charlatans.[41] It is one of the great tragedies of history that the one who, above all, set his face steadfastly against any attempt to beguile the people by wonder-working, should in the end have been condemned as a false prophet and misleader. "By their fruits ye shall know them": that is his vindication. Certainly no man saw more clearly the terrible danger, or did more to try and avert it. The Day of Deliverance was a secret hidden with God alone; it was for those who wished to particip-ate in it to prepare themselves by doing His will.

The great speech drew to its close. Into its brief compass Jesus had incorporated all that was of real import for the material and spiritual welfare of his people. He had cleared away the shifting sands, and got down to bed-rock, enunciating those abiding principles upon which alone the Community of the Kingdom of God could be securely founded. He concluded with a parable, with which in various forms his audience was familiar.

> "Whosoever heareth these my words, and doeth them, is likened unto a wise man, which built his house upon the rock; and the rain descended and the floods came, and the winds blew, and beat upon that house: it fell not, for it was founded upon the rock. But whosoever heareth these my words, and doeth them not, is likened unto a foolish man, which built his house upon the sand; and the rain descended, and the floods came, and the winds blew upon it, and

beat upon that house: it fell, and great was the fall of it."

So; it was finished. Logically, inexorably, he had dealt with point after point, facing every issue squarely, charming, persuading, admonishing, his voice now modulated, now resounding, adding the value of a perfect delivery to the simple wisdom of what was spoken. What was to be the response?[42]

Jesus rose wearily, and slowly began to descend from the height; but the radiance of the truths he had uttered still shone in his countenance, and lent majesty to his person. The multitudes awed into momentary forgetfulness of their physical ills gave back as from the presence of Moses coming down from the vision of God on Sinai. They were astonished at bis doctrine; for he taught as one having authority. Before they were aware Jesus attended by his disciples had passed out of sight by the rocky defile that led downwards to the Vale of Arbel, Arbel where the Messiah would manifest himself.

Suddenly there issued from one of the caverns a leper, and flung himself down before Jesus, lifting up imploring hands and crying, "If thou wilt, thou canst make me clean!" Jesus, still far away in thought, saw in the man a symbol, and touched with quick tenderness he laid a hand upon him before he realized what he was doing, and said, "I will; be thou clean!"

Those words! It was long ago in the Temple at the most solemn moment of the ritual of the great Day of Atonement. The high priest had come forth from the holy place having sprinkled the blood of expiation, and in a clear voice he had pronounced the Ineffable Name of God while the priests and the people kneeled and fell upon their faces and blessed the Name of the Lord. And when the high priest had finished uttering the Name in sanctity and purity, he had said, "Ye shall be clean...."

It was the supplicant gratefully and joyously blessing God for deliverance that startled Jesus out of his reverie. He spoke harshly, and pushed the man from him. "See thou tell no one: but be off, show thyself to the priest, and offer for thy cleansing those things which Moses commanded for a testimony!"

Returned once again to Kefar-Naum Jesus was met by a delegation of elders who desired to enlist his help on behalf of a Roman centurion, whose favourite slave was sick. Lest he should refuse to attend a Gentile, they hastened to declare that the officer was most worthy. "Truly he loveth our nation," they said, "and he hath built us a synagogue." It was enough. Jesus went with them. But before they reached the house there came friends of the centurion with a message: "Lord, trouble not thyself: for I am not worthy that thou shouldest enter under my roof: wherefore neither thought I myself worthy to come unto thee: but speak the word of power, and my servant shall be healed. I myself have to take orders, and under me are soldiers, and I say unto one, 'Go,' and he goeth; and to another 'Come,' and he cometh; and to my servant, 'Do this,' and he doeth it."

Jesus received this message with astonishment, and turning round to the elders and his disciples, he exclaimed, "Know ye, I have not found so great faith, no, not in Israel!" And it is recorded that they that were sent, returning to the house, found the servant well that had been sick.

That day there were many asking, "Who can this man be, who speaks with such authority?"

CHAPTER XI

Mercy, Not Sacrifice

There were certain ears upon which the words of Jesus had not fallen pleasingly. In his speech he had not been sparing in his denunciations, and he had been exceedingly outspoken in his revelation of abuses. He had painted the portrait of the hypocrite with such disturbing faithfulness that those whom the likeness convicted stood in mortal fear of recognition. Vanity, pride, and self-esteem whispered a message of hatred to receptive hearts. Even sincerity rose up in arms against the blow to party prestige. What the speaker had said might be true, reasoned some of the Pharisee scribes who had been present, but it could do no possible good to promote internal dissension by making the masses suspicious of the system which was their only bulwark and defence. Once let it be believed that there were weak spots in the Pharisaic "Maginot Line," and all hopes of a united front to the enemy must be abandoned. Israel would perish.

Jesus could not recognize any such consequence as inevitable. There was a world of difference between healthy and unhealthy criticism. Healthy criticism was the criticism of evils; unhealthy criticism was the criticism of individuals. For him the collective security of Israel was endangered by censoriousness, which invited and encouraged an artificial conformity. Of what use was a wall which, while it gave an impression of solidity, had sections which were hollow within? At the first general assault the weak spots would be discovered, and a breach effected. Then indeed the people might perish.

Jesus said, Let there be no outward seeming, but inward reality. What a man does matters infinitely less than what he is. It was in this sense that the great rabbi, who became the chief interpreter of the teaching of Jesus, argued: "Do we then make void the Law through faith? God forbid! Yea, we establish the

Law."

The Nazarene who had spoken so boldly on the mount, and with such a definite assumption of authority—his "I say unto you"— was not one of the fellowship which formed the kernel of Pharisaism; he was not even the acknowledged disciple of any of the fraternity: this made his strictures harder to bear, and provoked a spirit of contradiction among those duly qualified to teach, even where the power and essential truth of the message was appreciated. There is nothing more galling to professionalism than to be told its business by apparently self-constituted authority, and nothing more exasperating than the public disclosure by an outsider of professional shortcomings and inconsistencies. Let the statements and the criticisms be never so valid, they are none the less offensive. Unfortunately at this stage of his activity Jesus was precluded from disclosing his status. How could the listening scribes, injured in their amour-propre, be expected to guess that the fellow who expressed himself with such blatant egoism in defiance of hallowed tradition was none other than the Lord's anointed, or claimed to be such? Had they known, the spirit of grace and supplication might miraculously have been poured upon them. At least their attitude towards the message would have been conditioned by their acceptance or rejection of the claim. As it was, they were required to do a thing most difficult, to subordinate their considered judgment to that of an arbitrary authority, and the very presumption of such a suggestion was enough to make repudiation inevitable.

It was a tragic necessity, which at this early stage thrust the most influential body of prospective supporters into opposition. It was with a sense of foreboding in the minds of some, and of bitter antagonism in others, that the accredited representatives of popular religion withdrew themselves.

From whatever motives—and there were many that lay between the extremes of good and bad—the policy of Galilean Pharisaism shaped itself from this time into a settled endeavour, now friendly, now hostile, but in any case determined, to discredit Jesus, to find the gap in his armour, to undermine his influence, lest this misguided, dangerous, or too-enlightened preacher—according to personal opinion—should bring disaster on the nation.

Had Jesus been free to declare himself publicly the course of history might have been changed; but this, as we have seen, he was unable to do; otherwise there would have been an end of his ministry.

It may be said that he should have taken some of the rabbis into his confidence and won them to his side. But even if he had attempted this his chances of being received and accepted would have been as slender as if in our own day he were to present himself at any of the theological colleges. A Messianic, or Christian, expectation is a very different thing from a flesh and blood reality. All sorts of questions would be asked with growing scepticism, ending inevitably with bland disbelief. So far removed is a purely mental concept from actual fact. And in the most unlikely event of recognition, the prospect of success would not have been improved. Instead of being the undefiled vehicle for the voice of God, Jesus would have become the controlled instrument of sectarian policy. He would, so to speak, have been run for Messiah on a party ticket.

Nevertheless, the open heckling, the uncomplimentary stage- whispered asides, the sarcastic innuendos, the critical crosstalk, which were the weapons employed by the scribes to embarrass Jesus, to provoke him, to force him to play into their hands by some unconsidered act or utterance, could not fail to be in the highest degree irritating even to a less sensitive soul. Jesus was both irritated and angry; but he was sufficiently master of himself not to fall into any of the traps that were laid for his feet. He did not make the mistake of underestimating the power of his opponents, and he fully appreciated that behind the game they were playing, undignified and irreverent as it seemed, there was a cold strength of purpose for what was to them a just cause that matched his own. They were bent on extinguishing him, and he on convicting them, with the salvation of Israel as the stake. The scribes were to discover that they were dealing not, as they at first thought, with an unconventionally religious man-of-the-people, but with a personality of a mental and spiritual calibre that went far towards endorsing the authority he asserted. He was really dangerous.

Jesus, contrary to expectation, did not stumble and fall into confusion at the barbed words of the trained dialecticians; he turned and met them with a righteous indignation: he even deliberately multiplied by his sayings and actions the opportunities for them to exercise their skill at his expense, and then brought home to them by an apt question or remark the falsity of the position they had adopted even according to their own standards. By these means he extracted for the benefit of the populace the maximum of spiritual illustration out of each encounter. The attackers found themselves reduced to the position of valuable foils for the penetrating judgments of the untutored Galilean. Instead of discrediting him, they were only succeeding in enhancing his reputation. And their impotence did nothing to mollify the bitterness of their discomfiture.

There may be those who are tempted to think and to say, especially at this distance of time, that all these theological disputations to which we are treated seem to be purely academic, and undeserving either of the prominence which they are given or the passion and heat displayed. It is known of course that pundits, and particularly religious pundits, are capable of a virulence in polemic which is pitiably disproportionate to the value of the point at issue. But it would show a definite lack of understanding of the situation to suppose that the conflict between Jesus and his adversaries had no deeper justification than a desire to secure a technical triumph. The immediate cause for which they contended was the soul and the physical continuity of the nation, and if the duel was a outrance it was because both parties believed that the danger of the dissolution of the soul of Israel and of the body politic was imminent. There was also an awareness of larger issues, the mediatorial mission of the Elect People as an essential part of God's plan for the salvation of the world. The objectives on either side were broadly identical, but the processes by which they were to be attained which were considered constructive by the one were regarded as destructive by the other. The pressing nature of the problems and the restricted and unhelpful circumstances in which a solution was demanded provided no possibility for reasonable discussion. The available opportunities permitted only of quick-fire question and answer, which proved exacerbating and estranging instead of integrating. This too was part of the great tragedy, a tragedy which the course of events has prolonged by nineteen centuries. There was no time then, and ample time since has not been able to compensate.

In the records upon which we have to depend for our information there is a grouping of incidents, representing a selection from among many that might have been set down, which effectively illustrate the beginnings of the conflict between Jesus and the scribes of the

Pharisees. We are shown the conditions, and the respective tactics of the protagonists. It must be remarked, however, that these preliminary skirmishes were almost entirely domestic: they took place largely in private and between two groups—treating Jesus and his disciples as a group—which would naturally associate, and which had very much in common. Indeed, it was the common ground and the common ideals that magnified the differences, and engendered a more implacable hostility, rather than any fundamental disagreement in principle.

Neither the Government nor the Established Church was as yet involved, or in any way concerned, and when subsequently these were forced to take cognizance of Jesus and his doctrine and to proceed against him, their measures were initially dictated by considerations of State expediency more often than by personal antagonism. Yet the Romans, the Herodians, and the Sadducean hierarchy were worlds removed from Jesus in outlook, as compared with the Pharisees.

The scene of the incidents which follow is laid in and about Kefar-Naum, which Jesus had made his headquarters; and the events apparently took place shortly after his return there from his first preaching tour which had culminated in his mountain discourse. In two cases the Fourth Evangelist has transferred the locality to Judea and Jerusalem, as he has done in other instances in order to appeal to the south, which invited the northerners to "search and see that the Prophet cometh not out of Galilee," and he has coloured his narrative accordingly.

In a remarkably short space of time Jesus had achieved an extraordinary popularity, mainly it is true through a widespread belief in his healing powers, and it was now most difficult for him to secure any privacy at all. He was certainly safest from mobbing in Kefar-Naum, since it was a customs station with a Roman garrison, where people had to be cautious about congregating in large numbers. Here, in Peter's house or with other friends, he could enjoy comparative quiet. There was never absolute peace, for neither houses nor doors were proof against the determined onslaught of parental and filial affection which filled the limited space indoors with the sick and their relatives and blocked the narrow thoroughfare outside.

There was no lack of initiative about the four who, finding other means of access impossible, conveyed a paralytic up to the roof, opened a part of it, and let the man down on his mattress into the presence of Jesus. The faith that had inspired such enterprise could not fail of its reward, but the provocative words that Jesus used were, "Son, thy sins be forgiven thee." At this there was a significant exchange of looks on the part of the scribes sitting by, as who should say, "Why doth this man speak blasphemies? Who can forgive sins, but God alone?" Jesus perceived their thoughts. It may be that he had said the words intentionally; for he was very ready with his answer. "Why reason ye these things in your hearts?" he challenged. "Whether is easier, to say, thy sins be forgiven thee, or to say, rise up and walk? But that ye may know that the Son of Man hath power on earth to forgive sins"—he turned to the paralytic—"I say unto thee, arise, and take up thy couch, and go thy way into thine house."

And immediately the man received strength and rose up before them all, and departed to his house, glorifying God. There was general amazement joined with feelings of uneasiness, for Jesus had too closely linked the man's physical restoration with release from the bondage of sin for anyone's personal comfort. And those who were most disturbed were loudest in vociferating the formula: of benediction to the Almighty. As for the scribes, they were left on the horns of a dilemma. Not yet did they dare to suggest that Jesus had effected the cure by the aid of evil spirits.

They were given little time to resolve the problem set them, or to plan a fresh attack. Jesus took the offensive in a most unexpected manner. He seemed determined to force them into a position where they had to choose with disconcerting promptness between submission to his authority or open opposition. The task before him was too big for qualified approval or qualified criticism. Action must come first and discussion afterwards. Jesus asserted a spiritual dictatorship, and the Pharisees, who were the champions of democratic religion, were bound to rebel against the insistence on an immediate decision.

Jesus could be infinitely patient, but he could not tolerate procrastination. His method was to take a point, face it, deal with it, and have done with it. The Pharisees, on the other hand, wished every possible contingency, likely and unlikely, to be taken into consideration. This truly made for mildness in judgment; but the judgment though mild might in the end prove harsher on the very account that every mitigating circumstance and eventuality had been advanced. It left no loop-hole, because no conceivable situation had been neglected. Perhaps the harshness would operate in only one out of a hundred cases, and in the other ninety-nine the application would be mild. But still there was the one case, and it was this one—the lost sheep—that Jesus had come to seek and to save.

What was lacking in the judgment of the Pharisees, as in most human judgments, was regard for the personal element, the psychology of the individual soul. Jesus held that no judgment is of universal validity. Not only the time, and the place, and the circumstances, and the motive, must be weighed, but also the man himself, who is being judged. This, however, would require that the judge himself should be gifted with Divine insight; and just because his is the necessarily lower function of administering the law Jesus could not accept the office, for morally in the sight of God the law cannot put any man outside the law.

There came one to Jesus, saying, "Master, speak to my brother, that he divide the inheritance with me."

Jesus answered, "Man, who made me a judge or a divider over you?"

Then he turned to the company, and admonished them, "Take heed and beware of covetousness, for a man's life consisteth not in the abundance of the things which he possesseth." And he told this story.

"The ground of a certain rich man brought forth plentifully; and he thought within himself, 'What shall I do, because I have no room where to bestow my fruits?' And he said, 'This will I do: I will pull down my barns, and build greater; and there will I bestow all my fruits and goods. And I will say unto my soul, Soul, thou hast much goods laid up for many years; take thine ease, eat, drink, and be merry.' But God said unto him, 'Thou fool, this very night thy soul shall be required of thee: then whose shall those things be which thou hast provided?' So is he that layeth up treasure for himself, and is not rich toward God."

At another time when Jesus was teaching, the scribes of the Pharisees brought to him a woman taken in adultery. And having set her in the midst, they asked him, "Master, this woman hath been taken up in adultery, in the very act; and in the Law Moses commanded us that such should be stoned: what therefore dost thou say?"

Jesus seemed not to have heard; he had bent his head, and was drawing industriously with his finger in the dust. But as they persisted with their question, he raised himself, and replied, "He that is without sin among you, let him first cast a stone at her." And again he bent down and scrawled in the dust.

There was a pregnant silence, while the judges judged themselves. Then, beginning with the oldest, they departed one by one; for there is not a righteous man upon earth who has not sinned. And Jesus was left alone and the woman standing there.

No one had been put to an open shame by eyes of accusation. Only when all had gone did the man who refused to judge again look up; and then he inquired mildly of the woman, "Mistress, where are they? Hath none condemned thee?" "None, sir," came the timid answer. And Jesus said, "Neither will I condemn thee; go, and from this time no longer sin."

Jesus had to tell the Pharisees plainly: "Ye judge after the flesh; I judge no man. But if I did judge, my judgment would be true, for it would be aided by the Father that sent me."

There was the weakness in all law, that it was capable of justifying injustice. To be strong it had to be reinforced by a knowledge of God's ways. On two occasions within a few days, when either Jesus himself or his disciples broke through the fence of the Pharisaic code, he had to make clear his position by reiterating the words of Hosea.

"Go ye and learn what this meaneth, 'I desire mercy, and not sacrifice;' for I am not come to call the righteous, but sinners."

"If ye had known what this meaneth, 'I desire mercy, and not sacrifice,' ye would not have condemned the guiltless."

The tactics which Jesus adopted to illustrate his attitude was to go down to the customs station at Kefar-Naum and invite a Jewish tax-collector to become his disciple. He knew perfectly well what he was doing in selecting a man technically regarded as utterly immoral and irreligious, a man excluded from all hope of the world to come. It was a courageous and also a dangerous gesture, liable to be misunderstood not only by the scribes of the Pharisees, but also by the more patriotic of his own adherents. But it was a risk that had to be taken. The worth of the individual over and above every other consideration had to be demonstrated boldly. The Kingdom of God would consist of a redeemed society, not of a party, or a class, and certainly not alone of those commonly called the righteous.

It would be wrong to suppose that the Pharisees held that a Jew who followed an immoral occupation was necessarily an abandoned person, though he was generally assumed to be so. Such a man, however, by the performance of one noble act might be restored to the congregation, and counted worthy to intercede with God for the people in time of trouble.

Matthew the son of Alphaeus, the tax-gatherer, was perhaps entitled to the honourable name of *Halevi*, the Levite. Whatever circumstances had driven him to follow such a detested calling it is evident that he had not lost all self-respect or consciousness of his privileged status in the community. Any old associate who might address him as *Halevi*, would be told with a gruffness that masked his pain, "My name is Matthew, Matthew the tax-collector, Matthew the transgressor!" And the friend would pay the due, and remark with a sigh, "The Lord send thee repentance— Matthew."

That night would see Matthew roistering in low company, drinking and shouting to conceal his deep sense of shame. Time and again the urge came upon him to redeem himself, to be done with the life of a pariah, but always the will power was lacking. It demanded a strong external influence to extricate him from his position, and that influence had not come into his life until the day that the wonderworking teacher, of whom he had heard marvellous tilings, came to him, looked into his heart, and said, "Follow me!" Then suddenly the bands were snapped, and Matthew rose up with alacrity, and followed him.

With what joy the ex-publican made a great feast for Jesus in his house. The gains of the unrighteous Mammon were heaped up, translated into good cheer, and demolished in one last lavish entertainment in payment of a willing tribute, answering for every unjust and extorted claim. To the happy Matthew it seemed the most appropriate atonement, and as such Jesus accepted it without question. It was not in the power of Matthew to seat the pious and respectable at his table. The guests perforce were his former boon companions, hardly the most savoury element in Kefar-

Naum society. But this did not deter Jesus; he reclined in the place of honour and was the centre of good feeling and friendliness.

The news of the teacher's conduct got round, and soon came the censorious, inquisitive and unctuous, inquiring of the disciples in shocked tones, "Why eateth your master with publicans and sinners?" And when Jesus was told, he sent word with his usual laconism, "They that are whole need not a physician; but they that are sick." The proverb was to the point. But the inquirers persisted, with apparent concern, that surely such worthy service demanded a life of austerity. One fasted and prayed that the spirit of penitence might be given to sinners, as did the Pharisees and— significantly—the disciples of John. One did not have to eat and drink with them. Would it not be more suitable if the master's disciples also fasted? In saying "disciples" they were, of course, using the indirect speech of the Eastern, meaning respectively John and Jesus.

With equal Orientalism Jesus responded, "Can the friends of the bridegroom mourn while the bridegroom is with them?' That is to say, the bridegroom does not mourn on his wedding day. And he added: "There is no one who would put a patch of raw cloth on an old robe, for it would drag at the robe, and the rent would be worse than before. Neither do they put new wine into worn out wine-skins, for the wine-skins would be split, and the wine spilled: but they put new wine into new wine-skins, and both are preserved." You cannot rescue people long sunk in degradation by displaying a hard and chill morality; for you will only drive them further away and complete their ruin. You must enter into relations with them in a friendly and sympathetic manner, and then you may wean them from their evil ways.[43]

The group of Pharisees who had constituted themselves as a local vigilance committee took their departure; but they determined that some of their number should henceforth watch every move made by Jesus and his men. Presently this unorthodox and cocksure teacher, who always had a ready answer, would overreach himself, and then they would have him.

Thus it came about that on an early Sabbath there were witnesses, who marked that as Jesus and his disciples walked through a field of standing corn some of them began to pluck the ears, rub them, and eat the grain. Immediately, they confronted Jesus with this evidence of sinful conduct. "Behold, thy disciples (i.e. you, yourself) do that which is not lawful on the Sabbath day." But the answer was again ready. "Have ye not read what David did, when he was an hungered, and they that were with him? How he entered into the House of God, and did eat the shewbread, which was not lawful for him to eat, neither for them which were with him, but only for the priests? The Sabbath was made for man, and not man for the Sabbath."

That same day he himself saw a man working on the Sabbath, and stopped to address him. "Man," he said, "if thou knowest what thou doest, blessed art thou, for the son of man is lord of the Sabbath; but if thou knowest not, thou art accursed, and a transgressor of the Law."[44]

And he came into the synagogue. And there was a man there who had a withered hand. And he cried out, "I was a mason, seeking a living by the use of my hands. I beseech thee, Jesus, that thou restore me to health, that I may not shamefully beg for food."[45]

The vigilants were on the alert to see what Jesus would do, and they muttered, "It is not lawful to heal on the Sabbath." Jesus heard them, and called to the man, "Rise up, and stand forth in the midst!" Then he looked about him in anger, and asked, "What man of you having one sheep, if it fall into a pit on the Sabbath, will not lay hold on it, and lift it out? And is not a man of more worth than a sheep? Wherefore it is lawful to do good on the Sabbath." Turning to the former mason, he said sharply, "Stretch forth thine hand!" And suddenly the man found its use restored to him, and he stretched it out.

Burning with resentment against the upstart who got the better of them on every occasion, and who now, through their own persistence, had made them look foolish in public, the clique of Pharisees hurried from the building followed by not a few jeering remarks.

The position, as it had developed, was more than flesh and blood could stand. Here was this new teacher, scholastically untrained, without respect for persons or institutions, setting up his own authority, and by a glib tongue, an appealing manner, and the gift of healing, winning over the people to religious anarchy. It had always been difficult to bring the Galileans under the yoke — they were a proud and independent stock—and now it was going to be ten times more difficult. What this Jesus was aiming at was not yet evident; but it would be incredible to think that he was working up such a large and enthusiastic following out of simple goodness of heart. No doubt he had some deep laid scheme. It was always the way with these demagogues: they began with a great show of concern for the rights of the poor and the oppressed, and when they had obtained the power for which they craved, then they threw off the mask and revealed themselves in their true character. Then woe to those who had given them the power; for they would be the first victims of tyranny. The movement must be crushed in its inception and its leader put out of the way; for once it had reached greater proportions its ultimate collapse might drag the whole nation down to ruin with it. The governor would dearly love an excuse to punish the Jews for disloyalty, and he would be deliberately blind to distinctions. At present the affair was localized, and was outside Pilate's jurisdiction. This, therefore, was the time to act. The Herodians must be persuaded that this Jesus was planning a revolt, and they must get the tetrarch Antipas to order that he be arrested, as John the Baptist had already been arrested on a charge of incitement to rebellion.

So argued the disgruntled group of Pharisees, as they took counsel together. But either they did not know, or they wilfully ignored, that Herod Antipas had confined John in the fortress of Machaerus not because he feared the outcome of the prophet's wild denunciations, but because his wife Herodias hated him for saying that her marriage was illegal.

It went much against the grain for the Pharisees to have anything at all to do with the Herodians, the scoffers and yoke breakers, whom they detested only slightly less than Jesus. But there was no help for it. They themselves were powerless.

A representative was chosen to wait on Chuza, Herod's chancellor. He was received in due course with cold politeness, and told his story. It was useless to accuse Jesus of having infringed the Pharisaic code, for the Herodians were very liberal in their Judaism. It could only be claimed that he was fomenting disaffection. The chancellor thanked his caller somewhat cynically for his anxiety for the welfare of the government, which must have been very riling for the Pharisee, and inquired, "What has this Jesus of Nazareth said or done?" The Pharisee had to admit that Jesus had not yet said or done anything of a subversive character; but he was stirring up the people and recruiting a large following, surely that was something to consider. "Perhaps," agreed the chancellor noncommittally. "But I cannot recommend the arrest of this man merely on suspicion. If you want me to intervene you must produce better evidence than that."

When the Pharisee had gone, Chuza called his secretary. "There is a certain Jesus of Nazareth who seems likely to cause trouble. It would be well to keep him under observation."

That evening the chancellor related the incident to his wife Joanna with some amusement, and he was greatly astonished when she besought him earnestly not to listen to anything that was said against that good man. "Why, I did not know that you knew the fellow," he exclaimed. "He is a mighty teacher," she declared, "and has healed many of the sick. I beg you to leave him alone." The chancellor shrugged his shoulders. "Well, he is safe from me as long as he does nothing seditious. I don't want to interfere with him, especially as the Pharisees are against him. But do be careful, and don't mix yourself up with any political nonsense. I don't want to lose my place."

Next day Joanna, a charitable and benevolent lady, sent secretly to Jesus. "You have enemies. Be on your guard." She also sent a substantial present for the Master's needs. The same day the emissary of the Pharisees was reporting to those who sent him, "Chuza will do nothing without definite evidence." It was agreed that the evidence would have to be obtained. But this was going to be no easy matter. They had had sufficient taste of the skill of Jesus in debate to recognize that they could not draw him readily into making an indiscreet remark in public. If only they had a spy among the disciples, who might learn of his secret intentions...

Strangely enough, about this time, there entered the service of Jesus a man who might have served their purpose, and who in the end was the instrument of his destruction. Judas the son of Simon the Zealot joined the new movement with his father. Nicknamed —though it is not now known why—the Iscariot, he was a man with nothing to lose, a sombre brooding spirit, who had long identified his people's wrongs with his own. Mentally unstable, morbidly egotistical, and with a certain cunning and petty avarice, he yet had his points. He was deeply religious, and in his own fashion he was a patriot, hating the sinners in high places, and with a detestation of foreigners that amounted almost to mania. Judas disliked physical violence and the shedding of blood: this had kept him from enlisting under the banner of the Zealots, although his sympathies, like those of his father, were with them. The teaching and the methods of Jesus and his followers struck a responsive chord in his being. There was the revivalist fervour, the power over demons, the wandering life, the crowded gatherings, the communal sharing, the outspoken denunciations of the evils of the generation, the promise of a new order with riches and glory.... The Christian message has always attracted men of this type, pathological compounds of good and bad. They seem to be more usually found in the extreme evangelical bodies where there is a minimum of Church government.

No record exists of the first interview between Jesus and Judas. The Master must have recognized that here was a soul passionately desiring to serve the highest ends, but labouring under a sense of persistent frustration. He would not have dreamed of rejecting him; for his policy was, "Him that cometh unto me I will in no wise cast out." He may have hoped that example, occupation, and responsibility, would straighten out the bends in the character of Judas, and convert him into one of the most valuable of his followers. If it was folly that induced him to make Judas one of his chosen apostles, it was a sublime folly. So the son of Simon the Zealot was numbered with his father among the Twelve.

Jesus acted promptly and without ostentation on receiving the warning of the plot against him. He could not afford to risk arrest at this early stage of his work, even on a false charge. The damage to his cause would be incalculable. He therefore withdrew quietly from Kefar-Naum with his disciples, and proceeded to a retired spot by the lakeside near Bethsaida. There he instructed Peter to arrange that shipping should always be in readiness, if need arose. It would then be easy, in case of emergency, to escape across the water to sanctuary in the territory of Philip.

At present it was the friendly populace which constituted for Jesus his chief source of danger. Some of the poor people, either in hysteria or in gratitude, were continually acclaiming him in extravagant and compromising terms. With all the authority at his command he called upon them to refrain; but in this thing few would obey him.

CHAPTER XII

Judgment unto Victory

Jesus had to face the fact that he had not only opponents, but personal enemies, who were working actively for his downfall, and he had to review his position in the light of this knowledge. His conduct before he learned of the conspiracy of the Pharisees shows few signs of planning. One looks in vain for any clear evidence that he was proceeding by any pre-arranged method towards a definite goal. Behind the seeming inconsequence of his activities, however, there must have been at least the broad outlines of a programme. Manifestly, he could not look very far ahead: he had to be guided very largely by circumstances as they arose, and certainly he regarded his immediate business as an extension of the work of John the Baptist in calling the people to repentance in preparation for the coming of the Kingdom of God. His single distinctive contribution towards the establishment of that Kingdom had been his statesmanlike speech on the mountainside. The demands on his time as a healer had been so unexpectedly overwhelming that they had forced him to limit his field of operations to the few miles between Kefar-Naum and Nazareth. He had toured the intervening towns and villages, teaching as he had opportunity, but he had made no effort as yet to extend his campaign to other parts of Galilee, much less to Judea, Samaria, Paraea, and the Decapolis. It is very doubtful if Jesus had visited Judea since his baptism, and still more doubtful if he had gone up to Jerusalem. We have already remarked that the Fourth Evangelist sometimes gives a southern setting to Galilean events. Everything related in the Synoptic Gospels is against the view that Jesus declared himself at this stage in the deliberate maimer that John suggests that he did. We have the impression that there had been nothing in what he had either said or done remotely to suggest the initiation of a movement on a national scale, or indeed, of a movement of any sort. Among the stock descriptions of him one that appears to be very remote from the truth is "the Founder of Christianity." This decidedly was the difficulty felt by the local interests whom he had antagonized: they did not know where he stood, or what were his objectives.

Until now there had been no cause for undue haste or anxiety. Even if there was intention to pursue a particular course, he could afford to bide his time. To quote his own words: "Mine hour has not yet come." In the meantime it was left to destiny to shape his ends. He had placed himself unreservedly in the hands of God: it was for God to show the way, and for him to follow. We have already noticed that Jesus had set himself steadfastly against acting precipitately. He had schooled himself to patience. He read the history of his people as a continual object lesson on the folly of exceeding instructions, and he had long ago determined that his motto should be "Implicit Obedience." He was the Servant of the Lord, and it is for the servant to obey without question. It was this quality in him that was found to have tremendous import. By the disobedience of Adam every evil had come upon the human race, and the doom of death. By the obedience of the Messiah the disintegrating process was reversed, and loving submission triumphed in resurrection life.

There are some men who, while they are mentally alert and extraordinarily quick-witted, are incapable of playing a leading part in affairs because they distrust a policy of action. They are so keenly aware of the many sides to every question that they are sceptical of their own power to sustain a fixed part for any length of time. They are amused at the blundering idiots who go at life head down regardless of obstacles or consequences, and they find the brutal determinist, who deliberately excludes from consideration everything but the end in view, a distinctly unpleasant fellow.

Jesus possessed a breadth of vision and a depth of insight which made leadership extremely difficult. He was not so much opposed to action as afraid of its dangers if uncontrolled by the directing hand of God. He could lead, therefore, only in so far as he was conscious of being led. He had made one mistake in the synagogue at Nazareth and the lesson from it had been salutary. Another mistake of the kind might prove fatal. He did not fear to die; but he did fear to be unfaithful to his calling. He had to be cautious for the Kingdom's sake. He believed that by Divine appointment the hopes of Israel, and through Israel of the World, were vested in his person. Such responsibility was so grave that he dared not take a single step, much less a risk, unless he was assured that it was in the line of God's will. To an extent that may appear fantastic to many people he relied on "Guidance;" but he did not degrade this form of inspiration by bringing it to bear on petty things; he reserved it for matters of moment, and especially for the conduct of his mission. Yet he was in no sense a puppet of Providence, quiescent except when the invisible spiritual strings were pulled. He had, as we have seen, strong emotions, amazing vitality, and a powerful intellect, and he employed them all with a freedom that revealed him as a personality of sturdy independence, even while he exhibited what has been called sanctified common sense.

It was common sense that emphasized the necessity for taking certain precautions to prevent any disruption of his work and to avoid any premature disclosure of his status. The forces ranged against him had to be circumvented so that he could carry on: he had to fight a delaying action until it was revealed to him how he should proceed. At the same time the existence of the opposition made him aware that the first stage in his public career had ended, and another one more intense and perhaps decisive had begun. The new situation demanded not only the arrangement of certain safeguards, but a speeding up of his efforts and particularly the wider diffusion of his message.

The initial step was to secure his retreat in case of need. This he had done by never going very far from the shores of the lake, and providing for a ship to be always in readiness to take him and his disciples to at least temporary safety on the farther coast.

The second measure was to choose out twelve of his men according to the number of the tribes of Israel, and to instruct them more closely in the principles of the Kingdom. He intended shortly to send these out to all parts of the country, to regions where it was not advisable as yet that he should come in person. In this way the message of the Kingdom would be spread far and wide. There would be dangers; but not so great as those which threatened him. He had never minimized the risks, it might even be said that he exaggerated them, and he had invariably pointed out that his service offered few attractions. There had come to him one of the scribes, saying eagerly, "Master, I will follow thee whithersoever thou goest." And he had answered warningly, "The foxes have holes, and the birds of the air have nests; but the Son of Man hath not a floor[46] whereon to lay his head."

As his own situation became more precarious, he painted discipleship in still less pleasing colours. Those who joined him must regard themselves as without family, without property, without any expectation of life, condemned rebels ever on the road to execution, carrying about with them daily the crosses on which they must suffer. There was no encouragement for the weakling or the fainthearted. "Whosoever will save his life shall lose it: but whosoever will lose his life for my sake shall find it. For what is a man profited if he shall gain the whole world, and lose his own soul?'

And the admonition which Jesus gave to his individual followers, he conveycd also to the crowds that thronged after him.

"If any man come to me, and hate not his father, and mother, and wife, and children, and brethren, and sisters, yea, and his own life also, he cannot be my disciple. And whosoever doth not bear his cross, and come after me, cannot be my disciple. For which of you, intending to build a tower, sitteth not down first, and counteth the cost, whether he have sufficient to finish it? Lest haply, after he hath laid the foundation, and is not able to finish it, all that behold it begin to mock him, saying, 'This man began to build, and was not able to finish.' Or what king, going to make war against another king, sitteth not down first, and consulteth whether he be able with ten thousand to meet him that cometh against him with twenty thousand? Or else, while the other is yet a great way off, he sendeth an ambassage, and desireth conditions of peace. So likewise, whosoever he be of you that forsaketh not all that he hath, he cannot be my disciple."

These are not the words of one who had any illusions. Jesus was fully cognizant of the dangers he was facing. He had counted the cost for himself, and he wished those who threw in their lot with him to be no less sure what they were doing. They had the opportunity to turn back if they wished. No one was compelled to enter his service, and those who did so realized the desperate nature of their calling, and could be depended upon to play their part.

The third measure which Jesus adopted, intended to obviate the risk of arrest on a charge of sedition, was to use the popular Galilean medium of the parable through which to convey his teaching. He had been warned that the civil authorities were interested in his activities, and that meant that in addition to his declared enemies there would be official spies among the crowds listening in the hope of hearing something that would justify the government in taking action.

The parable lent itself admirably as a method of circumventing the informer. Only those with sympathetic discernment would understand the purport of the stories which Jesus told, as he indicated by the admonition, "He that hath ears to hear, let him hear." But those of slow wit, of spiritual apathy, or who were expecting a very different message, would be baffled as they heard what seemed a perfectly innocuous comparison of the Kingdom of God with aspects of the common life of the people, with the workings of nature, and with incidents of constant occurrence which decidedly had no political significance. They were pointedly told that these were dark sayings concealing an inner meaning: they might invent a meaning that chimed with their suspicions; but it would be impossible to verify that the speaker intended the interpretation which they put upon his words. It was not that Jesus had anything seditious or subversive to say in relation to the regime; this is made clear by his private interpretations, even though we have not the whole truth. At the same time the doctrine was strongly messianic, and to that extent anticipated the growth of a new order and society, and we have already shown that

Jesus dared not as yet avow any messianic pretensions. He had made a beginning of doing so in the synagogue at Nazareth, and in a more guarded manner in the Sermon on the Mount, and the consequences had taught him present caution.

Teaching by parables had its drawbacks, for the disciples — devoted but somewhat obtuse—were left as much in the dark as anyone else, and were forced privately to ask for enlightenment.

In these various ways Jesus sought to safeguard his position and secure continuity for his message, while he gained time to educate his own company and to develop his hold on the people. He showed himself to be an excellent tactician.

The local fellowship of Pharisees observed with dismay both his caution and his growing popularity, and, feeling the need for more expert minds than their own, they sent for some of the famed

Doctors of the Law from Jerusalem. Surely they would be more than a match for the upstart.

The welcome reinforcements arrived and, having listened gravely to a statement of the situation, they joined the company about Jesus in time to witness a man who was blind and dumb from a paralytic stroke receive sight and speech. There was an outburst of enthusiasm, and someone remarked wonderingly to his neighbour,

"Is not this the Son of David?" The teachers from Jerusalem were startled. The matter was indeed as serious as they had been given to understand. One of them roughly caught hold of a man who was chanting in a kind of ecstasy, and swung him about. "Do you not know," cried the Pharisee, irefully, "that he casteth out demons by Beelzebub the prince of the demons?" The man thus challenged gaped at the rabbi, who let him go. But those nearest made a murmur of protest. The rabbi raised his voice, and with more courage than sense repeated his assertion. This time the murmur swelled to an angry roar, and the nature of the disturbance came to the ears of Jesus. He quieted the people with a gesture, and turned on his accuser.

"Every kingdom divided against itself is brought to desolation; and every city or house divided against itself shall not stand. If Satan cast out Satan, he is divided against himself. How then shall his kingdom stand?

"And if I by Beelzebub cast out the demons, by whom do your disciples cast them out? Therefore they shall be your judges. And how can a man enter into the strong man's house to plunder his goods, except he first bind the strong man? Then he will plunder his goods. Whosoever is not with me is against me; and he that gathereth not with me scattereth.

"And therefore I say unto you, every sin and blasphemy shall be forgiven a man; but the blasphemy which is against the spirit shall not be forgiven. And every man that saith a word against the Son of Man, it shall be for-given him; but he that saith a word against the Holy Spirit, it shall not be forgiven him, neither in this world, nor in the world to come."

The scribe was abashed, but his companions cried out derisively, "Rabbenu (our master), we wish to see a sign of thee."

In his indignation Jesus very nearly made the slip for which his opponents had been waiting.

"An evil and adulterous generation seeketh a sign," he cried, "but no sign shall be given it except the sign of Jo-nah the prophet. The men of Nineveh shall arise in the Judgment with this generation, and shall condemn it: for they repented at the preaching of Jonah, and, behold, a greater than Jonah is here. The queen of the south shall arise in the Judgment with this generation, and shall condemn it: for she came from the uttermost parts of the earth to hear the wisdom of Solomon, and, behold, a greater than Solomon is here."

Jesus pulled himself up, and continued more calmly. "When the unclean spirit is gone out of a man, it goeth through dry places, seeking rest, but finding none, Then it saith, 'I will return unto my house from whence I came out.' And it cometh, and findeth it empty, cleaned out with shovels, and adorned. Then it goeth, and taketh seven other spirits more wicked than itself, and they enter in and dwell there; so the latter end of that man is worse than the beginning. Even so shall it be with this wicked generation."

This was turning the tables with a vengeance. "Out of the abundance of the heart the mouth speaketh. The good man bringeth forth good things out of his good store: but the evil man bringeth forth evil things out of his evil store." These men had once cast forth the evil spirit from within them, that they might serve God: they had cleansed the temple of their soul. But now they had allowed the evil to return sevenfold, and the words of malice and hatred that fell from their lips testified that the unclean spirit dwelt in their hearts. Let them be the judges as to who was activated by Beelzebub.

The next attack came from a quite unexpected quarter, and proved far more trying than any opposition by strangers. The relatives of Jesus had become alarmed, and attempted to extricate him from a dubious position which reflected on their own orthodoxy. "He has taken leave of his senses," they said, and went in a body to bring him away. But the pressure of the crowd proved too strong for their purpose, and they did not wish to make their identity known. A family conference followed, at which the mother of Jesus and his brothers were present. After the Nazareth incident they had spent a short time at Kefar-Naum, either because they could not bear the scandal, or in the hope of persuading Jesus to relinquish his activities, or perhaps for both reasons. Later they had returned home, and tried to reorganize their lives under the new conditions. The strange aberration of the head of the house had been a shattering blow, and the younger brothers were very bitter about it. Only Mary would hear no evil spoken of her firstborn. Grief and anxiety had drawn her nearer to him now than in all the years that she had experienced his daily presence. In her own rather superstitious and unintelligent way she believed in him. She felt lost and lonely. Now pressure was being put upon her by offended kinsmen to make another attempt to put a stop to what they regarded as a family misfortune. Her younger sons added their voices to the insistent appeal. She agreed to go, though she was quite sure it would be useless. At least she would see him again....

A man pushed his way through the tightly packed throng, and after a struggle of several minutes reached the side of Jesus. "Behold," he panted, "thy mother and thy brethren stand without, and seek to speak with thee." Jesus looked away across the sea of heads towards the little group on the outskirts of his seated audience, and a spasm of pain passed over his face. He remembered his mother's words at Cana: "Whatsoever he saith unto you, do it!" Now she was being used against him, and he must stand firm. While inwardly he prayed that she might understand, he spoke almost harshly to the messenger, "Which is my mother, and who are my brethren?" And he stretched forth his hand towards his disciples, and cried, "Behold my mother and my brethren! Everyone that doeth the will of my Father which is in heaven, the same are my brethren, my sisters, and my mother."

Mary went her way, and James and Jose, Simon and Judas, comforted her.

It may have been the same day that Jesus, concerned at the continual and varied efforts to frustrate his work, adopted the precaution of veiling his teaching in parables. He took the further precaution of using his waiting ship as a pulpit, while the multitude lined the shore. He could not know whether at any moment his words might be rudely interrupted. If there was an attempt to arrest him, the crowd was likely to fight. But he did not want bloodshed, and safely on board the ship there was no need for anyone to defend him, and the authorities would have no excuse to injure the people.

He began to speak in a pleasing, yet indirect fashion of the Kingdom of God, comparing its worth and its growth with the familiar things of country and village life. He revealed his keen observation, and called to his service the nature studies of the years of waiting at Nazareth. The visit of his family had quickened his memory and revived thoughts of those bygone days when he had imitated his father as he strode along the furrow casting in the seed. The beauty of his diction and the poetry of his utterance laid a spell upon his audience.

> "Behold, the sower went forth to sow his seed; and as he sowed, some of them fell by the way side, and the birds of the air came and ate them up. And others fell upon the rock, where there was not much earth: and forthwith they sprouted, because they had no depth in the earth: but when the sun was risen, they were

dried up; and because they had no root, they withered away. And others fell among the thorns; and the thorns grew up, and choked them. But others fell into good ground, and brought forth fruit, one an hundredfold, and another sixty, and another thirty-fold. He that hath ears to hear, let him hear."

Vividly the images succeeded one another. Parable followed parable; the lesson of the Wheat and the Tares, of the Natural Action of the Soil, of the Mustard Seed, and of the Leaven. Later, to his disciples only, he put forth the parable of the Hidden Treasure, of the Pearl of Great Price, and the parable of the Draw-net. In all of these he enshrined an aspect of the mystery of the Kingdom of God.

To the disciples, who had received no warning, this sudden concentration on allegorical teaching came as a great surprise. It appeared to them to be one of those mystic vagaries of the Master, for which they could never account. His words made it clear that there was an inner meaning to these simple-seeming tales; but they could not fathom what it might be. Intrigued and piqued, they asked him, "Why dost thou speak with us in parables?" Jesus answered, "Because it is given unto you to understand the secrets of the Kingdom of God; but unto them that are without it is not given: for my secrets are for me and for my household.'[47] Still they were no wiser, and required him to explain. Jesus had to come down to their level, and offer an interpretation, apt and comprehensible so far as it went, but touching only the surface of the subject.

The secrets of the Kingdom, as they were revealed to Jesus, are secrets still. With a sigh of regret he told his little company: "Many prophets and righteous men have desired to see what ye are seeing, but have not seen; and to hear what ye are hearing, but have not heard."

At last the long day, so full of emotional and mental strain, drew to a close. Jesus was possessed of an overpowering weariness: he must have rest. "Send the people away," he requested, "and let us cross over to the other side." He retired to the stem of the vessel, laid his head on a cushion, and almost instantly he was asleep.

Darkness fell while they were still a great way from the farther shore. Suddenly a storm arose. Gusts of wind came whistling through the mountain gorges and churned up the water into angry waves. The fishermen were helpless. It did not appear that the ship could survive the fury of the elements. But Jesus, utterly exhausted, slept on, deaf to the shrieking of the tempest.

At last the fears of the disciples would suffer him to rest no longer. They shook him urgently by the shoulder, and shouted at him reproachfully, "Master, carest thou not that we perish?"

Jesus rose on his elbow, stared at the ring of panic-stricken faces, and inquired mildly, "Why are ye fearful, O little of faith?"

They gave back as he climbed slowly to his feet, and stood there swaying, while the wind reached out and tore at his robes and the spray lashed him in the face. "Peace, be still!" he cried imperatively with arm outswept in a gesture that included sky and sea and the cowering men.

With dramatic abruptness, as so often happened on the lake, the storm died away, and there was a great calm. But to the superstitious crew it seemed as if a miracle had happened, and as they bent to their oars they muttered furtively, "Who is this, that even the winds and the sea obey him?"

CHAPTER XIII

What Went Ye Out to See?

The region to which Jesus had come to recuperate was no pleasure ground. Gaulanitis, or the Golan, afforded over a large area excellent pasturage for cattle; but that part of it which bordered on the eastern shore of the lake was harsh and almost arid, a high plateau, which broke off abruptly at the water's edge, intersected by clefts and ravines. Here there were few inhabitants, and though Graeco-Roman influence had given to the neighbouring city of Gergesa a semblance of civilization and culture, the natives were of a rather wild and debased type. They cultivated a few crops in the fertile rifts, and bred hogs which nuzzled the scrubby soil for roots.

The welcome which Jesus received was in keeping with the character of the coast. The sun had not yet risen above the horizon when he and his disciples landed from the ship. Suddenly the stillness was broken by a horrid only half-human sound, and from the shadows there ran out upon them a fierce and pitiful creature, stark naked, who screamed at them and waved his arms from which hung a few rusted links of an iron chain. The poor lunatic imagined that the strangers had come to seize and confine him as the Gergesenes had several times attempted to do. At a short distance he stood his ground, and as they approached he cried in anguished tones, "I adjure ye by God, that ye torment me not!"

"I am not come to torment thee," replied Jesus compassionately. "What is thy name?"

"Legion," answered the madman. He fell upon his knees and besought Jesus that he would not send him out of the country. It was now quite light, and the morning glory shining full upon the stranger made him appear like an angelic visitant. Trembling in every limb, he suffered Jesus to draw near. Gently the Master laid a hand upon him, and commanded the unclean spirit to depart. The lunatic shivered at the touch, let out one terrible cry, and collapsed. Startled at the awful and penetrating noise, which echoed and re-echoed among the rocks, a herd of hogs just turned loose to feed stampeded, and rushed in panic flight down a steep declivity, and were drowned in the lake. The swineherds fled back to the city, and told an incoherent story of what had happened; and presently there issued forth a motley throng curious to learn the truth of the business.

When they reached the scene they saw the man who had been mad sitting at the feet of Jesus, clothed, and in his right mind; and they were afraid. Earnestly and humbly, lest offence be given, they besought the Jewish magus to leave their coasts, and to bewitch no more of their hogs, for they were a poor people.

So Jesus returned with his company into the ship. But the former lunatic ran down to the water's edge and begged that they would take him with them. Jesus shook his head. "Go home to thy friends," he said, "and tell them how great things the Lord hath done for thee, and hath had compassion on thee."

They came again to the other side of the lake, having had little of rest or refreshment. Their reception, however, was in striking contrast to that of the Gergesenes. The crowds flocked down to the shore crying out a glad welcome. As Jesus landed, one of the rulers of the synagogue, whose name was Jair, hastened to meet him, and in the broken accents of a deeply distressed father entreated him: "My little daughter lieth at the point of death. Come, come and lay thy hands on her, that she may be healed and live."

There could be no refusal of such a request, and Jesus followed him at once as rapidly as the dense throng would permit. Many wished to delay him, to be cured of their own illnesses, and pressed towards him from every side. Among them was a woman, who for twelve years had been a miserable sufferer from a continual haemorrhage. Hope had lent her an access of vitality, and she squeezed herself desperately through the crowd, confident that she had only to touch the fringe of the rabbi's robe, and she would be relieved. But being ritually unclean she dare not face him, knowing that her contact was defiling. She therefore crept up behind and touched him surreptitiously. Her faith brought its own reward, for at once she felt within herself that the bleeding had ceased.

The hyper-sensitiveness of Jesus made him turn round sharply. "Who touched me?" he exclaimed.

Peter exploded, "Thou seest the multitude pressing upon thee on every side, and sayest, 'Who touched me?'"

"Someone did touch me," Jesus answered, and he looked about him keenly to discover who it might be. Certain that she would be found out, the woman in fear and trembling threw herself at his feet, and confessed. He did not rebuke her. "Daughter," he said, "thy faith hath made thee whole. Go in peace."

While he was speaking there came servants from the house of Jair, and reported to the distracted father, "Thy daughter is dead. Trouble not the Master."

Jesus heard them, and replied, "Be not afraid; only believe." He hastened to the house, having already ascertained the nature of the illness. He felt sure that the girl had only sunk into a coma. When they reached the place the professional 'mourners were already in attendance, weeping and wailing, and creating a din with their instruments. "Make way," he cried, "for the damsel is not dead, but sleepeth." They laughed him to scorn. Nevertheless, at his request, Jair had them sent away. Jesus went immediately to the inner room where the patient was lying, taking with him only Peter, James and John, and the girl's parents. He lifted the limp hand, and held it, letting his strength and warmth flow through the limb to the brain. Then he bent down and spoke sharply into her ear, *"Talitha cumi* (maiden arise)!" Her eyelids flickered and opened, and she sat up, to the great astonishment of her parents. Jesus told them to give her something to eat, and went his way, not waiting for their profuse thanks.

At his headquarters at Kefar-Naum he prepared again to set out on a short tour. And he came to Cana and to the region about Nazareth; but he would not enter his native town. They were still unbelieving there, and all that he might do was to lay hands on a few sick folk, and heal them.

The time was ripe for him to broaden the field of his operations. He looked upon the people, helpless, and leaderless, and pointed out to his disciples, "The harvest truly is plenteous, but the labourers are few. Pray ye therefore the Lord of the harvest, that he will send forth labourers unto his harvest."

He had chosen twelve of his followers, after the number of the tribes of Israel, and as well as he might he had taught them the principles of the Kingdom of God. They should now assume part of the responsibility for proclaiming the message of salvation throughout the land of Israel. He proposed to dispatch them two and two as his envoys, and on their return he would know best how to order his course. His final instructions before their departure were precise.

"Go not into the way of the Gentiles, and enter ye not into the cities of the Samaritans: but go ye unto the perishing sheep of the house of Israel. Go and cry, 'Turn ye, turn ye, for the Kingdom of Heaven is nigh at hand.' Provide neither gold, nor silver, nor lesser coin in your girdles. Pack not for the journey, either two coats, or sandals, or staves: for the labourer is worthy of his food. And into whatsoever city or town ye shall enter, inquire who in it is honourable; and there abide until ye go forth from thence. And when ye obtain entry into an house, ask after its peace, saying, 'Peace be with this house.' And if the house be honourable it will give you peace again. But if any man will not receive you, neither hearken to the sound of your words, go forth outside of the house or city, and shake off even the dust from your feet. Truly, I say unto you, it shall be more tolerable for the land of Sodom and Gomorrha in the Day of Doom, than for that city. Behold, I send you forth as sheep in the midst of wolves: be ye therefore subtle as serpents, and simple as doves.... He that receiveth you receiveth me, and he that receiveth me receiveth Him that sent me. He that receiveth a prophet as a prophet shall receive a prophet's reward; and he that receiveth a righteous man as a righteous man shall receive a righteous man's reward. And whosoever shall give to drink unto one of these little ones, even a single cup of cold water, as a disciple, truly, I say unto you, he shall in no wise lose his reward."

When the twelve had left on their mission, Jesus himself set forth on a more extended Galilean tour. The district to which he turned his attention was Upper Galilee, the stronghold of Zealotism, which he preferred to visit unaccompanied by his nearest disciples, who might have embarrassed him by their sympathies with the followers of Judas of Galilee, and precipitated a crisis. Among the places which he entered in this wild mountainous country, with its fanatical inhabitants, must have been Gishcala and Meiron, names familiar in Jewish history of the time. It is tempting to speculate that the high rock near the latter was even in those days called *Kissë haMashiah* (Messiah's Throne). No record remains of what Jesus said or did in the Zealot country; but when he returned to the neighbourhood of Kefar-Naum, after a short and not very satisfactory stay at austere Chorazin, he had familiarized himself with the viewpoint of the ardent nationalists.

It was at this juncture that a deputation or embassage came to Jesus. The facts are rather difficult to ascertain. According to the records of *Matthew* and *Luke*, John the Baptist, having heard in prison reports of the activities of the man whom he had initiated into the new fellowship of Israel, sent two of his disciples with the direct question, "Art thou the destined to come, or do we await another?" Manifestly this was a question to which Jesus was forced to return an inconclusive answer. He replied therefore, "Go ye and tell John what ye have heard and seen: the blind receive their sight, the lame walk, the lepers are cleansed, the deaf hear, and the poor are made happy, and happy is he that is not offended in me.

Mark omits this incident altogether: but *John*, combining what apparently occurred with a much later event which took place at Jerusalem, has a curious story of the Pharisees and chief priests sending officers to arrest Jesus while he was teaching in the Temple on the feast of Tabernacles. The confusion is due to a similarity of features, and is discerned by reference to other traditional material never previously utilized in a life of Jesus. On the basis of this material, and in the absence of any certainty, it is possible to attempt no more than a conjectural reconstruction of the circumstances.

The Pharisee opponents of Jesus had been watching his movements anxiously, and they feared the worst from his incursion into the Zealot country, where they, had not followed him. What had he been plotting? They knew of the sending forth of the Twelve; and they deemed it opportune to take advantage of his comparative unguardedness—now that he was again among them—to have him brought before the district Sanhedrin for interrogation. This court, to be distinguished from the Great Sanhedrin at Jerusalem, held its sessions at Sepphoris. One of its members, who was also a member of the higher court, was Nicodemus. There was no question of arrest, as there was no charge against Jesus; but he could be invited, more or less peremptorily, to appear and answer inquiries about his recent movements and intentions. He could not of course be compelled to incriminate himself. Accordingly it was decided to send two emissaries—their names are given in one version as Ananias and Ahazias[48]—accompanied by an escort of horsemen, to require his attendance at Sepphoris.

They came upon Jesus while he was teaching by the lake north of Kefar-Naum. There was immediate evidence of the hostility of the crowd, which would not let them through, and not a few threats of open violence. Jesus strove to pacify the people by crying, "Fight not, but trust ye in the power of my Father which is in heaven." It is not clear whether the emissaries were able to deliver their message; but in the end they were forced to retire with the warning of Jesus, "Go ye, and report what ye have seen. These are the same words that he is said to have used to the Baptist s disciples.[49]

The officers sought to justify to the court their failure to produce their man, by describing the extraordinary sway which he wielded over the multitude. "Never man spake like this man," they said. "Are ye also deceived?" was the scathing comment. "Have any of the magistrates or of the Pharisees believed in him? It is only these plebeians, these *amme-haaretz*, which knowing not the Law are accursed." Nicodemus ventured a mild protest. "Doth our Law judge any man before it hear him, and know what be doeth? He had a lively recollection of his interview with Jesus, with whom he had been greatly impressed. They rounded on him, their anger no whit abated by the fact that to hear Jesus and know what he was doing, was what they had been unable to achieve. "Art thou also of these Galileans?" they challenged their colleague rudely. "Search for thyself, and see that the Prophet cometh not out of Galilee."

In the meantime, after the officials had gone, Jesus addressed the crowd, which Luke describes as "an innumerable multitude of people, insomuch that they trod one upon another." He said: "Beware ye of the leaven of the Pharisees, which is hypocrisy. For there is nothing covered, that shall not be revealed; neither hid, that shall not be known. Whatsoever has been spoken in darkness shall be heard in the light, and that which hath been whispered in the ear in closets shall be proclaimed upon the housetops. And I say unto you, my friends, be not afraid of them that kill the body, and after that have no more that they can do. But I will forewarn you whom ye shall fear: fear him, which after he hath killed hath power to cast into Gehenna; yea, I say unto you, fear him."

Jesus pointed to some children, who, free of care, were modelling birds out of clay,[50] and asked: "Are not five sparrows sold for two farthings, and not one of them shall fall to the ground without your Father? Even the very hairs of your head are all numbered. Fear not, therefore, ye are of more value than many sparrows. Whosoever therefore shall confess me before men, him will I confess also before my Father which is in heaven. And whosoever shall deny me before men, him will I also deny before my Father which is in heaven. Think not that I am come to send peace on earth: I am not come to send peace, but the sword. For I am come to divide a man from his father, and the daughter from her mother, and the daughter-in-law from her mother-in-law. As it is written, 'A man's enemies shall be the men of his house.' And whoso loveth his father and mother more than me is not worthy of me; and whoso loveth son or daughter more than me is not worthy to be with me in the Kingdom of Heaven. And when they bring you into the synagogues, and unto magistrates, and powers, take ye no thought how or what ye shall say; for it shall be put into your mouths what ye shall answer. For it is not ye that shall speak, but the Spirit of your Father shall speak in you." There is considerable foreboding about this speech. The opposition had made a concrete move. More drastic action would almost surely follow. The controversy would be even unto death before the messianic reign was established.

Some of the Galilean disciples of John the Baptist came forward and put the definite question to Jesus, was he the Messiah, or no? They had every right to do so. That they had been sent by John all the way from the southern fortress of Machaerus, where he was incarcerated, seems improbable: but the stern and uncompromising prophet had many adherents among the Galilean highlanders. They had the same slogan, "No King but God!" The Baptist had spoken of the one who should come, and now Jesus had been among them preaching in very similar terms. His words invited a demand for certain knowledge. But he could only answer by inference. The stage was not yet set for the denouement.

When these had taken their departure, Jesus began to speak of John to the crowd with his experiences among the Zealots fresh in his mind. His bantering tone was belied by the earnestness of his manner.

"What went ye out into the wilderness to see? Was it a reed (*kanah*) shaken with the wind (i.e. a Zealot—*Kanna* —moved with passion)?

"But what went ye out to see? Was it a man clothed in soft raiment (i.e. surrounded with flatteries)? Behold, they that be clothed in soft raiment are in kings' houses.

"Only what went ye out to see? The prophet? Yea, I say unto you, he was more than a prophet. For he it is, concerning whom it was written, 'Behold, I send my messenger, which shall prepare the way before me.' Truly, I say, among them that are bom of women there hath not arisen a greater than John the Baptist: howbeit he that is least in the Kingdom of Heaven is greater than he. Only from the days of John the Baptist until now the Kingdom of Heaven is raped, and the forceful despoil it. For all the Prophets and the Law prophesied until John. And if ye will receive it, this is Elijah, which was to come. *He that hath ears to hear, let him hear.*"

The glance of Jesus rested again on the children at play. "Whereunto shall I compare this generation?" he continued. "It is like the children sitting in the market, which call unto their companions, and say, 'We have played merrily unto you, and ye have not danced; we have played mournfully, and ye have not lamented.' For John came neither eating nor drinking, and they say, ' He is possessed of a demon.' The Son of Man came both eating and drinking, and they say, 'Behold the man, a glutton and a drunkard, and a friend of publicans and sinners.' But wisdom is justified of her children."

He felt a sense of frustration, and spoke with a touch of bitterness.

"Woe unto thee, Chorazin! woe unto thee, Bethsaida! (cities of fanatical nationalism) for if the mighty works were done in (alien) Tyre and Sidon, which were done in you, they would long ago have turned from evil in sackcloth and ashes. Surely, I say unto you, it shall be more tolerable for Tyre and Sidon in the Day of Judgment, than for you.

"And thou, Kefar-Naum (home of indulgence), art thou not raised up to heaven? Thou shalt be reduced to Gehenna. For if the mighty works were done in (selfish) Sodom, which were done in thee, doubtless it would have remained unto this day. Truly, I say unto you, it shall be more tolerable for the land of Sodom in the Day of Doom, than for thee."

Jesus was overwrought: he missed the comforting support of the Twelve. It had been a day of alarms. There was imminent danger of the interruption of his activities. Why could not the people see, as he did, that the time was short? Why did they make so little response? Why did they not realize the urgency for repentance? He had allowed his anxiety to find vent in warning, sarcasm, and invective. Why were they so terribly obtuse when it came to the one thing that mattered? Truly it seemed as if their eyes were blinded, their ears deaf, and their hearts hardened. They craved physical healing, but thought nothing of their soul's salvation. Of what use to go on?

Thankfully he accepted the suggestion of one of the Pharisees that he should dine with him. It was a God-sent opportunity to relax, and for a brief space to forget. His host appeared to regard his invitation as a religious duty, the bestowal of a pious kindness, rather than as a privilege, for he took no pains—as Jesus noted—to show his guest any of the customary courtesies.

While they were reclining at table, however, there came a prostitute of the city, having learned where the teacher was, bringing with her an alabaster box of ointment. She came as a living lesson to Jesus himself that the message of repentance meets with a response in the most unlikely places, a lesson which later found an echo in his declaration to the self-righteous, "The publicans and the harlots go into the Kingdom of Heaven before you." The woman now stood behind him weeping, bathing his feet with her tears, and wiping them with her long tresses. Having dried his feet, she kissed them, and anointed them with her ointment.

The Pharisee was amazed that he accepted these services. Surely, if this man were a prophet, he would have known what manner of woman this was, and not suffered her to defile him with her touch.

Jesus perceived what was passing in his mind, and remarked suddenly, "Simon, I have somewhat to say unto thee."

"Say on, master."

There was a certain creditor which had two debtors: the one owed five hundred pence, and the other fifty. And when they had nothing to pay, he frankly forgave them both. Tell me, therefore, which of them will love him most?"

"I suppose he to whom he forgave most," replied the puzzled Pharisee.

"Thou hast judged rightly," Jesus approved, and indicated his ministrant. "Seest thou this woman? I entered into thine house, thou gavest me no water for my feet: but she hath washed my feet with her tears, and wiped them with the hairs of her head. Thou gavest me no kiss: but this woman since the time I came in hath not ceased to kiss my feet. My head with oil thou didst not anoint: but this woman hath anointed my feet with ointment. Wherefore I say unto you, her sins, which are many, are forgiven; for she loved much: but to whom little is forgiven loveth little."

He turned to the woman graciously: "Thy sins are forgiven. Go in peace."

And that peace which went with the woman, as she drew her robe across her burning tear-stained face and moved away, remained also in the comforted heart of him who had bestowed it.

When Jesus took his leave his despondency had entirely vanished. Food and drink had warmed and cheered him. But more than these, his body had been soothed by the harlot's ointment, while her penitence had been as balm to his soul. In her person his erring people, astray from their God, had anointed his feet: soon, perhaps, it would be his hands, his breast, and his head. The proud waters that sought to engulf him had been repulsed. Surely they would be stayed while he set to work with renewed energy to rescue the sheep that were perishing. The presence of women in his own company was a great solace. Their faith might be instinctive, even superstitious; but it was loyal, and grateful, and abiding. Others might forget to-morrow what the Lord had done for them; but not they. There was Mary of Magdala, out of whom seven demons had been driven, and Susanna, and more significantly Joanna the wife of Herod's chancellor, who now had thrown in her lot with him, and several others. He thought of them with an affection in which there was nothing sensual as the mothers and sisters whom God had given him in his need, to replace those he had lost.

CHAPTER XIV

Sufficient Unto the Day

The fortress of Machaerus glowered from its commanding height upon the lesser mountains of Moab, and regarded disdainfully the opposing hills across the Dead Sea divide. The Watch Tower of Arabia, last outpost of Herod's tetrarchy in the south, was in no way concerned with Galilee's strivings after freedom: it contended with the wiry sons of Ishmael, and found itself fully engaged. Yet at this moment Machaerus must needs be the grim custodian of many northern hopes, for in its dungeon languished the Prophet John the son of Zacharias, called the Baptist. A scorned woman had placed him there, Herodias the wife of Antipas, because he had denounced her marriage as unlawful. Death would have ended his incarceration long since, if she could have had her way, but so far the tetrarch had refused to yield to her repeated solicitations, fearing a rising among his subjects.

This night there was feasting and revelry in the luxurious palace set on a neighbouring height, with which the fortress communicated by a causeway. Here everything was in utmost contrast both with the prison and the primeval landscape. It was a marvel how such magnificence had been transported to and erected upon so unpromising a site. It was the anniversary of Herod's accession, and he was making merry with his lords and captains. At the crown of the festivities, when the wine had circulated freely, the lithe and beautiful Salome, young daughter of Herodias by her former marriage, came in and danced, and so delighted the tetrarch that he swore to give her whatever she desired. This was Herodias's opportunity. Quickly she told the girl to ask for the head of John the Baptist. Herod was drunkenly grieved; but he would not go back on his oath, and sent an executioner to the fortress. Presently he returned bearing the grisly guerdon on a dish.

Some of the disciples of John, ever at hand to serve their master, heard the direful news, and begged for the body. They interred it in a rocky cavern amidst the fierce solitude of the mountains which looked away to the distant green prospect of the Jordan valley, and then they journeyed north day and night to tell Jesus.

The younger prophet was deeply moved at the tidings. His path and that of the Baptist had crossed but once; but this had been the supreme moment of his life, and he had lived ever since in the glory of that ineffaceable experience. Memory vividly recalled the scene, the multitudes, the stem and strangely garbed preacher, the water, the thunder, the lightning, the dove, the Voice.... And now a burning and a shining light had been taken out of the world, and the world grew dark and cold. "The Kingdom of Heaven is at hand!" At hand—oh God!

A harsh voice broke in upon his musings. "Master, why tarriest thou? Escape for thy life! It was for this we came swiftly to warn thee."

Jesus did not delay, but took ship and fled across the northern end of the lake to a desert place alone. Here for the time he was safe in the territory of Herod Philip, half-brother of Antipas, and the discarded husband of Herodias. As it happened the tetrarch of Galilee was disinclined to make inquisition for him. He had heard reports of a new prophet proclaiming a similar message to the one he had executed, and effecting miraculous cures. A momentary remorse made him declare superstitiously, "It is John the Baptist: he is risen from the dead, and therefore the powers are working in him." But reason recognized that this was another, and Herod was relieved, for as long as the people had a substitute prophet they would not be inclined to cause a disturbance over the death of John. He had quite enough trouble on his hands because war was threatened by Aretas king of Petra, whose daughter he had divorced in order to marry Herodias. One day he would satisfy his curiosity by seeing the new prophet and comparing him with John; but that could wait.

Word was brought to Jesus in his retreat that his twelve envoys had returned, and he came back secretly to meet them. The Twelve were full of their adventures, and told him gleefully, "even the demons were subject unto us." Their exuberance of spirits was heartening and contagious. "I beheld Satan as lightning fall from heaven," ejaculated Jesus thankfully, and added soberly, "Notwithstanding in this rejoice not, that the spirits are subject unto you; but rather rejoice, because your names are written in heaven." In fulness of gratitude for this further token of God's guiding hand, he lifted up his soul in praise:

"I give thanks unto thee, O Father, Lord of heaven and earth, which hast concealed these things from the wise and prudent, and hast revealed them to the despised. Yea, O Father, for so was Thy will before Thee."

He turned a radiant face upon his disciples, and spoke in the mystical language which he used when his being was exalted. "All hath been given me of my Father. And no man knoweth a son like a father; neither knoweth any one the Father as a son knoweth Him, and to whomsoever the son willeth to reveal Him. Come unto me, all ye that labour and are heavy laden, and I will satisfy you. Take my yoke upon you, and learn of me, for I also am driven out and depressed in spirit; and ye shall find rest for your souls. For my yoke is gentle, and my burden is light." Practical considerations made it inadvisable to continue. The spot was frequented, and it might be dangerous to linger here too long. "Come," he said, "into a desert place, and rest a while." As unobtrusively as possible they took ship, and made for the coast near Bethsaida Julias, where Jesus had been living in seclusion.

But he had been seen and recognized, and his going marked by some of the people. Swiftly the tidings circulated that Jesus had landed and left again with his disciples. A large number, therefore, ran out and, watching the direction of the vessel, hurried round the head of the lake, and made such good time that they were there to greet Jesus on his arrival. He was deeply touched, because they were as sheep not having a shepherd, and straightway he began to teach them.

Thus occupied, the evening drew on, and the disciples anxiously noted the lengthening shadows. Still Jesus continued, absorbed in his discourse. At last they could contain themselves no longer, and approached him: "This place is desolate, and the hour is already past; take leave of the crowd, therefore, that they may go into the villages, and buy themselves food."

"There is no need for them to go," said Jesus. "Give ye them to eat."

"Wouldst thou have us go and buy two hundred pennyworth of bread to feed this multitude?" they protested.

"How many loaves have ye? Go and see."

They reported on inquiry that there were five small barley loaves and two pickled fish, the remaining stock of a boy vendor.

"Bring them hither to me," Jesus commanded. He ordered the people to sit down in rows on the grass. Then he took the loaves and the fishes, and lifting up his eyes to heaven, he said the blessing, and broke the food, and distributed it to his disciples, and they in turn to the crowd. And the story tells that all did eat and were satisfied; and there were left over twelve baskets full of the fragments. And the number of them that did eat were five thousand men, beside the women and infants.

It is vain to deny that the canonical records intend us to understand that a miracle took place, and that there was a mysterious multiplication of the food. It is equally vain to attempt to explain the miracle scientifically or mystically so as to bring it within the bounds of our comprehension. Such multiplications are familiar in Jewish legend. As late as the days of the Maccabees it is said that when Judas purified the Temple from heathen abominations only one cruse of pure oil for the lighting was to be found, and that this was miraculously multiplied so as to last for eight days until new oil could be procured.

It is more important to recognize that the essential event lay outside the sphere of the miraculous. Popular report has not been able altogether to conceal the direction of true emphasis. The description of the Fourth Gospel, with its mention of a discussion about the manna in the wilderness and "the bread from heaven," allows it to appear that Jesus performed one of those "magical" or symbolic acts with which the prophets of old were wont to dramatize their message. Other traditions enable us partially to make good a very definite loss.

The incredulous disciples asked, "Will God prepare a table in the wilderness?"1 Jesus reminded them of Isaac's blessing on Jacob, promising the dew of heaven, and the fatness of the earth, and plenty of com and wine. He played on the word *rov* (plenty), reading *ribu* (10,000) and pointed forward to the fulfilment of the blessing, when they should eat and drink at his table in the Kingdom, and sit on twelve thrones judging the twelve tribes of Israel. "The days will come," he said, "in which vines shall grow, each having ten thousand stems, and on each stem ten thousand branches, and on each branch ten thousand shoots, and on each shoot ten thousand bunches, and on each bunch ten thousand grapes, and each grape when pressed shall yield twenty-five measures of wine; and when one of the righteous shall lay hold of one of these bunches another will Cry out, 'I am a better bunch; take me, and through me bless the Lord.' Likewise also a grain of wheat shall bear ten thousand ears, and each ear shall have ten thousand grains, and each grain shall yield ten pounds of fine wheaten flour. So shall it be with every fruit, and seed, and herb; and every beast that feedeth thereon shall dwell in peace the one with the other, and shall be subject unto the dominion of men."[51]

But Judas Iscariot murmured, "Shall the Lord indeed do these things?"

Jesus answered him, "They shall see who come to those times."[52] Afterwards he taught the multitude, "Labour not for the food which perisheth, but for that food which endureth unto the life of the world to come, which the Son of Man shall give unto you." If he did not quote the words of the prophet Isaiah, they were certainly present in his mind:

> "Wherefore do ye spend money for that which is not bread, and your labour for that which satisfieth not? Hearken diligently unto me, and eat ye that which is good, and let your soul delight itself in fatness. Incline your car, and come unto me: hear, and your soul shall live; and I will make an everlasting covenant with you, even the sure mercies of David. Behold, I have given him for a witness to the people, a leader and commander to the people."

This doctrine marks a turning point in the public career of Jesus. In face of the danger in which he stood the time for reticence was passing away; the messianic message could become more definite. He was now determined to return and face his enemies: it did not become him to skulk in wilderness retreats. He therefore urged his disciples to take ship and return round the head of the lake to Bethsaida, while he sent the people away.

It was not easy to get rid of the multitude, for they had understood some of the implications of his words, and they would have taken him by force and made him king. Only with great difficulty were they persuaded to leave him: and he, having committed himself to a bolder policy, went up into a mountain to pray.

The night advanced, and still Jesus remained in prayer. The course that he proposed to follow might lead to his death, or to victory. The future was as dark as the skies above, as filled with trouble as the rising tempest. But his resolve was confirmed. John had been faithful unto the last; how could he exhibit cowardice or fear?

Coming down from the height, he took his way along the border of the lake towards Kefar-Naum. In the ship his disciples had made little progress against the head wind, which bad forced them inshore. They were bending at their oars, toiling in rowing, and were closer to the bank than they thought. Suddenly the figure of Jesus rose up before them in the shallows. Failing to recognize him in the dim light, they cried out in fear, "It is a *mazik* (a malignant spirit)!" Jesus answered, "Have confidence: it is I; be not afraid." He went on board, and shortly after the wind dropped, and they were able to make good speed to Gennesaret.

On their arrival there was an extraordinary bustle and activity, as they were recognized. There was a rush to bring the sick to be cured, and there were many entreaties that they might only be allowed to touch the fringe of the Master's robe. All that day Jesus ministered to the sufferers, until the invitation of a Pharisee to dine made him aware of his need of refreshment.

Tired and abstracted, he went into the house just as he was without washing his hands. The host wondered at this breach of the prescribed conduct, but made no remark. There were scribes there, however, who did not hesitate to inquire, "Why do thy disciples (implying, why dost thou) eat bread without washing the hands?" Jesus came to himself, and, as was his habit, answered the question by asking another. "And why do ye transgress the commandments of God by your decrees? Is it not written in the Law, 'Honour thy father and thy mother?' Moreover it is written, 'And he that curseth his father and his mother shall surely die.' Yet ye say, 'Whosoever saith unto father and mother, It is a *corban* (a dedicated gift), whatsoever of mine might profit thee, he shall be free,' though he honoureth not his father and his mother. Thus have ye made void the commandments of God by your decrees. Ye hypocrites, Isaiah did well indeed to prophesy concerning you, 'This people honoureth me with mouth and lips, but its heart is far from me, and their fear toward me is become a taught commandment of men.'"

"It is the same God that made outside and inside," said Jesus to his host. "If thou bestow alms as thou art able, all things shall be clean to thee." He may have said much more, as Luke suggests, for his nerves were on edge after the day's exhausting labours. At the end he rose abruptly, and went out, and called the people to him. "Hear, and know," he declared, "that whatsoever entereth into the mouth defileth not the man; but that which proceedeth out of the mouth, that defileth the man."

Then came his disciples, rather perturbed, to tell him, "Knowest thou that the Pharisees which heard this saying were annoyed?" And he answered, "Every plant, which my Father in heaven hath not planted, shall be rooted up. Leave them alone: for they be blind, and leaders of the blind. And if the blind lead another blind, both of them shall fall into the ditch."

But when he had gone home, Peter asked him, "Explain unto us this parable."

"Are ye also without understanding?" Jesus complained. "Do ye not understand, that whatsoever entereth into the mouth entereth into the belly, and is cast out in excretion? But those things which proceed out of the mouth, they proceed from the heart; and these are the things which defile the man. For from the heart proceed evil thoughts, murders, adulteries, fornications, thefts, false witness, and blasphemies: these are the things which defile the man: but that he should eat without washing his hands defileth not the man."

Jesus speedily recovered his equanimity. It was hardly possible to awaken to the wonder of a Galilean morning in early spring without sunshine in one's own soul; and this was lovely Gennesaret, where the birds and rills made music, the flowers flashed their colours, and the thick foliage gave grateful shade—the Garden of Princes.

Strolling with his disciples by the estates of the nobles with their bams and storehouses protected by fencing, he told the story of the rich man, who was so avaricious that he kept putting off the day when he would peacefully enjoy his possessions until too late. "Thou fool," God said to him, "this very night thy soul shall be required of thee, and whose then shall all these tilings be?"

"Lay not up for yourselves stores upon earth," Jesus continued, "where caterpillar and moth devour, and where thieves break through and steal; but lay up for yourselves stores in heaven, where caterpillar and moth waste not, and where thieves do not steal: for there where your store is, there your heart will be also.

"And therefore I say unto you, be not anxious for your souls, in what ye shall eat, or in what ye shall drink; or for your bodies, wherewith ye shall be clothed. Is not the soul more than food, and the body more than raiment? See the birds of the heavens; they sow not, neither do they reap, nor gather into their bams; yet your Father which is in heaven feedeth them. Arc ye not much better than they?" He smiled gaily. "Which of you by taking thought can add even a single cubit (eighteen inches) to his stature? Why, then, are ye anxious about raiment (Will you suddenly grow right out of your clothes)?

"Consider the lilies of the field (the wild narcissus), how they grow; yet they toil not, neither do they spin. Truly, I say unto you, that not even Solomon in all his glory was arrayed hke one of these. Wherefore, if God so clothe the herb of the field, which to-day is, and to-morrow is cast into the oven, how much more so you, O little of faith.

"Be not anxious, therefore, saying, 'What shall we eat?' or 'What shall we drink?' or 'What shall we wear?' For after all these tilings do the Gentiles seek: for your Father which is in heaven knoweth that ye have need of all these things. Seek ye therefore at the first the sovereignty of God, and His righteousness; and all these things shall be added unto you. And be not anxious for the morrow: for the morrow's day shall be anxious for itself. Sufficient unto the day is the evil thereof."

An interesting fact about this teaching is that it consists of a string of Jewish proverbial pearls, which Jesus has most fittingly strung together. It shows how well known to him was the wisdom of his people, and thus throws a valuable sidelight on his educational equipment, which for one of his upbringing is quite remarkable. Most of the parallels have been noticed by scholars; but there is one which appears hitherto to have escaped attention. The writer of the *Letter of Aristeas*, living a century before Jesus, has put this speech into the mouth of the high priest Eleazer: "The priests who rule the Egyptians, and have closely investigated many things and been conversant with the world, call us (Jews) 'men of God,' a designation which does not belong to the rest of mankind (the Gentiles), but to him only who reverences the true God: but they are men of meat and drink and raiment, for their whole nature finds its solace in these things. But with our countrymen these things are counted of no worth, but their reflections throughout their whole life concern the sovereignty of God."[53]

CHAPTER XV

Whom Say Ye that I Am?

The year which now opened proved to be one of intense activity and increasing drama, during which Jesus progressively abandoned his non-committal attitude, and revealed himself clearly as the Messiah first to his disciples, then to other persons, later to the people, and finally to his enemies. This same year was one in which Jewish religious and political feelings were exacerbated by the high-handedness of the procurator Pontius Pilate, who, planning to bring a supply of water to Jerusalem by means of an aqueduct, raided the sacred treasury of the Temple, and seized the corban money to defray the cost. There was an outbreak at Jerusalem, probably at the Passover early in April, A. D. 30, which had wide repercussions.

That Pilate should have chosen to obtain funds for a quite meritorious enterprise in this typically stupid and ruthless fashion in the very year that Jesus purposed to manifest himself publicly as the Messiah is one of those strange conjunctions of circumstances in which history abounds. Under normal conditions a man who claimed to be the Messiah, and who yet neither attacked the government, incited to sedition, nor raised armies, might have been allowed to go his way deluding himself, as unbelievers would say, and his wretched dupes, until he came to a natural end or his followers tired of him. He might have become the venerable and venerated head of a quasi-mystical Jewish sect, with a series of elected successors, for as long as the group held together. The Nazarenes, or Christians, so far as they were heard of at all, would have been set down as religiously eccentric and politically harmless. But all of these possibilities were ruled out by the highly inflammable state of popular feeling. A Messiah, any sort of Messiah, was a menace to the peace of the country, and it was almost inevitable that the authorities should take steps to dispose of him. The procurator of Judea had the wrath of Caesar to fear if the Jews revolted; the tetrarch of Galilee had to fear for his position and revenues if his turbulent subjects got out of hand; the high priest had to fear for the very life of the nation if the Zealots took the bit between their teeth. The fate of hundreds of thousands of innocent people would require the speedy death of this one man, and that man as it happened was Jesus of Nazareth.

There was no one who saw this more clearly than Jesus himself as the eventful year wore on.

At present he was unaware either of the necessity for, or the imminence of, what he came to regard as his voluntary sacrifice. He had already determined, however, no longer to evade his antagonists, and by this determination he had acquired a liberty of movement which had been lacking hitherto. His previous preaching tours had been of very limited extent, never more than a short radius from his base at Kefar-Naum. So long as it was practicable he now intended to cast loose from his lakeside anchorage, and dispense with his former precautions. He would follow up the initial journeys of his six pairs of envoys, and gradually cover the whole country. Before turning his face towards the south, he planned to complete his circuit of Galilee: this required that he should visit the extreme north-west and north-east. Nowhere is there any indication that he thought of overstepping the boundaries of the land of Israel. He had no direct mission to the Gentiles: his task was to rescue the lost sheep of his own people. It was through a redeemed Israel that the world at large would be saved and brought to a knowledge of the One God and Father.

The international knowledge of Jesus was not much greater than the average individual's knowledge of the extra-terrestrial universe. He was acquainted with Roman and Syrian as such individuals are acquainted with sun and moon, and he knew Greek, Egyptian, and Arab as they know the Great Bear, Venus, and the Milky Way. For the rest, there were Gentiles in the aggregate, ruled by the kings of the earth, as the universe is ruled by the planets. It was a geocentric system, with the *ge* very literally the *land* of Israel. The inhabitants of the earth were of two orders, the dwellers in the Land and the dwellers outside the Land. It was to this effect that the rabbis taught. "A man should always strive to dwell in the land of Israel, even if it be in a town where the majority are Gentiles, rather than to reside outside the land, even in a place where the majority are Israelites; for he who dwells in the land of

Israel is like one who has a God, and he who dwells abroad is like one who has no God, for it is said, 'To give you the land of Canaan, to be your God.'"[54]

The new series of excursions may partly have been intended to gain information about the state of the people in the different localities, their spiritual and social condition, and the nature of their messianic expectation. Jesus may also have purposed to visit the homes of certain Jews, whom his disciples in their travels had discovered to be of those who waited for the Redemption. It is not too much to imagine that a secret list of sympathizers had been compiled, some of whom later were to form the nucleus of the numerous Nazarene communities which sprang up rapidly, and were to be found dotted all over Galilee and the Decapolis, and as far north as Damascus. Tradition has recorded a few names of these adherents; but usually we hear of "houses" into which Jesus and his disciples might safely come. These were the propagating cells of the Kingdom of God. There was such a house somewhere on the borders of Tyre and Sidon in the zone of Syro-Greek influence to which Jesus now went, "and would have no man know it."

It is clear from this reference that there was nothing foolhardy or venturesome about these tours, in spite of the change of policy which made them possible. Jesus proceeded most circumspectly, more so indeed than during his campaign in the Zealot country. Messianically, he was travelling incognito, and he appears to have refrained from any public proclamation that would draw

the crowds about him. He was a stranger to these regions, and their potentialities were unknown: it was
wiser therefore not to take risks which might place him
in a false position, and perhaps result in imprisonment,
exile, or death. In any case the tangible results of his
public teaching, first boldly and then veiled in parables,
had been poor, almost negligible. There had not been
even the violent expressions of contrition which had attended the ministry of John the Baptist. His appeal had
lacked the revivalist fervour of the ascetic prophet: it had
been addressed to the reason rather than to the emotions. His popularity had rested on his fame as a doctor,
body-doctor and spirit-doctor. It was patent to Jesus
that he was sought after for his benefactions and not for
his doctrines. After all that he had said, the Kingdom of
God remained for most men a shadowy hope, perhaps
more shadowy now for being so much talked about. Who
knew what the Kingdom really was, and how it would
function? Who could tell, except the Zealots, of a way by
which it might be called into existence? He had explained what manner of men they would be that should
enter the Kingdom; but he had not revealed how they
might achieve that standard of virtue.

Had Jesus failed because he did not yet know the answer
to these vital questions? It still remained for him to discover that he himself was the way to the salvation which
he preached. All his experiences had been calculated to
impress upon him how little he commended his message; and his was too sensitive a nature not to be keenly
aware of his handicaps and limitations. His origin, upbringing, trade, and personality, were all against him. He

possessed neither beauty of face nor grace of form to make him a darling of the people. He knew that his mode of expression gave offence, that some of his qualities were not likeable. Even as a boy the other boys were not over anxious to have him as a playmate. He was alternatively preoccupied and disconcertingly outspoken. There was something about him that made it difficult to respond to the welcoming smile, the kindly eyes, and the compassionate voice. He could create trust and confidence; but he could not readily inspire affection. Men did him homage out of gratitude, or reverential awe; but none thought to embrace him except an errant disciple in the act of betrayal. There was genuine distress in the cry, "Betrayest thou the Son of Man with a *kiss*?" Too often those upon whom Jesus conferred benefits hastened swiftly away without pausing to give thanks. "Were there not ten lepers cleansed?" he asked sadly on one occasion. "But where are the nine? There are not found that returned glory to God, save this stranger." The solitary exception was a Samaritan. His followers were uneasy in his presence. Close association with the Master had modified, but had not dispelled, a curious feeling of oppression like that which is experienced when a storm is gathering. There was superstitious fear, there was a measure of faith, but there was little love. Perhaps it was that truth in itself is not lovable. It is not easy to love the lightning and the sharp two- edged sword, and by his own words Jesus had confessed that he had come to send both these visitations. And he did not make truth palatable: he did not coat it with honey. He presented it abruptly, often rudely, so that it hurt. He had received the advances of Nicodemus with apparent incivility. The antagonism of the Galilean Pharisees had arisen out of his pointed and biting remarks about hypocrites. Towards the end many of his disciples went back, and walked no more with him, because they could not bear his hard sayings.

Some women loved Jesus: they were those who knew intuitively how he was starved of human love, and their nature answered the call of his need. Of his male intimates, only two, so far as we know, loved Jesus unfeignedly: they were Peter and the Unknown Disciple. The love and the loyalty of Peter appears in a dozen incidents. It was a doglike attachment, whereas that of the other was filial. It was these two, when the body of Jesus after his burial was reported missing, who cared most to discover what had become of his mortal remains. Just so, little children and animals loved Jesus: they recognized the depths of love in him, and their innocence was not offended in him. But adults on the whole found it hard to esteem him at his real worth; and the knowledge of this, while it saved him from self-pride and vanity, and made him direct the hearts of all men to the Heavenly Father, also interposed a barrier which was only broken down by his death.

Those who speak of the winsomeness of Jesus are speaking of an idealized figure, a refined, spiritualized, and radiant being, and not of the Jesus of history. Those who were acquainted with him on earth were reminded of the words of Isaiah, "He hath no form nor comeliness... there is no beauty that we should desire him." The faith of the Church could only thrive by ceasing to know Jesus after the flesh. The end of physical contact made it possible to fashion a frame after the likeness of his inner imperishable loveliness, spiritually discerned, which was hidden from most of his contemporaries.

A psychological study of the early life of Jesus makes many things about him intelligible, though it cannot account for every phase of his complex personality. The effects of his long and enforced self-repression were bound sooner or later to manifest themselves, as they did both in fits of moodiness and gusts of anger. Only his discovery of a life in God helped to correct the balance and enabled him to control undesirable impulses. There could have been no Temptation in the Wilderness for anyone less temperamental and highly-strung. The victory of the spirit was revealed by the absence of surliness in the times of abstraction, and of malice in the anger, and more than anything else by his normal poise and gentleness. But his abnormalities had certainly become aggravated by the conditions of his public career.

Since the call at Jordan Jesus had been prodigal in his expenditure of physical and nervous energy. He had lived on the capital of his strength, and with every month that passed he became a more difficult man with whom to deal. He had never been what is called polite: he had never tried to fit himself for Society; but now under the burden of the continual strain even his customary self-possession frequently forsook him. He suffered badly from insomnia. His condition manifested itself in asperity and exasperation, and unconscious sarcasm. But he would not desist from his strenuous activities: he was driven on by his destiny. "I must work the works of Him that sent me, while it is day: the night cometh, when no man can work." His belief in his Divine election did not falter, but rather grew stronger, and induced strange dreams and visions. Where before he had expected that the coming of the Kingdom would be a gradual process by the permeation of the spirit of repentance; now he tended to imagine it established by a sudden cataclysm. Of his own generation only those would be saved who were elect, as he was elect. God had elected him, and he had elected his companions, and they in turn would bring in those other elect, who would be found worthy to stand before the Son of Man in the Day of Doom. At times he spoke with mystic meaning, but not in mystic language, about his relationship with God the Father; and his phrasing of the stuff of Essene apocalyptic about his pre-existence and future glorification sounded to the ordinary devout mind not a little blasphemous. He began to dwell on the idea of suffering in a way that was perilously near to being morbid, and to envisage his future power and majesty with a suspicion of megalomania. The manner in which he would dazzle and confound his startled enemies appears in his later parables, in that of the Wicked Husbandmen, of the Sheep and the Goats, and of the Talents (or Pounds).

"Whosoever shall fall on this stone—rejected of the builders— shall be broken: but on whomsoever it shall fall, it will grind him to powder."

"When the Son of Man shall come in his glory, and all the holy angels with him, then shall he sit on the throne of his glory: and before him shall be gathered all nations...."

"Those mine enemies, which would not that I should reign over them, bring hither, and slay before me."

These are expressions which, even in parable, are rather unhealthy. In fact the evidence covering the later part of his career makes obvious, what anyone could safely have predicted, that Jesus was on the verge of a nervous collapse.

The spaces in which he could recruit his strength and restore his peace of mind grew fewer during this last year of his life. Even so far away from the centres of conflict as he was now, somewhere in the north-east of Palestine, he was not free from molestation. There came a woman out of those coasts, a Syro-Phoenician, begging healing for her afflicted daughter. Jesus took no notice, and at last his disciples entreated him, "Do something for her, and send her away; for she crieth after us." Jesus responded, "I was not sent but unto the lost sheep of the House of Israel." The woman, however, reading hope in the petition being made on her behalf, hastened forward, and cast herself at his feet; but he continued adamant, and told her harshly, "It is not fitting to take the children's bread, and to give it to the dogs," a saying which tradition has paraphrased, "It is not lawful to heal the Gentiles, who are like to dogs on account of their using

various meats and practices, while the table in the Kingdom has been given to the Children of Israel."[55] But the
woman was quick-witted, and replied, "Truth, certainly,
lord: but the dogs, even they, eat of the fragments which
fall under their master's table." It was a confession that
no heathen could have made, and as such Jesus accepted
it appreciatively. "O woman," he said, relenting, "how
great is thy faith! Be it unto thee even as it is in thine
heart."

The poor canine has figured in the uncomplimentary
epithets of many nations. "Thou hast the face of a dog,"
meant in Palestine in those days, "Thou art like a Gentile." No doubt the Gentiles also spoke then as since of
"Dogs of Jews."

Tradition has more to tell us of the woman. Her name
was Justa, or she took that name, and she obtained healing for her daughter because already she was living after
the Jewish manner. This, indeed, is likely, not only from
her words, which suggest that she was a proselyte, but
because it is improbable that she would have heard of
Jesus and his powers except through close association
with Jews. Subsequently she was driven from home by
her pagan husband, and with her daughter joined the
Nazarene community.[56]

Shortly after Jesus had returned to the Sea of Galilee
there approached him both Pharisees and Sadducees,
tempting him, and asking that he would show them a
single sign from Heaven. Jesus made an exclamation of

disgust, and answered them according to the folly of the question. "When it is evening, ye say, 'It is destined to be fine by the heavens: for the heavens are ruddy.' And at daybreak, 'It will be stormy: for the heavens are lowering in their ruddiness.' And, behold, ye know how to judge the face of the heavens; but ye cannot discern the signs of the times. An evil and lewd stock seeketh a sign; and no sign shall be given it, but the sign of Jonah the prophet." And he turned on his heels and left them.

Almost immediately he took ship with his disciples to the head of the lake, and so abrupt was his departure that they had forgotten to furnish themselves with a supply of bread. And he said to them, "See and beware of the leaven of the Pharisees and Sadducees." The disciples imagined that he must be referring to their neglected purchase. "What are ye thinking, O little of faith," Jesus interrupted their whisperings, "that it is because ye have taken no bread? Why do ye not understand that it was not concerning loaves that I said to you, 'Beware of the leaven of the Pharisees and Sadducees?'" Then it dawned on them that by leaven he meant doctrine.

The road of Jesus now lay northward. Over the flower-carpeted hills he led them, and the favoured valleys, past the little lake called the Waters of Merom, traversing the rich Hula lands, and coming at last into the extreme limits of the Decapolis, into the parts about Caesarea Philippi, where the slopes of Hermon begin to mount to his snowclad summit, and pagan Pan presides over the birth of Jordan.

Walking there, and drinking in the health-laden breezes, Jesus fell to meditating on the strange riddle of his life and mission. The train of his thought made him turn suddenly to the Twelve, and ask, "What do men say of the Son of Man, who is he?" They answered, "Some say John the Baptist; and some say Elijah; and others again, Jeremiah, or another of the prophets." His voice rose sharply, "And ye, whom say ye that I am?"

There was silence, until Peter cried out impulsively, "Thou art the Messiah, the Son of the living God."

The strained expression vanished from the face of Jesus. Surely this was a *Bath Qol*, an inspired utterance. Warmly, he exclaimed, "Happy art thou, Simon bar Jonah, for flesh and blood did not reveal this unto thee, but my Father which is in heaven! And I say unto thee that thou art Kepha (the rock), and upon this rock will I build my kingdom, and the gates of Hell shall not prevail against thee.[57] And unto thee will I give the keys of the Kingdom of Heaven; and whatsoever, thou shalt bind on earth shall be bound in heaven, and whatsoever thou shalt loose on earth shall be loosed in heaven." And he charged his disciples that they should tell no man that he was the Messiah.

According to popular belief there were three gates to Hell, one in the desert, one in the sea, and one in Jerusalem. It was more particularly of the third gate that Jesus was thinking.[58]

He began to make known to them that he needs must go to Jerusalem, there to be rejected by the chief priests and elders and scribes, and to be slain; but on the third day he would rise again from the dead. For so it was written in Hosea: "I will be unto Ephraim as a lion, and as a young lion to the house of Judah.... I will go and return to my place, till they acknowledge their offence, and seek my face: in their affliction they will seek me early. Come, and let us return unto the Lord: for he hath tom, and he will heal us; he hath smitten, and he will bind us up. After two days will he revive us: in the third day he will raise us up, and we shall live in his sight. Then shall we know, if we follow on to know the Lord: his going forth is prepared as the morning; and he shall come unto us as the rain, as the latter and former rain upon the earth." Jesus viewed the prophetic necessity for his fate with equanimity. He actually found solace in the prospect of his ordained suffering. Just now he would not abate one whit of the penalties which should issue in glorious victory. He was in exalted martyr mood ready to caress the stake and lave his hands in the flames. But Peter experienced no such exaltation. His human devotion tore miserably at the fine meshes of the net in which the Eternal Fisherman had caught his beloved master. He laid hands on Jesus, as if to shake him free from the enveloping folds, chiding him as if he were a fractious child, saying over and over again, "Far be it from thee, lord: all this shall not be unto thee."

But the spirit of Jesus could not be grasped and held. He turned on the distressed apostle, and ordered him, "Follow me, satan! Thou art an offence unto me; for thou savourest not of the things that be of God, but of those that be of men." And he said to them all, "Whoever will follow me, let him reject self, and take up his cross, and follow me. For he that desireth to save his soul shall lose it; but he that shall lose his soul for my sake shall find it. For what shall it profit a man, if he gain the whole world, and in his own soul receive injury? Or what exchange shall a man give for his soul? The Son of Man shall surely come in the glory of his Father with his angels, and then shall he pay every man, each according to his deeds. Truly, I say unto you, there be those standing here, which shall not taste death till they see the kingdom of the Son of Man that cometh."

Six days later Jesus took Peter, James, and John, and led them up Mount Hermon. Peter's misery had affected him more deeply than he showed, and he wished as far as possible to prepare the minds of these loyal friends, who had been with him from the beginning, for the ordeal which he was convinced was to come. "The hour is at hand," he told them, "that the Son of Man should be glorified." And he explained, "Except a com of wheat fall into the ground and die, it abideth alone: but if it die, it bringeth forth much fruit." He strove to persuade them to bridge the dark gulf of the valley of death, and to look beyond, as their eyes might do even now, up to the majesty of the heights sparkling in the sunshine. He was only partially successful, for their minds could not reach out and seize the grandeur of the conception. Something more was needed, needed too at heart by Jesus himself, for their persistent regard for the gloomy side had sent a chill into his own soul. He decided to spend the night on the mountain, and while his disciples slept he would commune with the Heavenly Father in the solitude.

Long after the trio had fallen into a troubled slumber, Jesus sat reflecting on the things that had been uppermost in all their thoughts during the day. Fragments of prophetic and apocalyptic ideas danced in his brain.

It was written that in the last days, "the mountain of the Lord's house shall be established in the top of the mountains, and shall be exalted above the hills; and all nations shall flow unto it." It was said that God would take the mountains of Sinai, Carmel, and Tabor, and pile them on top of one another, and set New Jerusalem on the summit.[59] There would come a great multitude to fight with the Son of Man, and he would cut out a lofty mountain, and fly with the clouds of heaven, and stand upon it; and the multitude would wither away at the fiery breath of his mouth. And he would call together another peaceable multitude, the lost tribes of Israel.... [60]

In the early dawn an urgent hand was laid on the shoulders of Peter and his companions. Jesus stood before them. His face was radiant. The rising sun streamed upon him through the haze, making his garments glisten like the snow, and transforming him into a being from another world. His words smote strangely on heavy ears. "Just now," he said, "the Holy Spirit lifted me by a lock of my hair, and carried me away to the top of Mount Tabor. And, behold, it had become a very great mountain.[61] And I stood on the height thereof, and drew all men unto me. And there came Moses from Sinai and Elijah from Carmel, and spake with me of my exodus at Jerusalem. And the glory of the Father was there, and He glorified me with His own glory, saying 'This is my beloved Son, with whom I am well pleased; hear ye him.'"

Not yet fully released from the thrall of sleep, the vision communicated itself to the half-conscious minds of the disciples as if they were actually participating in it. Peter, scarce knowing what he said, murmured, "Master, it is good for us to be here: if thou wilt let us make three tabernacles; for thee one, for Moses one, and for Elijah one."

A heavy mist swirled down and hid Jesus completely from view. The disciples were overcome with fear as they entered into the cloud, and hid their faces in their robes. Was the Spirit about to transport the Master, or all of them, to the dizzy altitude where God dwelt? Jesus approached and touched them. With relief they heard the familiar voice, saying, "Arise, and be not afraid." And when they had lifted up their eyes, and looked about, the mist had dispersed, and to their surprise there was no one there except Jesus only with themselves.

As they came down from the mountain Jesus charged them, "Tell no man the vision, until the Son of Man be risen from the dead." They looked at each other blankly, unable to comprehend what this rising from the dead should mean, and not daring to ask him. An easier question offered itself; it concerned his public manifestation as Messiah, which the vision had foretold. "Why say the scribes that Elijah must first come?" Jesus, assured by his recent experience, answered them, "Elijah shall surely come, and restore all things. And I say unto you, that Elijah is come already, and they knew him not, but have done unto him whatsoever they chose." Then they understood that he spoke of John the Baptist.

So they came to the rest of the disciples, and found a heated discussion going on between them and some of the scribes round a man who had brought his epileptic son to be cured. With one accord they turned to Jesus, and the man came eagerly forward, and began to pour out a long story of his boy's afflictions, how he kept falling into the fire and into the water; and the upshot of it was that he had brought him to the Master's disciples, but they could not cure him.

"O stubborn and perverse generation," exclaimed Jesus with a renewal of his old fire, "how long shall I be with you, how long shall I suffer you? Bring him to me." He rebuked the demon, and the boy was cured the same hour.

When the visitors had gone away, the disciples gathered about Jesus, and asked, "Why could not we cast the demon out?" He replied, "Because of your lack of faith. Truly, I say unto you, if ye have faith as a grain of mustard seed, and shall say unto this mountain here, 'Remove hence!' it will remove immediately; and the thing shall not be withheld from you. But such a demon as this is never cast out without prayer and fasting." The words show how greatly he was restored in health and spirits. "Uprooter of mountains" was a stock expression for one who overcame difficulties. To-day Jesus felt equal to shifting the mass of Hermon.

Unostentatiously, as he had come north, Jesus returned to Kefar-Naum, arriving there about the middle of March when the official money-changers were in session in the country towns to receive the half-shekel of the Temple tribute. The collectors approached Peter, inquiringly, "Doth your teacher pay the didrachma?" 'Certainly," said Peter, without hesitation. But when they reached the door of the house, Jesus barred his way. "How seemeth it to thee, Simon? Of whom do the kings of the earth receive custom and tribute, of their own subjects, or of foreigners?" "Of foreigners," replied Peter. "If so," said Jesus, "the subjects are free. Nevertheless, give to them, like the foreigner."[62] When they had entered the house Jesus asked the Twelve, "What was it that ye disputed among yourselves by the way?" They were silent; for they had been arguing which of them should be greatest in the coming kingdom. As so often, Jesus might appear to be completely self-absorbed; but all the time his senses were keenly alive to what was going on around him. Frequently he surprised both his disciples and his critics by catching up a remark which they had not intended to be overheard. His powers of perception and observation were remarkably acute, and very little escaped him. Now he sat down, and calling to him a child of the household, he took him in his arms, and said to them, "Truly, I say unto you, unless ye repent, and become as children, ye

shall not enter the Kingdom of Heaven. Whoever therefore shall humble himself as this boy, the same shall be
greatest in the Kingdom of Heaven. And whoso receiveth
one such boy as this in my name receiveth me."

Said John: "Master, we saw one casting out demons in
thy name; and we forbad him, because he followeth not
with us."

Jesus answered, "Forbid him not: for he that is not
against us is for us. And whoso offendeth one of these
little ones which believe in me, it were better for him that
an upper-millstone were hanged about his neck, and that
he were cast into the depth of the sea. Woe unto the
world because of offences! It must needs be that offences
come; but woe to that man by whom the offence
cometh." "Master," asked Peter, "how many times shall
my brother sin against me, and I forgive him? Till seven
times?"

"I say not unto thee, till seven times," was the emphatic
rejoinder, "but until seventy times seven times; for even
in the prophets, after they were anointed by the Holy
Spirit, the word of sin was found.[63]

"And therefore the Kingdom of Heaven is likened unto a
man that is a king who wished to make a reckoning with
his servants. And when he had begun to make a reckoning, one was brought unto him, which was due to render
him ten thousand minas. And as he had not wherewith
to pay, his lord commanded that he be sold, and his wife

and children, and all that he had, until full payment should be made of what was due to him. Then that servant fell down and entreated him, saying, 'Give me time, and I will pay thee all.' And the lord had pity on his servant, and let him go, and forgave him his debt.

"But this servant went forth, and found one of those who were servants like himself, and this one was due to render him an hundred meahs. And he seized him, and held him fast, saying, 'Pay what thou owest me.' Then that servant fell down, and entreated him, saying, 'Give me time, and I will pay thee all.' But he would not; and went and cast him into prison, till he should pay all his debt. So when the other servants saw what was done, they were exceedingly grieved, and came and related to their lord all that had happened.

"Then his lord called unto him, and saith unto him, 'Servant of Belial, I forgave thee all the debt, because thou didst intreat me and shouldst not thou also have had pity on thy fellow-servant, even as I had pity on thee?' And his lord's anger was kindled, and he delivered him to the prison, till he should pay all his debt. So likewise shall my Father which is in heaven do unto you, if ye from your hearts forgive not every man his brother their trespasses."

After this Jesus set his face steadfastly to go towards Jerusalem.

CHAPTER XVI

Tell That Fox

The Passover of A. D. 30 was at hand. Believing that it was necessary for him to suffer, and assured that his triumph would follow, Jesus was full of eagerness to offer himself. "I have a baptism to be baptized with; and how am I straitened till it be accomplished!" The Passover, with all its traditional significance, was so clearly the most appropriate Jewish festival at which to make his sacrifice, so that Israel might be delivered from a stronger bondage than that of Egypt, and begin a new life of freedom in the Spirit.

He elected to take the road through Samaria. He had no prejudice against the Samaritans. When set beside the great and eternal truths, which men esteemed so lightly, the schism of Gerizim seemed a very little thing. Coming now into the borders of the Cuthites, as the Jews termed the Samaritans, Jesus sent messengers ahead of him to secure lodging in one of the villages. But they would not receive him, as he was bound for Jerusalem. Stung by this insult to their Master, James and John, the turbulent, would have called down fire from heaven to consume the inhabitants. The displeasure of Jesus was with his hot-blooded disciples, not with the ignorant, if bigoted, people. "Ye know not what maimer of spirit ye are of," he rebuked them, "for the Son of Man is not come to destroy men's lives, but to save them." And they went to another village.

When they reached Judea, Jesus did not go direct to Jerusalem, but turned aside as he neared the city and, crossing Mount Scopus, he came down on the farther side of the Mount of Olives, and halted at the village of Bethany. Here a woman named Martha, who lived there with her sister Mary and her brother Lazarus, received him into her house.

At the festive season the environs of Jerusalem, especially on the eastern side, provided an extensive camping ground for pilgrims, who could have no hope of accommodation in the crowded city. Jesus preferred to make his temporary abode in a place where he could obtain some degree of quiet and privacy while he laid his plans. He was possibly influenced also by the gossip of the countryside which reported that all was not well in the Holy City. He learned that Pontius Pilate the procurator had outraged the feelings of all the religious parties, moderates and extremists alike, by seizing the Corban, the sacred funds of the Temple, in order to build an aqueduct to carry water from Solomon's Pools in the south into the city. The indignation was general, but in Jerusalem with the festival approaching there was likely to be serious trouble. Thousands were congregating from all parts, and if these were inflamed by fanatics, the consequences might rival the Black Passover of Archelaus.

It was manifestly inadvisable for Jesus to enter the city just now: his presence might be the means of provoking an outbreak against the Romans. The Galileans, as he knew from experience, were quite capable of setting him up as king, and making his Messiahship a rallying cry to rouse every loyal Jew to join in a holy war. Multitudes would be killed, and to no purpose. The people would have died in their sins, and the Kingdom of God would be farther away than ever. His own singular purpose would be wholly defeated. He might die, indeed, unmeritedly crucified or cut down by a Roman sword; but everything he had taught, and for which he had stood, would perish with him. His name would be only one more to add to the roll of heroes, or would earn the obloquy of a false prophet. To achieve its end, his death must stand out uniquely, and not lose itself in a holocaust of fruitless fury. His hour, it appeared, had not yet come.

Waiting developments, Jesus gave a remarkable exhibition of patience and restraint. Listening to his earnest, unhurried, teaching, no one could have realized how every nerve in his body was tingling with repressed excitement. Mary sat at his feet entranced. But Martha was of a different temperament. She was terribly worried over the situation, and tried vainly to conceal the fact by an excessive display of domestic zeal. She could not imagine how Mary could sit there placidly with all this going on. At last she could stand it no longer, and came to Jesus, and asked vexedly, "Master, dost thou not care that my sister hath left me to serve alone? Bid her therefore that she help me." Jesus understood her state of mind. Was he not enduring a greater torment? "Martha,

Martha," he said, "thou art careful and troubled about many things: but one thing is needful: and Mary hath chosen that good part, which shall not be taken away from her."

The best relief of all was prayer, and in those days Jesus was often at his devotions. Once when he had ceased, a disciple approached with the request, "Master, teach us to pray, as John also taught his disciples." It was a prayer for the Kingdom that he wanted; and Jesus responded with a variation of the well-known Aramaic words that concluded the prophetic preaching in the synagogue, and since known as the *Kaddish*.

"When ye pray, say, 'Our Father which art in heaven, hallowed be Thy Name. Thy kingdom come. Thy will be done, as in heaven so on earth. Give us to-day our needful bread. And forgive us our sins, as we release our debtors. And bring us not into temptation; but deliver us from the Evil One. For Thine is the kingdom, the power, and the glory, for ever. Amen.'"

"Bring us not into temptation; but deliver us from the Evil One." This indeed was a prayer that Jesus had made his own. Having brought himself into the proper frame of mind to meet his expected end, and having come so near to his goal, it was hard to hold back, and to conquer the urge to go on into Jerusalem, and to abandon himself, if need be, to the pressure of circumstances, to yield to the mad persuasion of the Zealots, to strive with them and—the Tempter suggested—to conquer. Never since

that night after his baptism had Jesus been so sorely be-set. Yet again, and more powerfully, he triumphed, and routed the Enemy of Souls. To God alone belonged the kingdom, and the power, and the glory.

Jesus soon had reason to know that his fears had not been groundless. When Pilate came up from Caesarea for the feast, as was the custom, he was assailed by the clam-our of the people, who cried out to him to cease work on the aqueduct, and to return the treasure to the Temple. Torrents of abuse were flung at his head, and the mob threatened to get out of hand. Neither were the Galileans averse to profiting by the occasion, and as usual took a leading part in the violent protest. Pilate refused to give way. This time he was not going to let these touchy Jews get the better of him with their foolish religious scruples. But in determining to quell the rioting, he was concerned to avoid any appearance of force which might offer an excuse for revolt. He therefore ordered his troops to cover their armour with the habits of pilgrims, and leav-ing their swords, to take staves in their hands, and mingle with the crowds in the Temple court. There should be nothing done, for which he might have to an-swer to Caesar.[64]

At a given signal his men set about beating the people, while in the inner court the Passover lambs were being slain; but so violently were his commands carried out by the soldiers that many of the worshippers were killed, and others were trampled to death. Pilate had had his re-venge for the business of the ensigns: but still there were some, incited by the Zealots, who overcame the garrison and seized the Tower of Siloam, which was the key to possession of the Ophel, the lower quarter of the city next to the Temple mount, and dominated the water supply from the Pool of Siloam in the valley. It was an abortive effort. The tower was isolated at a comer of the city wall. The men were ordered to surrender, and when they declined, battering rams were brought up, which eventually brought the masonry crashing down upon the defenders, eighteen of whom perished beneath the debris.

Among those arrested for taking part in the disturbances was one Jesus bar Abba, or bar Rabban. There is room for the opinion that the Galileans had deliberately used his name in order to give the impression that the prophet Jesus was with them. It may also be suggested that in ac-rimonious correspondence between Pilate and Herod Antipas, ruler of Galilee, arising out of the trouble, the tetrarch was told in no unmeasured terms to keep a firm hand on his unruly subjects, and he was advised that one of their ringleaders named Jesus had been taken pris-oner. The name, certainly, was not uncommon; but per-haps Herod assumed that this was the Jesus about whom he had heard so often. At any rate from that time there was enmity between him and Pilate.

The news quickly reached Bethany, and Jesus was told in detail about the disturbances, of the Galileans, whose blood Pilate had mingled with their sacrifices, and of those who had been buried in the fall of the Tower of

Siloam. He was much moved by the recital. How futile it was to expect that the Kingdom of God could be established by violence. He had raised his voice in warning before, and he must do so again. Such action could have only one ending. His pent-up feelings were released in a stormy outburst. "Suppose ye," he fired at his surprised informants, "that these

Galileans were sinners above all the Galileans, because they suffered such things? I tell you, nay: but, except ye repent, ye shall all likewise perish. Or those eighteen, upon whom the tower in Siloam fell, and slew them, think ye they were sinners above all men that dwelt in Jerusalem? I tell you, nay: but, except ye repent, ye shall all likewise perish."

They stared at him in amazement. Quickly he regained his self- control. He remembered that the mercy of God had granted him another year in which he might lead the people to repentance. Not this Passover, but the next, would be the great consummation. Who could tell what might happen in the interval. In calmer tones he told this story.

"A certain man had a fig-tree planted in his vineyard; and he came and sought fruit thereon, and found none. Then said he to the vinedresser, 'Behold, these three years I come seeking fruit on this fig-tree, and find none: cut it down; why cumbereth it the ground?' And he answering said unto him, 'Lord, let it alone this year also, till I shall dig it about, and dung it. Perhaps it will bear fruit. If not, after that thou shalt cut it down.'"

Jesus returned to Galilee, and again took up the threads of his work. It was not long before the tetrarch came to hear of it, and he imagined that Pilate had released him. Blaming him as the cause of his conflict with the procurator, he expressed himself in forcible language about prophets who fomented discontent and stirred up revolt. Certain of the Pharisees, who heard him, hastened to Jesus to warn him, "Get thee out, and depart hence: for Herod will kill thee."

Assured that he was now immune from death until the appointed time, Jesus made light of the threat, where a few months earlier he would have gone into hiding. "Go ye," he said, "and tell that Fox, 'Behold, I cast out demons, and I work cures to-day and tomorrow, and the third day I shall be perfected.' Nevertheless I must walk to-day, and to-morrow, and the day following; for it cannot be that a prophet perish out of Jerusalem."

It is not possible exactly to date a change of attitude; but after this episode even that section of the Pharisees which had been hostile to Jesus and his doctrines exhibited an altered behaviour. They had gone to great lengths to remove him by embroiling him with the civil power. They had seemed lost to all sense of decency and proportion, as often happens with men of learning and even piety when their cherished beliefs are assailed. But now that what they had schemed for was likely to come to pass without their instrumentality they forgave their rival all his hard words, and endeavoured to save him. A similar transformation had taken place in their attitude towards John the Baptist. As long as he had his freedom they attacked him with scornful criticism; but no sooner was he in the clutches of Herod than they began to champion him; so that when the tetrarch suffered defeat at the hands of Aretas king of Petra, they said openly that it was a punishment from God on account of his treatment of John.[65] Only a few decades later they again voiced their disapproval at the summary execution of James the brother of Jesus,[66] and took up the cudgels on behalf of the Apostle Paul. Their natural inclination was towards mercy and beneficence; and it was only the vehemence of their outraged feelings that made some of them so far forget themselves, a lapse which they endeavoured to repair when they realized its fatal consequences. More often now, when challenged, they held their peace.

Jesus laboured feverishly in the brief space which he felt remained to him to bring conviction to his hearers as he taught in house and synagogue. He had practically abandoned his open-air activities as a concession to the threat of the authorities. He had come so near to the valley of the shadows that he felt already like one who has returned from the grave. Where before he had striven earnestly for souls, now he wrestled for them mightily. All his gifts of speech, his powers of persuasion, his energy and strength, were thrown into the struggle. The urgency for decision was the keynote of his message.

"Strive to enter in at the narrow gate," he cried, "for I say unto you, many will seek to enter in, and shall not be able. When once the master of the house is risen up, and hath shut the door, and ye begin to stand without, and to knock at the door, saying, 'Lord, lord, open unto us;' and he shall answer and say unto you, 'I know you not whence ye are.' Then shall ye begin to say, 'We have eaten and drunk in thy presence, and thou hast taught in our streets.' But he shall say, 'I tell you, I know you not whence ye are; depart from me, all ye workers of iniquity.' There shall be weeping and gnashing of teeth, when ye shall see Abraham, and Isaac, and Jacob, and all the prophets, in the Kingdom of God, and you yourselves thrust out."

As he was dining one day, a fellow-guest, who had been attentive to his discourse, exclaimed, "Blessed is he that shall eat bread in the Kingdom of God!"

Jesus turned sharply, and related this parable. "A certain man made a great supper, and bade many: and sent his servant at supper time to say to them that were bidden, 'Come; for all things are now ready.' And they all with one consent began to make excuse. The first said unto him, 'I have bought a piece of ground, and I needs must go and see it: I pray thee have me excused.' And another said, 'I have bought five yoke of oxen, and I go to prove them: I pray thee have me excused.' And another said, 'I have married a wife, and therefore I cannot come.' So the servant came, and showed his lord these things. Then the master of the house being angry said to his servant, 'Go out quickly into the streets and lanes of the city, and bring in hither the poor, and the maimed, and the halt, and the blind.' And the servant said, 'Lord, it is done as thou hast commanded, and yet there is room.' And the lord said unto the servant, 'Go out into the highways and hedges, and compel them to come in, that my house may be filled. For I say unto you, that none of those men which were bidden shall taste of my supper.'"

Out of his heart and brain Jesus conjured up image after image to touch the consciences of his hearers. Yet the vivid and incomparable tales he told, which since have converted millions of erring souls, and still have not lost the force of their simple appeal, fell flatly on the dull ears of his own generation.

He described the joy in heaven over one repenting sinner. He envisaged God as the shepherd going after the lost sheep in the wilderness until he found it, and brought it home, rejoicing; as the woman sweeping out her house in search of her lost coin, and seeking diligently until she found it, and calling her neighbours to share her joy. He revealed God as the compassionate Father longing for the return of the prodigal, starving in a far country. Does there exist a more moving scene in any literature than the painting of the final reconciliation?

"I will arise," said the prodigal, "and go to my father, and will say unto him, Father, I have sinned against heaven, and before thee, and am no more worthy to be called thy son: make me as one of thy hired servants." And he arose, and came to his father. But when he was yet a great way off, his father saw him, and had compassion, and ran and fell on his neck, and kissed him. And the son said unto him, "Father, I have sinned against heaven, and in thy sight, and am no more worthy to be called thy son... But the father said to his servants, "Bring forth the best robe, and put it on him; and pur a ring on his hand, and shoes on his feet: and bring hither the fatted calf, and kill it; and let us eat, and be merry: for this my son was dead, and is alive again; he was lost, and is found."

Jesus praised to his disciples the business acumen of the unjust steward, who was about to be dismissed from his position. This man had the sense to make friends of his master's debtors, so that at least his future was secured.

"Alas," he said, "the children of this world in their generation are wiser than the children of light. He told the story of the rich man, who died and went to hell, and the beggar at his gate, who was carried to Abraham's bosom. "Send him to my father's house," the rich man besought the father of the faithful, "for I have five brethren; that he may testify unto them, lest they also come into this place of torment." Abraham saith unto him, "They have Moses and the prophets; let them hear them." And he said, "Nay, father Abraham: but if one went unto them from the dead, they will repent." And he said unto him, "If they hear not Moses and the prophets, neither will they be persuaded though one rose from the dead."

Nothing, it seemed, neither threats, nor bribes, nor entreaties, neither the warnings of Moses, nor the fulminations of the prophets, not even the voice of one back from the dead could awaken the drugged soul of Israel to a realization of its imminent and awful danger. Every effort was defeated.

CHAPTER XVII

Solomon's Porch

The summer passed, while Jesus still lingered in Galilee, loth to take leave of the land that he loved, afraid that never again in this life might he have the opportunity of testifying to its people.

The stimulus to part reluctantly from the familiar surroundings which held a thousand memories came from an unexpected quarter. Ever since their last attempt at intervention the brothers of Jesus had kept aloof from him, scandalized and ashamed. To their narrow orthodox minds the head of their house had committed unforgivable sins, and his continued presence in the neighbourhood where they were known was a constant source of irritation. They were not proud of his notoriety, and the praises of him that reached them were as the poison of asps. A more welcome report had it that their brother was wanted by the authorities in the south, and in this they saw an opportunity to be rid of him.

The pilgrim feast of Tabernacles would shortly be celebrated, and offered a convenient justification for approaching him. They sought him therefore in a body, apparently full of friendly and brotherly solicitude. "Depart hence," they said, "and go into Judea, that thy disciples there also may see the works that thou doest. For there is no man that doeth anything in secret, and he himself seeketh to be known openly. If thou do these things, show thyself to the world."

Jesus was not deceived by their stratagem, and answered curdy, "My time is not yet come: but your time is always ready. The world cannot hate you; but me it hateth, because I testify of it, that the works thereof are evil. Go ye up unto this feast: I go not up yet unto this feast; for my time is not yet full come."

Almost were James and Jude, Simon and Jose, guilty of fratricide, urging on their brother to what they believed might be his death. How deeply they afterwards repented of their criminal counsel is revealed by the fact that they were among the first to join the community of Nazarenes after Jesus had suffered. Indeed, the ascetic James, elder, and. no doubt the spokesman of the four, swore to heaven that from the hour of the crucifixion he would eat no bread until his brother was risen again from the dead.

A touching tradition relates that the first thing that Jesus did on his resurrection was to go to James in token of his forgiveness. "Bring a table and bread," he said. When these were forthcoming, he recited the blessing, the words of which now acquired a new significance, "Blessed art thou O Lord our God, King of the World, who bringest forth bread from the earth." Then he broke the bread, and offered a portion to James, saying, "My brother, eat thy bread, for the Son of Man is risen from among them that sleep in the dust."[67]

Truly was the sword piercing through the soul of the poor mother: her husband dead; her eldest son estranged from her and soon to be condemned as a malefactor; her other sons filled with black hatred against their own brother. It was pitifully alone that she went at the end to be near her Jesus in his last agonized moments. A tradition also says that in those moments his thought was for her, who had suffered only a little less than he; and that seeing his beloved disciple standing by, he said to her, "Woman, behold thy son!" and to him, "Behold thy mother!" And from that hour that disciple took her into his own house.

Nevertheless, at the time, Jesus took to heart what his brothers had suggested. It was true that he had already spent enough of his precious remaining days in Galilee. They were right when they said that there were others elsewhere who needed his presence. Therefore, when his brothers were gone up to Jerusalem, "then went he also up unto the feast, not openly, but as it were in secret."

The circumstances of what may be called the Judean ministry, which lasted from about October of A. D. 30 to January of A. D. 31, are derived from the unsupported testimony of *John's* Gospel; but the text has been so overworked by a later hand, and the dialogue has been so artificially expanded, that a great deal of it is worthless historically. It is possible, however, to glean something of what transpired.

Jesus probably made his home at Bethany, at the house of Martha, and from this convenient base he came frequently to Jerusalem into the Temple, and taught there in the customary place in the colonnades, and particularly in Solomon's Porch, which he had first visited as a boy. Here resorted the citizens of Jerusalem and visitors from other parts, especially those who loved religious discussion. The conditions were very different from those in Galilee. There was much theological argument, and speakers were frequently interrupted by questioners and habitual hecklers. Teaching often deteriorated into wrangling, and a large group would break up into a number of small groups, all of them debating a point with great volubility. After making due allowance for the partially fictitious character of the speeches and comments reproduced in the Fourth Gospel, the description given there does very effectively convey the modem Marble Arch or Glasgow Green atmosphere in an Oriental setting.

Among those in Jerusalem to whom the name of Jesus of Nazareth had already come to mean something there

was considerable whispered speculation when it was ru-
moured that he was coming up for the feast. Some said,
"He is a good man." Others said "Nay; but he deceiveth
the people."

When Jesus arrived quietly, and went into the colonnades to teach, immediately a crowd gathered round
him. Those who were versed in the intricacies of scribal
doctrine were amazed at his command of his subjects.
"How knoweth this man learning," they exclaimed, "having never studied?" Jesus answered, "It is God's doctrine, not mine." It was not long before he became
involved in the battle of tongues. He was not used to this
kind of thing, and the opposition to his views seemed to
his sensitive nature far more threatening than in fact it
was. Anticipating his ultimate fate, and associating it
with the present circumstances, he burst out, "Why go ye
about to kill me?" Not for a long time had the hecklers
had such a treat. "Thou hast a demon," they chorused
delightedly: "who goeth about to kill thee?" "Yet a little
while am I with you," declared Jesus, "and then I go unto
Him that sent me. Ye shall seek me, and shall not find
me: and where I am, thither ye cannot come." This set
the hecklers off again: "Whither will he go, that we shall
not find him? Will he go unto the dispersed among the
Gentiles....?"

There was much more of this sort of baiting on many
other occasions, which tried the patience of Jesus, frayed
his nerves, and ruffled his temper. His message, however, was not wholly without effect. There were those

who credited his words, and they encouraged him to persevere, ploughing this very difficult field, and sowing the seed.

An urban orator, used to the humorous attentions of hecklers would not have been in the least disturbed by the ridiculous remarks and caustic comments: they were all part of the game. He would have expected them and dealt with them in the same spirit. But with Jesus it was different. He was not used to such levity. His solemn Galileans did not joke about sacred things. Had he been a southerner, he would have been aware that the irresponsibility and lewdness of the citizens of Jerusalem were proverbial;[68] though they were neither better nor worse than the inhabitants of most big cities. In the event Jesus was as shocked as any Puritan visiting the aisles of Paul's Church in the days of good King Charles. The huckstering and the profanity called forth his utmost reprobation, worthy of the most fiery of divines. Exasperated by the foolish yapping, he cried out, "Why do ye not understand my speech? even because ye cannot hear my word. Ye are of your father the devil, and the lusts of your father ye will do. He was a murderer from the beginning, and abode not in the truth, because there is no truth in him. When he speaketh a he, he speaketh of his own: for he is a liar, and the father of it.... He that is of God heareth God's words: ye therefore hear them not, because ye are not of God." The baiters were hugely entertained, and responded cheerfully, egging him on to further flights, "Say we not well that thou art a Samaritan, and hast a demon?" It must have been hard for the ordinary unbiassed onlooker to repress a smile.

The truly devout, however, could not fail to pity Jesus's evident distress, and to be impressed by his earnestness and obvious sincerity. They had never had among them a preacher like this, who made personal claims that consorted so strangely with his simple provincialism. Some, who had been much exercised about him, waylaid him quietly as he was walking in Solomon's Porch during the Feast of Dedication, commemorating the exploits of the Maccabees. "How long dost thou keep us in suspense?" they said. "If thou be the Messiah, tell us plainly." But to this pertinent question Jesus would still give no direct answer. He suggested that if they had listened to him attentively, and believed the things that he said, they would have been able to draw the proper inference.

They could not know how he was trying to make the fleeting hours work for him, how he strained under the burden of the knowledge that his time was short.

Perhaps it was at this time that he conceived the idea of the dramatic public act which should disclose that he was the Messiah without any ambiguity.

So long as he continued in his present practices he was free from molestation. He was out of reach of Herod Antipas, who had no jurisdiction here, and Pontius Pilate had more important occupations than concerning himself about the niceties of Jewish law as debated by their scribes and teachers. Only the Temple authorities were watching Jesus carefully, to ensure that no breach of the peace occurred. There had been so many political and re-

ligious riots, the latest only a few months old, disorder-
ing the services, defiling the sacred enclosure with
bloodshed, endangering the very existence of the Jewish
nation, that the Temple police had received the most
stringent instructions to keep an eye open for any possible source of disturbance.

Their attention had already been drawn to the Galilean
preacher when he had first come to Jerusalem at the
Feast of Tabernacles. On the seventh day of the festival,
the day of the Great Hosanna, at the most solemn moment of the service, when the priest poured water from
Siloam out of a golden ewer into the funnel of the altar,
and the people were waving their branches of willow and
palm, there had been an incident. Jesus had been carried
away with emotion, and had cried out, "If any man
thirst, let him come unto me, and drink. He that believeth on me, as the Scripture hath said, out of his belly
shall flow rivers of living water." Some of the worshippers would have laid hands on him; but the police had
come along and warned him to be silent if he did not
wish to be ejected or taken before the Court.

Since then he had been under constant surveillance
while he was in the Temple precincts. The chief priests
were kept advised of his sayings. The man was possibly
somewhat deranged; but he was a Galilean, and Galileans were trouble-makers.

Complications did not arise, however, until about four
months had elapsed, when the sands, as Jesus believed,

had almost run out. That part of the heckling which was merely silly had tended to disappear once the novelty had worn off. Instead the opposition assumed a graver character, and became ugly and threatening, as

Jesus employed more extravagant expressions and similes in his anxiety to bring conviction to his audience. The following are fairly accurate samples of his language.

"All that ever came before me are thieves and robbers: but the sheep did not hear them. I am the Door: by me if any man enter in, he shall be saved, and shall go in and out, and find pasture. The thief cometh not, but for to steal, and to kill, and to destroy: I am come that they might have life, and that they might have it more abundantly."

"I am the good Shepherd, and know my sheep, and am known of mine. As the Father knoweth me, even so know I the Father: and I lay down my life for the sheep.... Therefore doth my Father love me, because I lay down my life, that I might take it again. No man taketh it from me, but I lay it down of myself. I have power to lay it down, and I have power to take it again." It is not surprising that many said, "He hath a demon, and is mad; why hear ye him?" Others more thoughtful replied, "These are not the words of one that hath a demon."

While Jesus offered no intelligible proofs that he was that unique teacher, the Messiah—for that would have been to place his head straightway in the lion's jaws—he

yet made increasing reference to his intimate relationship with the Father, which, unsupported by practical
evidence, began to sound to orthodox ears not a little like
profanation of the Name. At length matters came to the
pass that there was serious risk that he would be lynched
by some of his outraged listeners. Between those who
would have assaulted him and those who would have
him left alone a clash was imminent. The Temple police
may have been on the point of taking him into protective
custody to allay the excitement, when Jesus obviated the
necessity by slipping quietly away and abandoning his
labours. His disciples no doubt helped to hold the angry
crowd in check while he got clear of the Mountain of the
House.

During these months the Twelve had played an entirely
passive part. Among all these superior metropolitans
they had felt exceedingly uncomfortable and out of place,
and they were not in the least sorry to learn that the
Master was again going north.

Before they departed, Jesus stood upon the Mount of
Olives, and gazed wistfully across the valley towards the
scene of his abortive ministry. His features were sad and
careworn; but in his bosom burned the unconquerable
spirit of his Davidic ancestors. "O Jerusalem," he apo-
strophized the city, "Jerusalem, which slayest the prophets, and stonest them which are sent unto thee, how
many times would I have gathered thy children together,
even as a hen gathereth her chickens under her wings,
and thou wouldst not! Behold, your House is left unto

you desolate. And I say unto you, that ye shall not see me henceforth, till ye say, 'Blessed is he that cometh in the name of the Lord.'"

CHAPTER XVIII

Bethabara

The problem before Jesus was how to occupy himself for the next two months. He had said farewell to Galilee, and there were obvious reasons why he should not go there again. He felt deeply in need of rest, and desired to prepare himself both spiritually and physically for the coming ordeal. Prudence dictated that he should keep away from any region governed by the Fox. This disposed of Peraea as well as Galilee. He would not stay in Judea, and it would not be proper to make his abode in Samaria. There remained only the territory of Philip. Jesus had an inspiration: he would go to Bethabara by Jordan in the Decapolis, the place where he had been baptized by John, the place of the lightning, the dove, and the Heavenly Voice that had called him to begin his work. In that memorable spot he would renew himself. Bethabara (House of the Ford) was on the pilgrim route from Galilee. Here at the appointed time he would join the festive throng going up to Jerusalem for the Passover. Escorted by his own countrymen he could safely make the passage through Peraea, and they would be with him when he manifested himself as the Messiah.

Having reached this decision, Jesus took his journey through Samaria. We have imagined, as the details suit the occasion, that it may have been at this time that he came to Jacob's well by Sychar, and being wearied sat down to recover his strength. His nervous condition made him tire quickly, and he was grateful for the opportunity to ease his aching limbs, especially during the warmest part of the day, while his disciples went into the city to buy food.

During their absence, there came a Samaritan woman at this unusual hour to draw water. Jesus, always observant, noted the fact, and inferred from it that her manner of life made her desire to avoid the company of the other women of the city. All that he said, however, was, "Give me to drink." She knew at once from his accent that he was no Samaritan, and not being in the resorted to him, and said, "John did no miracle: but all things that John spake of this man were true." And many believed on him there.

There was a welcome absence of irritating incidents, and covert attacks. The local inhabitants were all friendly. His mind was composed, and trusting in God to bring him safely through the coming ordeal he was content to abandon himself to the full enjoyment of his present associations. The discussion of all kinds of subjects helped to fill the days. Among these was the problem of marriage and divorce. It was here that Jesus uttered the memorable words, "What therefore God hath joined together, man cannot put asunder."

Parents brought their children to receive the rabbi's blessing; and when the disciples would have turned them away, Jesus intervened, and mildly remonstrated with them. "Suffer the little children to come unto me, and forbid them not: for of such is the Kingdom of Heaven." And he took them up in his arms, and put his hand on them, and blessed them.

One day there came two rich men to Jesus, the elder of the two himself a rabbi. They had the same question to ask, "What shall I do to inherit the life of the world to come?" Said Jesus to the man of learning, "What is written in the Law, how readest thou?" He replied, "Thou shalt love the Lord thy God with all thy heart, and with all thy soul, and with all thy might; and thy neighbour as thyself." And Jesus said to him, "Thou hast answered rightly: this do, and thou shalt live." But the man was not satisfied: he wanted some task to perform, and pressed to know, "And who is my neighbour?"

Jesus perceived that he was looking for difficulties, and answered by a story. "A certain man went down from Jerusalem to Jericho, and fell among thieves, which stripped him of his raiment, and wounded him, and departed, leaving him half dead. And by chance there came down a certain priest that way; and when he saw him, he passed by on the other side (fearing the defilement of a dead body). And likewise a Levite, when he was at the place, came and looked, and he also passed by. But a certain Samaritan, as he journeyed, came where he was; and when he saw him, he had compassion on him. And went to him, and bound up his wounds, pouring in oil and wine, and set him on his own beast, and brought him to an inn, and took care of him. And on the morrow when he departed, he took out two pence, and gave them to the host, and said unto him, 'Take care of him; and whatsoever thou spendest more, when I come again, I will repay thee.' Which now of these three, thinkest thou, was neighbour unto him that fell among thieves?"

"I suppose he that showed mercy on him," said the lawyer dubiously.

"Go, and do thou likewise," commended Jesus.

The man of learning took his leave, pondering this conception, and his young companion came forward ingratiatingly. "Good Master," he began, "and what must I do to inherit the life of the world to come."

Jesus reproved him. "None is good but One, and that is God. If thou desirest to enter into the life of the world to come, keep the commandments of God."

"And which are they?" Jesus recited to him from the Decalogue. "But all these have I kept from my youth," protested the young man. "What lack I yet?"

"In that case," said Jesus dryly, seeing that he found the Commandments so easy to keep, "go and sell all that thou hast, and distribute it to the poor, and come, follow me."

The test was too much, and the self-righteous young magnate began to scratch his head in perplexity.

Jesus finished the lesson. "How sayest thou, 'I have kept the Law,' seeing that it is written in the Law, 'Thou shalt love thy neighbour as thyself.' And, behold, many of thy brethren, sons of Abraham, are clad with filth, dying of hunger, and thy house is full of much goods, and there goeth out therefrom nought at all unto them."[69]

The young man turned sadly away without another word. When he had gone, Jesus remarked with a sigh to Peter, sitting by him, "Simon bar Jonah, it is easier for a camel to enter through the eye of a needle than for a rich man to enter into the Kingdom of Heaven." "Who then can be saved?" asked the amazed disciples. Jesus told them, "On men's part this is impossible; but to God all such things are possible."

Peter bluntly spoke his mind. "Here are we; we have left everything, and followed thee; and what shall we have?"

Jesus answered earnestly and affectionately, "Truly, I say unto you, that ye which have followed me, in the new era when the Son of Man shall sit on his glorious throne, ye also shall sit on twelve thrones, and judge the twelve tribes of Israel. And whosoever leaveth house, or brethren, or sisters, or father, or mother, or wife, or chil-dren, or lands, on account of my name, shall receive an hundredfold, and shall inherit the sublime life. But many of the first shall be last; and the last shall be first.

"The Kingdom of Heaven is likened unto a man that is an householder, which went forth early in the morning to hire labourers to tend his vineyard. And when he had contracted with them at the rate of a zuz (i.e. *Zeus*, a denarius) for the whole day, he sent them into his vineyard. And he went out at the third hour (i.e. 9 a. m.), and saw others standing idle in the market-place, and saith unto them, 'Go ye also into my vineyard, and whatever is right I will give you.' And they went their way. Again he went out at the sixth hour and the ninth, and did likewise. And at the eleventh hour he went out, and found others standing, and saith unto them, 'Why stand ye here all the day idle?' And they said unto him, 'No man hath hired us.' And he saith unto them, 'Go ye also into my vineyard.'

"And when it was evening, the lord of the vineyard said unto his overseer, 'Call the labourers, and give them their wage, beginning from the first unto the last.' And when those came which came at the eleventh hour, they received each man a zuz.

"And when the first came, they thought that they should have received more than these; and they likewise received each man a zuz. And when they had received it, they murmured against the householder, saying, 'These last have laboured but one hour, and thou hast put them on a level with us, which have borne the burden of the day and the heat.' But he answered one of them, and said, 'Brother, I do thee no injury. Didst thou not contract with me for a zuz? Take what is thine, and go thy way: and as to my pleasure to give unto this last the same as unto thee, have I no right to do what I will in mine own sight? Or is thine eye evil because I am good?' So the last shall be first, and the first last."

At this point the Fourth Evangelist intervenes to furnish us with one of the most majestic of all the Nazarene legends. How much is fact, how much is fiction, the historian cannot determine. In the form in which it has been handed down the story records a miracle so tremendous that the mind reels beneath the shock of it. Yet even here there is room for the theorist, who can offer a rational explanation of the circumstances, if he will. Those who lived in the age of miracle thought the wonder they related less wonderful than the truth which it taught. That truth for them, dying for the Messiah's sake, was the fulfilment of the prophetic words, "He will swallow up death in victory; and the Lord God will wipe away tears from off all faces." But, apart from questions of doctrine or interpretation, the tradition is graphic enough to show that all its elements have not been invented.

While Jesus was at Bethabara a sad message from Martha and Mary of Bethany was privately delivered to him: it concerned their brother Lazarus, and was to this effect, "Master, behold, he whom thou lovest is sick." Here was a dilemma. Affection for his friend urged that he should go at once to his side, though something told him that it would be too late. On the other hand prudence represented the folly of putting himself in jeopardy, and risking the frustration of his carefully laid plans. If he were taken now, there might be no opportunity to make a public declaration of his Messiahship, and his self-sacrifice, designed to have a salutary effect on the nation, would be in vain. For two days he debated the problem and prayed for enlightenment. His decision, when it was made, was characteristic. No motive, however noble, could excuse him from undertaking an errand of mercy. To visit the sick was listed by the pious among those deeds which brought their reward both here and hereafter. Jesus himself exalted such ministrations as these in a famous parable:

> "... And then shall the King say unto them on his right hand, 'Come, ye blessed of my Father, and possess the kingdom prepared for you from the beginning of the world. I was an hungered, and ye gave me to eat: I was thirsty, and ye gave me to drink: I was a stranger, and ye entertained me: I was naked, and ye clothed me: *I was sick, and ye visited me.'...*"

Through such a service God would not allow His own cause to suffer. Therefore he said to his disciples quietly but decidedly, "Let us go again into Judea."

"Master," they protested, "the Judeans of late sought to stone thee; and goest thou thither again?"

Jesus answered, "Are there not twelve hours in the day? (This was but the eleventh hour.) If any man walk in the day, he stumbleth not, because he seeth the light of this world. But if a man walk in the night, he stumbleth, because there is no light in him." Then he explained: "Our friend Lazarus sleepeth; but I go, that I may awake him out of sleep.”

“But if he sleep, he shall do well,” they urged uncomprehendingly. “Lazarus is dead,” said Jesus, shortly, “nevertheless let us go to him.”

It was madness. If Lazarus was dead, what sense was there in Jesus dying also? But they knew by his set lips that his mind was made up.

Valiantly spoke up Thomas called Didymus, “Let us also go, that we may die with him.”

So they came again to Bethany. As soon as Martha heard that Jesus had arrived, she hastened to meet him, hoping against hope. “Master,” she greeted him half reproachfully, “if thou hadst been here, my brother had not died. But I know that, even now, whatsoever thou wilt ask of God He will give thee.”

Jesus answered gently, “Thy brother shall rise again.”

“I know,” said the grief-stricken woman, “that he shall rise again in the resurrection at the last day.” This was cold comfort.

At once he broke sharply through the ice of her despair with a challenge that has echoed down the corridors of time. In that moment he towered above all the frailties of mortality. “I am the resurrection, and the life: he that believeth in me, though he were dead, yet shall he live: and whosoever liveth and believeth in me shall never die. Believest thou this?"

Martha's careful mind, even in her distress, translated these amazing words into terms that she could conscientiously affirm. "Yea, Master: I believe that thou art the Messiah, the Son of God which should come into the world." Overcome by emotion, she turned away, and hurried into the house to find the sister who understood the Master so much better than herself. Stooping over Mary, as she sat with the mourners, she whispered, "The Master is come, and calleth for thee." At that, Mary rose hastily and went out. "Poor child," said her compassionate friends, "she is gone to weep at the grave:" and some of them followed her to give their comfort and support.

But it was at the feet of Jesus that Mary threw herself weeping. "Master, if thou hadst been here my brother had not died." It was the same complaint; but no words that man might speak could answer her, for here wept faith itself. Jesus moved restlessly, and asked of the company that had come out, "Where have ye laid him?"

"Sir, come and see." They led him to the sepulchral cave, sealed with a stone. Jesus wept.

"Behold how he loved him," said the onlookers. But Jesus was already in spirit in the presence of God, petitioning the invisible Majesty dwelling within the Light which is the effulgence of His Being.

A voice was heard, calm as the confines of outer space, commanding, "Take ye away the stone." Far away, as it seemed, there were murmurs of surprise and fear. Even reason tremblingly protested through Martha's lips. "Master, by this time he stinketh: for he hath been—there—four days... But now the stone was rolled away, and the mouth of Sheol yawned blackly.

Suddenly the voice gathered itself up, and launched itself like a bolt into the very heart of that darkness. "Lazarus, come forth!"

"And he that was dead came forth, bound hand and foot with grave-clothes: and his face was bound about with a napkin." But it was the figure from which the voice had emanated that swayed as at the recoil of a spring, and another, a different voice, said faintly, "Loose him, and let him go."

CHAPTER XIX

Jericho

Jesus dared not prolong his visit to Bethany. Without declaring his destination, which might embarrass his friends, he selected a city called Ephraim "near to the wilderness" as a place of temporary retirement, prior to crossing the Jordan to await the arrival of a pilgrim caravan from the neighbourhood of Kefar-Naum.

Rumour was already busy with his name. He was said to be somewhere at hand, and the comfort of the ruling hierarchy— remembering the disturbance created by his former presence in the Temple courts—was by no means increased by the prospect of having him in Jerusalem at the dangerous season of the Passover.

When the Sanhedrin met, two or three weeks before the festival, to discuss precautionary measures for the maintenance of order and the necessity for keeping a watchful eye on known agitators, the problem of Jesus of Nazareth was for the first time seriously considered. Some held that the man was a harmless religious enthusiast, and that it was folly to trouble about him. Others, however, took a different view. "He is a Galilean of the sect of Baptists," they reminded the Council significantly, "and he does not confine his preaching to the wilderness." The session became heated. "If you arrest him you will only make matters worse, and with what crime will you charge him?" Another senator retorted hotly, "You will wait, presumably, until he has gathered a large following, and then it will be too late. We shall be at the mercy of the Romans, who will suppress this Holy Place and destroy the last vestiges of our national liberty." Those who were most vehement in demanding action were of the Sadducean party. There must have been at least one Pharisee who dared to say, "And do you doubt that one day, by God's mercy, we shall regain our freedom, Romans or no Romans?"

Finally the high priest Caiaphas, president of the Council, made his voice heard above the uproar. "You know nothing whatever." he told the objectors, "nor consider that it is a matter of expediency that one man should die for the people, rather than that the whole nation should perish." But still there was opposition. "Is it one man? Will you begin to kill every patriot in Israel? I will have no hand in this business." Was it Joseph of Arimathaea or Nicodemus who expressed such sentiments, and left the assembly, followed by others? Caiaphas raised his eyebrows. "Our friends the Pharisees are too squeamish. It is fortunate that we do not depend on them for our protection." From that day the death of Jesus was determined.

Strict orders were issued to the Temple police. Every band of pilgrims coming up to the feast and entering the sacred enclosure was to be carefully scrutinized, to discover whether Jesus of Nazareth was among them. If necessary, questions were to be asked, to find out where he was lodging, so that he might be apprehended privately without causing a disturbance. "What think ye?" speculated the officers at their stations, after drawing a blank for nearly a week, "that he will not come to the feast?"

Meanwhile the object of so much solicitude had made his way unostentatiously to his chosen rendezvous with the caravan from the north.

Loud were the greetings, when the pilgrims arrived and found Jesus waiting for them. Hopes that in the past had been kindled by his stirring words about the Kingdom of God burst again into flame. Eager inquiries were showered upon him and upon his disciples. But Jesus would only agree that he was indeed going up to Jerusalem, and that he knew the things that should befall him there. It was enough to produce a fertile crop of suppositions, the most exotic of which was that at the chosen moment he would enter the city and drive out the Romans.

The Twelve could not fail to be affected by these furtive whisperings. Might there not be some truth in them? The Master was such a strange person, so variable in his aspect, so mysterious in his utterances, that it was impossible to be sure of his real intentions, or whether he meant his words to be taken literally. There were his extraordinary statements about his approaching death and resurrection. He had seemed a while ago to be confident that his end was at hand, and that he would be taken by the authorities, abused and executed: they had been alarmed and unhappy. But since then a year had gone by: he had been to Jerusalem; he had been in peril; and each time he had escaped. Might he not have received a fresh revelation? Might not the danger have passed? Might he not only have been trying their faith? Might he not have been speaking mystically?

Jesus, aware of their speculations, took an early opportunity while the caravan was on the road to take them aside and reaffirm his fate in precise terms. "Behold, we go up to Jerusalem, and all things that are written concerning the Son of Man shall be accomplished. For he shall be delivered unto the Gentiles, and shall be mocked, and spitefully entreated, and spitted on: and they shall scourge him, and put him to death: and the third day he shall rise again."

But they were wilfully obtuse. *Luke* writes, "They understood none of these things: and this saying was hid from them, neither knew they the things that were spoken." In fact they were encouraged by the talk of the pilgrims to take a deliberate stand against Jesus, and if need be to force him to play a part entirely at variance with his declared submissive intentions. He should be Messiah in reality, and all the world should know it. Once he was fully committed they were sure of success; for they believed that he truly was the Messiah, and they were convinced that when the moment for action arrived every loyal Jew would rally to his standard. After all they had their rights. They had companied with him in his tribulations, and they were entitled to the practical rewards that he had promised.

So they plotted, and grandiose visions filled their minds to the exclusion of all else.

Once they had set up a false image of the Kingdom, the inevitable consequence was a striving for power and privilege. Presently there would be an unseemly scramble for place and position, and ambitious motherhood thought it well to be first in the running. Salome shepherded her sons James and John before Jesus, and did him homage, craving a boon. "What wilt thou?" he asked. "Grant that these my two sons may sit, the one on thy right hand, and the other on thy left, in thy kingdom."

"Ye know not what ye ask," replied Jesus to this mon-strous request. "Can ye drink the cup that I shall drink of, and be baptized with the baptism that I shall be bap-tized with?"

"We can," said the Boanerges stoutly.

Jesus shook his head. "Ye shall drink indeed of my cup, and ye shall be baptized with the baptism that I shall be baptized with: but to sit on my right hand, or on my left, is not mine to give you, but for whom it is prepared of my Father."

When the rest heard, they were greatly incensed at this attempt to steal a march on them. But Jesus called them to him and endeavoured to correct their perspective. "Ye know," he said, "that the chiefs of the Gentiles rule over them, and their great ones exercise authority among them. It shall not be so among you: but whosoever among you wisheth to be great, let him be your minister; and he among you that wisheth to be first, let him be your servant: even as the Son of Man came not to be ministered unto, but to minister, and to give his soul a ransom for many." He was not for one moment ignorant of their scheming, which, had they been aware of it, as-sisted him in his own plans. Up to a point he proposed to countenance their contrivances to demonstrate publicly that he was the Messiah. He would even assist them; for so the authorities would be forced to take action. But while the disciples had no clear idea as to how their end was to be attained, Jesus had long been, maturing a programme which would ensure the result he desired to bring about.

The caravan had now crossed the Jordan by the ford, and was approaching Jericho.

On the outskirts of the city a well-known local character, the blind beggar Bar Timai, sat by the highway soliciting alms. These festive seasons yielded him a bountiful harvest. Company after company passed his pitch in beneficent mood. Rich men and nobles riding on horses or borne in litters might even bestow on him a piece of gold. The sound of a multitude was the signal for him to inquire who of consequence was in the train. This time they told him Jesus of Nazareth is passing by. Few things escape the sharp ears of the blind beggar, whose livelihood depends on his adroitness and long memory. Bar Timai now recalled in a flash the reports that had reached him in market gossip concerning this Jesus, reputed a prophet, and perhaps something more, something that it was dangerous to speak aloud. But what has the blind beggar to lose? Give a prospective benefactor the most august title, was his motto; for flattery opens the purse of charity. Therefore the dust-laden air was suddenly rent with the startling cry, "Jesus, Son of David, pity me! Jesus, Son of David, pity me!"

Some of the pilgrims ran to him angrily and fearfully. "Hold thy peace, fool!" they hissed.

But nothing would stop the son of Timai once he knew that he was on the right track. His high-pitched whine rose again and again, carrying far, "Son of David, pity me!"

Jesus heard, and stopped, and ordered him to be called. Some of the disciples went to him, and told him, "Comfort thyself, rise; he calleth thee."

The blind man rose with alacrity, gathered his rags about him with as much dignity as he could muster, and was led to where Jesus stood. "What wilt thou that I should do for thee?" the Master asked. "Lord," answered the blind beggar half humorously, half earnestly, "that I might receive my sight."

"Receive it, then," said Jesus. "Thy faith hath saved thee." Bar Timai, struck with amazement, rubbed his hands over his eyes. He blinked: it was true; he could discern the white road, and a dark moving mass receding along it. He staggered out into the highway, one hand clutching his robe and staff, the other clawing towards the distance, while his voice grew hoarse with calling out blessings.

The caravan entered and passed through Jericho without halting, making for the camping ground beyond the city, rich Romanized Jericho, with its palace, its villas, its amphitheatre and hippodrome, beloved of Cleopatra and Herod the Edomite! No place this for Galilean patriots. Yet among the pampered inhabitants was a manikin, a sharp, bird-like creature, with twinkling deep-set eyes that darted here and there inquisitively out of a wizened parchment face. It was Zacchaeus, wealthy chief collector of Jericho's ample revenues. Attracted from his house nearby to the approaching procession, he joined the rush of people on learning that it was Jesus the prophet of Nazareth, called the friend of publicans, whom everyone was anxious to see. But his size was against him, and he could not get near because of the press. Nimble of body as of wit, he ran on ahead, and spying a sycamore by the road side he climbed into it with surprising agility. Here he had an excellent view. There were growls beneath him, and not a few cursed his name; but he was used to such attentions and took no notice.

Jesus overheard the abuse, looked up and saw the cause of it, and for the second time that day he stood still. Here was a challenge that he could not refuse, the challenge of popular hostility towards a soul cut off from the religious life of the community, one moreover who had been to much trouble to see him. "Zacchaeus," he called out, "make haste, and come down; for to-day I must abide at thy house."

Overcome by emotion at being thus acknowledged and honoured, the tax-collector descended hurriedly from his vantage point, and received Jesus gladly. The crowd, however, murmured its disapproval that he should go to be the guest of a sinner. Zacchaeus stood fearful and penitent, his beady eyes shifting nervously from the mob to his protector. "Behold, lord," he twittered, "the half of

my goods will I give to the poor; and if I have taken anything from any man by false accusation, I will restore
him fourfold."

Jesus calmed the little man by addressing him indirectly,
loudly enough to be heard by the objectors, "This day is
salvation come to this house, forsomuch as he also is a
son of Abraham."

Before these boldly spoken words of reclamation and
forgiveness the complaints died away.

With new arrivals, and those who had already reached
here, some hundreds, possibly thousands, of pilgrims
were now assembled amidst the luxuriant semi-tropical
surroundings of the City of Date Palms. Swiftly the report spread from group to group that Jesus the prophet
of Nazareth was come, and other more thrilling news
concerning his purposes was whispered covertly.

What were the thoughts of Jesus himself that night? Did
he remember that his namesake of old had set forth from
this place to conquer the Promised Land? Did he take
courage from pondering the ancient vision?

And it came to pass, when Joshua was by Jericho, that
he lifted up his eyes and looked, and, behold, there stood
a man over against him with his sword drawn in his
hand: and Joshua went to him, and said unto him, "Art
thou for us, or for our adversaries?" And he said, "Nay;
but as captain of the host of the Lord am I now come."

This time the victory would be won without the sword, and it would be a greater victory.

At early dawn, before the sun had topped the mountains of Moab, the mighty camp was astir. The baggage was hastily packed, a meal was eaten, and the multitude put itself in line of march to begin the steep ascent towards Jerusalem, singing joyously.

CHAPTER XX

Hosanna, Son of David!

The winding road climbed steadily out of the Dead Sea depression amidst scenes of rugged grandeur. On the left was the howling wilderness of Judea; on the right was the impressive ravine of the Wadi Kelt. The region was a famous haunt of robbers, and it was necessary for the caravan to send forward an advance guard to keep a sharp look out. Entering this forbidding area, the songs faded on the lips of the pilgrims, and even conversation languished. Those who spoke told direful tales of sudden attack, rape, and slaughter, and pointed in illustration to the mingled bones of men and beasts that lay by the wayside.

This day, mercifully, the wild men of the hills kept their distance, and the caravan arrived safely at the khan which had figured in the parable of the Good Samaritan. The worst of the journey was now over. Spirits rose, tongues were loosed, and everyone appeared anxious to make up for the enforced silence of the morning. Once again thoughts were centred on the Holy City, and often heads were turned speculatively towards one who sat apart surrounded by his disciples. Would this be the great Passover, the Feast of Freedom and Triumph?

Jesus caught snatches of talk among his immediate following which showed him that some of them at least were in expectation that the Kingdom of God was on the very eve of being established. Abruptly he addressed them.

"There was a certain man which went abroad, seafaring, which called his servants, and delivered unto them his substance. Unto one he gave five talents, to another two, and to another one; to every man gave he according to his ability; and straightway took his journey.... And it came to pass that after a long time that lord returned, and made a reckoning with them. So he that had received the five talents drew nigh, and brought yet other five talents, saying, 'Lord, thou deliveredst unto me five talents: and, behold, I have added unto them yet five others.' And his lord said unto him, 'Oho! In that thou hast been a good servant and faithful over the little; come: and I will give thee charge over much. Go enter into the joy of thy lord.'" And so it befell with him that had received the two talents. "Then he also that had received the one talent drew nigh and saith, 'Lord, I knew that thou art a hard man, and reapest where thou hast not sown, and gatherest where thou hast not scattered: and I was afraid, and went and hid thy talent in the earth. Behold, thou hast what is thine.' And his lord answered and saith unto him, 'Thou evil and slothful servant, thou knewest that I reap where I have not sown, and gather where I have not scattered: thou oughtest to have delivered my money to the bankers, then, surely, at my coming I should have received mine own with increase. Take now the talent from him, and give it unto him that hath the ten talents. For unto him that hath shall be given, and he shall have abundance; but from him that hath not even what he seemeth to have shall be taken away. And the idle servant, cast ye him into the darkness outside, where there shall be weeping and gnashing of teeth.'"

But though Jesus had spoken of the lord returning after a long time, his audience did not grasp the implication.

There was no opportunity for comment, for the caravan was preparing to go forward. Some miles of waste and rocky country had still to be covered before the last stage of the journey was reached, and the delightfully named villages of Bethany and Bethphage—the place of dates and green figs—came into sight, nestling at the eastern base of the Mount of Olives.

To-day Jesus would not leave the company to turn aside to Martha's house. But as they approached the neighbour villages, he prepared to put into execution an arrangement, which unknown to his disciples he had planned during his long sojourn of the previous winter. His heart beat faster as dramatically he issued his orders to his disciples. "Go, two of you, to the village over against you: and as soon as ye be entered into it ye shall find an enclosure and there an ass's colt tied, whereon never man sat; loose, and bring him unto me. And if any man say aught unto you, ye shall say, the Master hath need of him, and straightway he will send him hither."

Wonderingly they obeyed him, and found the enclosure at the crossroads, and the colt tied by the door. As they were untying him they were challenged by the owners; but on repeating the words of Jesus, they were allowed to take the animal away.

Returning, they laid their garments on the ass for a saddle, and mounted Jesus on his back. Their first thought must have been that he was fatigued with the journey: but suddenly someone had a flash of insight. Excitedly he quoted from the prophet, "Tell ye the daughter of Zion, Behold, thy king cometh unto thee, lowly, and riding upon an ass, even upon the foal of an ass."

The word ran along the pilgrim line to those in front and those that came after, "Jesus is truly our Messiah! The prophecy is fulfilled: he has mounted on his ass. *Hedad!* God save the king!"

For a few minutes the wildest confusion reigned. Back and forth ran the people to where Jesus sat, throwing themselves on the ground in utter abandon, acclaiming him ecstatically. Jesus sat still amidst the din created by his fervent subjects; but the light of a great gladness shone from his eyes. This experience alone was worth all the years of toiling and waiting, worth too the fate that was stretching out cold hands towards him.

At last he gave the signal to set forward. Some of his ardent followers had already claimed the privilege of grasping his bridle; the others grouped themselves solidly around him. They began to move.

At this the enthusiasm doubled its intensity. The people tore off their cloaks and veils and spread them before him, so that the feet of his ass, or at least his shadow, might fall upon them. Many hastened to pull down leafy branches from the trees, and to carpet the way. Thus proceeding in triumph they ascended the Mount of Olives until Jerusalem and the Temple burst on their view. The emotion which Jesus had striven to suppress could no longer be stifled, and the tears rolled down his cheeks as he gazed again upon the city. "Oh, if thou hadst known," he cried, "even thou, at least in this thy day, the things which belong unto thy peace! But now they are hid from thine eyes." Vain lamentations!

On went the multitude with Jesus in their midst, down the slopes of Olivet, shouting aloud their jubilation. "Hosanna, Son of David! Blessed be the king that cometh in the name of the Lord! Hosanna in the highest!"

Pedestrians on the road stared dumbfounded or, carried away by the demonstration, raised their voices in unison with those who set the echoes ringing. Shocked Pharisees called out in horrified tones, "Master, rebuke thy disciples." Jesus smiled at them happily, though his face was still streaked with the stain of tears. "I tell you," he replied, "that if these should hold their peace, the stones would immediately cry out."

And so the king came to his capital.

Jerusalem was familiar with the songs of the pilgrim bands arriving for the festivals, and it was not at first realized that there was anything unusual about the procession approaching the valley gate. The frowning walls, however, seemed to cast a gloom over the joyous throng; for the shouting became sporadic and uncertain as they advanced up the Street of the Cheesemongers. But Jesus still sat on his beast, and looked neither to right nor left. "Who is this?" questioned the curious, as he went by; and they were answered, "It is Jesus the prophet, from Nazareth of Galilee." The concourse here had considerably diminished in numbers, as some slipped away shamefacedly into the side streets. It appeared singularly foolish now to be crying Hosannas. But others remained, and continued less heartily their messianic acclamations. These were enough to set the old city seething, as the urchins took up the words they heard, without appreciating their import, and ran up and down the steps of the narrow thoroughfares piping, "Hosanna, Son of David!"

At one of the Temple gates Jesus alighted and, followed closely by his disciples and a multitude that pressed after them, he strode into the Court of the Gentiles. At last he was free to carry out a long intended task. Stooping swiftly, he gathered up a bunch of cords which had tethered some of the sacrificial beasts, and wielding this impromptu whip he advanced upon the hucksters and bankers, laying about him lustily. There was nothing of the simple teacher of righteousness about the man with blazing eyes, who drove all before him: he moved with the decided steps of a conqueror. Overturning the tables of the moneychangers and the stalls of the dove sellers, he cried imperiously, "Take these things hence. It is written, 'My House shall be called a house of prayer;' but ye have made it a den of robbers." He was brought up short by a distracted group of the market licencees. They waved impotent and gesticulating hands at him: "What token showest thou unto us, seeing that thou doest these things?" They received their answer. "Destroy this temple, and in three days I will raise it up." Evidently they were dealing with a madman. "Forty and six years was this Temple in building, and wilt thou rear it up in three days?"

Meanwhile the children were enjoying themselves hugely sporting among the wreckage, and shouting gleefully, "Hosanna, Son of David!"

The onslaught had been so daring and so unexpected that some minutes elapsed before the scandalized custodians, after a hurried colloquy, confronted the disturber. "Hearest thou what these say?" they demanded, hoping, at any rate, to obtain a denial of messianic pretensions. But Jesus retorted, "Have ye not read, 'Out of the mouths of babes and sucklings thou hast founded strength------------'"

Mentally they completed the quotation: "because of thine enemies, to silence the enemy and the avenger:"

and their thoughts were murderous. Before they could decide on the next move, Jesus had left the Temple.

Thus ended this notable day.

Departing from the city, Jesus went to lodge at his old quarters in Bethany. Not only was he safer there, because of the pilgrims camped round about; but it would have been difficult to find lodgings in the city owing to the calls upon all the available accommodation.

There was no question now of evading the authorities. He had challenged them publicly. Their careful plans for arresting him quietly had been brought to nothing by his boldness in entering the city and the Temple with the maximum of publicity. They had set their traps, expecting that he would attempt to sneak in unobserved. But with so much attention focused upon him they were powerless to touch him lest they should precipitate an outbreak. They would have to think of some other means of getting him into their hands.

In the morning Jesus presented himself again in the Temple, and began to teach the people. Such effrontery was amazing; but the authorities "could not find what they might do; for all the people were very attentive to hear him." Nevertheless it was impossible that the fellow should be allowed to continue to comport himself in the Temple as if he were master of it. They must at least do something to assert their position, or the Sanctuary would speedily be given over to mob rule. It was a feeble enough effort they made, but calculated to exercise a certain moral effect, and to show that they were not to be intimidated by such outrageous conduct. A phalanx of impressive and unbending dignity advanced to where Jesus stood, and a voice accustomed to immediate obedience made itself clearly heard. "By what authority doest thou these things, and who gave thee this authority?" Jesus did not give back an inch. "I also will ask you one thing," he said. "Answer me that and I will tell you by what authority I do what I am doing. The baptism of John, whence was it, of Heaven, or of men?" What insolence the fellow had! But it was a poser. "Answer him, thou Boethusian!" jeered an onlooker, observing the hesitation, and the cry was taken up from every side. The phalanx wavered, and was evidently agitated. Haughty heads came together in consultation. "If we say, Of Heaven; he will say, Why then did ye not believe him? But if we shall say, Of men; we shall be in danger from the people: for they are convinced that John was a prophet." Better to be non-committal. "We cannot tell," answered the spokesman truculently, and a great shout went up.

"Neither do I tell you by what authority I do these things," replied Jesus. But he did not leave the matter with this negative result: he followed up his advantage.

"But how seemeth it to you? There was a certain man which had two sons; and he approached the first, and said, 'My son, go work to-day in my vineyard.' But he answered and said, 'I will not go:' but after that he repented, and went. And he approached the second, and said likewise. And he answered and said, 'I go, sir;' but he went not. Which of these two did the father's will?" "The first," they said, wondering what he was driving at. "Truly, I say unto you," announced Jesus, "that the publicans and harlots precede you in the Kingdom of Heaven. For John came unto you in the way of righteousness, and ye believed him not: but the publicans and harlots believed him; and ye, when ye had seen, repented not after that, to believe him."

Even so, he had not finished with them. "Hear ye another parable," he said.

"There was an householder, which planted a vineyard, and surrounded it with a hedge, and digged a winepress in it, and built a tower, and delivered it to vinedressers to cultivate it, and went abroad. And when the time of the fruit drew near, he sent his servants to the vinedressers, to receive the fruits. But the vinedressers seized his servants, and beat one, and slew another, and another they stoned. Again he sent other servants more than the first; and they treated them in like manner. At last he sent unto them his son, saying, 'Perhaps they will reverence my son.' But the vinedressers, when they saw the son, said among themselves, 'This is the heir; come, let us kill him, and his inheritance will be ours.' And they seized him, and brought him outside the vineyard, and slew him. Think for yourselves, when the lord of the vineyard is come, what will he do to those vinedressers? I will tell you what he will do, he will destroy those wicked vinedressers in their wickedness, and will hire out his vineyard to others, which shall render him the fruit in its season."

There was no mystery about this parable, deliberately recalling the saga of Isaiah. His point was self-evident. Indeed, it told them many things. It told them that this glib-tongued Galilean adventurer claimed definitely to be the Messiah, that he was fully ahve to their intentions, and that he actually dared to threaten them to their faces.

How they itched to fulfil his words. Jesus read their thoughts like a book., He knew that they would have their hour; but they should know that their triumph would be shortlived. Retribution would surely follow. Sternly, he warned them; "Have ye not read in the Psalms, 'The stone which the builders rejected is become the head of the comer. This is from the Lord, it is wonderful in our eyes?' And whoso falleth on this stone shall be broken; but on whomsoever it shall fall, it will grind him to powder."

With these words ringing in their ears the deputation departed. As long as he had the populace behind him, backing him up, it was both useless and undignified to bandy further speech with the knave, puffed up with his own conceits. It would go hard with them if they could not match cunning with cunning, and devise a way of getting him into their power without a riot, which must be avoided at all costs. They glanced almost involuntarily towards the Antonia tower, which housed the Roman garrison. No! Between the excitable and easily deluded masses below, and the insatiable Eagle hovering there above, life was by no means easy for the religious guardians of the nation. Let the one move, and the other would pounce, and that would be the end: the Sanctuary violated, the State disrupted, all pleasant things turned to dust and ashes. Lord God, what a heavy responsibility! And this mountebank, this miracle man, this messianic pretender, was just the one to bring the whole carefully supported edifice toppling down. Calling himself 'the head of the corner' when he was undermining the very foundations!

The Council sat long in debate that day on how the peril should be met. Open arrest was out of the question for the present, and even a secret arrest might bring repercussions which would be just as fatal. While the man had the popular sympathy he was inviolate. There was therefore only this possibility, to alienate the people from him. Mobs are fickle things, rending one day where they have worshipped the day before. These crowds were of many parties and opinions; he could not satisfy them all. If he valued his own skin and could be made to speak in favour of the Roman regime he would antagonize the Zealots. If he identified himself with the doctrines of either of the other principal parties, Pharisees or Sadducees, the consequence would be to distract the crowd and weaken his influence by raising a theological discussion divorced from dangerous issues. Whatever he was planning would then inevitably fail. The Zealots were the most combustible element Obviously, therefore, the first attempt must aim at turning these against him. They could not approach the fellow again officially; but they could send those who would assume the guise of party supporters, feigning to be seekers after truth, who would put the pertinent and appropriate questions which they would construct. This should be done on the morrow.

Thankful to have solved the difficult problem, the Council broke up with feelings of deep relief.

CHAPTER XXI

The Day of His Coming

In the morning of the third day of the week, as soon as it was learned that Jesus was again in the Temple, the Council's plan was put into operation. Their agents mingled with the crowd ready to take up his words according to the answers he should give to the questioners, and either to denounce him as an enemy of the people or to claim him as a sectarian, and so to divide his supporters.

Presently there was a movement among those who surrounded Jesus, and a man came forward humbly. "Rabbi," he said, "we know that thou art sincere, and teachest the way of God in truth, and art not influenced by any man; for thou regardest not the face of man. Tell us therefore, how seemeth it to thee? Is it right to pay tribute to Caesar, or not?"

A hush fell upon the audience. Did the questioner know what he was asking? What would the prophet reply?

Jesus regarded the group from which his interrogator had emerged. Their acting was not quite good enough. "Ye hypocrites," he said, "why tempt ye me? Show me a denarius." The coin was produced. He would not touch it, for that would have offended the Zealots, but asked, "Whose is this likeness and this inscription?"

"It is Caesar's," they answered.

"Then," said Jesus, "render unto Caesar what is Caesar's —and to God the things that are God's."

An excited babble broke out. The saying could be interpreted to mean that we have distinct duties to God and to Caesar: they do not conflict. It could also mean that God is our only king. It is plain that we can give nothing to Caesar if we give all our allegiance to God. In fact, as the emissaries of the Council suspected, the words and the action of Jesus expressed subtle contempt for the priestly plotters. Here was a denarius; it bore Caesar's portrait, was inscribed TIBERIUS CAESAR DIVI, divine Caesar. Let those who claimed to serve the God of Israel reconcile it with their consciences how far they were prepared to acknowledge the theistic pretensions of Caesar.

The first question had failed, and the questioners withdrew, marvelling.

Later came those who spoke for the Sadducees, saying, "Rabbi, Moses said, 'If a man die, and have no son, his brother shall take the wife of the dead unto him to wife, that he may raise up seed to his brother.' Now there were seven brethren; and the first, when he had married a wife, died and, having no issue, left his wife to his brother. Likewise the second, and the third, until the seventh. And after that the woman died also. In the resurrection whose shall she be, because all the seven were husband to her?"

The question was frivolous, but Jesus chose to treat it as a serious matter. "Ye do err," he told them mildly, "not knowing the Scriptures, nor the power of God. For in the resurrection they marry not, neither are they betrothed, but are as the angels of God in heaven. And concerning the resurrection of the dead, have ye not read what God spake to Moses in the bush, saying, 'I am the God of Abraham, I am the God of Isaac, I am the God of Jacob.' God is not the God of the dead, but of the living."

Again the attack was foiled. Jesus had answered like a Pharisee, and with a simplicity and cogency that left no room for dispute.

Finally, a Pharisee question was put. "Rabbi, which is the greatest commandment in the Law?" Jesus replied without hesitation. "'Thou shalt love the Lord thy God with all thy heart, and with all thy soul, and with all thy might.' This is the greatest commandment in the whole Law." But he added pointedly, "And this is the first, but the second is like unto it, 'And thou shalt love thy neighbour as thyself.' On these two commandments hang all the Law and the Prophets."

Victory was now complete. They dare not ask him any more questions. But he had still a question to put to them before they left him. "How seemeth it to you concerning the Messiah, whose son is he?" Failing to see the trap, they answered immediately, "He is the Son of David."

"And how then doth David by the Holy Spirit call him lord, saying, 'The Lord affirmed unto my lord, Sit thou on my right hand, till I make thine enemies the footstool of thy feet.' If David then call him lord, how is he his son?" They were nonplussed; for they had received better than they had given. The thrust was two- edged: it brought forward a text that promised the triumph of the Messiah over his enemies, and at the same time established that he was accountable to no one, neither to courts, nor high priests, nor kings, nor governors, seeing even that King David in spirit paid homage to him as his superior. In effect Jesus warned them that no person or body on earth had the right to try or judge the Messiah. Therefore whatever action the authorities might be contemplating against him would be illegal.

The usual interpretations of this question entirely ignore the situation and are quite irrelevant to it. Jesus was not trying to prove either that he was Divine, or that he could still be the Messiah though not descended from David. He was really adopting much the same attitude as was maintained sixteen centuries later by King Charles the First of England, who refused to recognize the authority of the court which tried him, or to offer a defence. The explanation now given reveals why Jesus kept stubbornly silent before all his judges, and would not plead, and would only answer such questions as dealt with his identity as Messiah, the King of Israel.

When the false scribes had retired, Jesus launched forth into a diatribe against all hypocritical religious professors. The text has been unduly amplified in *Matthew's* record; but it is quite possible that Jesus may have repeated some things which he had said elsewhere. The other Gospels make it clear, however, that he did not specifically mention the Pharisees or any sect by name.

Never had Jesus appeared more like one of the prophets of old as he stood there, the very incarnation of avenging truth. The words poured from his lips like a stream of liquid fire, and the common people heard him gladly.

"On Moses's seat sit the scribes: all therefore that they say unto you, observe and do; but do not ye according to their works, for they say, but do not. For they bind up heavy and importable burdens, and put them on men's shoulders; but they will not stagger about with them themselves. And so all their works they do that they may be seen of the children of men: for they make broad their frontlets, and enlarge the comers of their mantles, and love the principal couches at the suppers, and the chief seats in the synagogues, and benedictions in the market, and to be called of men, rabbi. But ye shall not be called rabbi; for one is your rabbi, and that is the Messiah; and all of you are brethren. Also be not ye called father upon the earth; for one is your Father, which is in heaven. Neither be ye called teachers; for one is your teacher, and that is the Messiah. He that will be greatest among you let him be your minister. For whoso exalteth himself shall be abased; and whoso abaseth himself shall be exalted.

"Woe unto you scribes, hypocrites! which close the Kingdom of Heaven against the children of men; for ye enter not yourselves, neither do ye allow them that are eager to enter. Woe unto you scribes, hypocrites! which devour widows' houses in order to pray lengthy prayers; and therefore shall receive a lengthy judgment. Woe unto you scribes, hypocrites! which compass sea and land in order to make one proselyte, and when he is made, ye make him twofold more a son of Gehenna than yourselves. Woe unto you, blind guides, which say, 'Whosoever sweareth by the Temple, it is nothing; but he that sweareth by the gold of the Temple is guilty!' Fools and blind: whether is greater, the gold, or the Temple that sanctifieth the gold. And, 'Whosoever sweareth by the altar, it is nothing; but he that sweareth by the gift that is upon it is guilty!' O blind: whether is greater the gift, or the altar that sanctifieth the gift? He that sweareth by the altar, sweareth by it, and by all things thereon. And he that sweareth by the Temple, sweareth by it, and by that which abideth therein. And he that hath sworn by heaven, sweareth by the throne of God, and by Him that sitteth thereon...."

Even the elements seemed to gather themselves to listen, as if compelled by his utterance. The skies became overcast, and distant thunder pealed out an amen. Some cried out superstitiously, "An angel spake to him."

But Jesus said, "This voice came not because of me, but for your sakes. Now is the judgment of this world: now shall the prince of this world be cast out. And the Son of Man if he be lifted up from the earth, will draw all men unto him."

In this mood of fierce exaltation the crowd could no longer follow his meaning. "We have heard out of the Law that the Messiah remaineth for ever; and how sayest thou, 'The Son of Man must be lifted up?' Who is this Son of Man?"

In the semi-twilight of the shrouded and fading day they were answered enigmatically. "Yet a little while is the light with you.

Walk while ye have the light, lest darkness come upon you: for he that walketh in darkness knoweth not whither he goeth. While ye have the light, believe in the light, that ye may be the children of the light."

With these words of farewell he himself passed into the shadows, and was hidden from their sight for ever.

The way of Jesus lay through the inner Court of the Women, and it was there that he beheld a poor widow casting her two mites into the treasury chests; and he told his disciples that she had made a greater sacrifice than all those who gave, however liberally, of their abundance. Hers was perhaps the last sacrifice of that decisive day; for the short evening service, held before sunset, was now over, and the time drew near for the gates to be shut.

For Jesus it was indeed farewell, for never again would he enter those massive portals, never again would he teach in those colonnades, never again would he join in the worship of the Sanctuary. The skies had cleared now, and the rays of the dying sun struck blood red upon the great stones, while the chill shadows crept eastward in his train, as if they would catch and imprison his feet as his steps rang hollowly upon the paving.

There is nothing more terrifyingly desolate than the mighty edifices of man standing deserted in the twilight. Here remains but the mouldering shell from which the spirit has fled. God has gone, because life which is the evidence of His Presence has gone, and the unclean whispers that linger are but the false life of insubstantial ghosts.

Suffering from nervous reaction after the excitement of the past hours, and being peculiarly sensitive to impressions, the sense of desolation communicated itself to the soul of Jesus, and his mind was filled with depressing images bound up with the fate of his people. The dark visions of Isaiah and Jeremiah of the last days of Babylon merged imperceptibly into the gloomy predictions of the apocalyptists.

And Babylon, the glory of kingdoms, the beauty of the Chaldees' excellency, shall be as when God overthrew Sodom and Gomorrah. It shall never be inhabited, neither shall it be dwelt in from generation to generation; neither shall the

Arabian pitch tent there; neither shall the shepherds make their fold there: but wild beasts of the desert shall lie there; and their houses shall be full of doleful creatures; and owls shall dwell there, and satyrs shall dance there. And the wild beasts of the islands shall cry in their desolate houses, and dragons in their pleasant palaces: and her time is near to come, and her days shall not be prolonged.... My people, go ye out of the midst of her, and deliver ye every man his soul from the fierce anger of the Lord. And let not your heart faint, neither fear ye for the rumour that shall be heard in the land; a rumour shall both come one year, and after that in another year shall come a rumour, and violence in the land, ruler against ruler....

Most of his disciples, less imaginative, were impervious to such sensations. They could only marvel rustically at the splendours of construction so sharply etched by the sunset. "Master," they intruded on his reverie, "see what manner of stones and what buildings are here!" A muffled answer reached them. "Do ye regard all these things? Truly, I say unto you, there shall not be left here one stone upon another, that shall not be thrown down." The mood was still upon Jesus as silently they crossed the valley and ascended Olivet. He sat down upon a boulder and, sinking his head upon his hands, gazed long and earnestly upon the city and Sanctuary as the darkness spread slowly over the prospect. He pondered the words of the seers, who spoke of the messianic plagues. It was not alone he who would suffer, but the faithful, and this whole cosmos would be swallowed up in endless night.

"Ask him, speak to him," begged the rest of the disciples of Peter, James and John, as they stood at a little distance, made anxious and uncertain by the Master's fateful saying. The three intimates went forward hesitatingly. "Master," they pleaded, "tell us, when shall these things be, and what will be the sign when these things are to come to pass?"

Jesus lifted his head and answered them with deep solemnity, "Let no man deceive you: for many shall come in my name, saying 'I am Messiah,' and shall deceive many. Ye shall hear of wars and rumours of wars. See that ye be not dismayed. It needs must be that such things be done; but the end is not yet. For nation shall rise against nation, and kingdom against kingdom; and there shall be pestilence, and famine, and earthquake, in every place. And these are but the beginning of the plagues.

"Then shall they give you over to the tribulation, and shall slay you, and all nations shall hate you on account of my name. And then shall many be offended, and a man shall betray his neighbour, yea, a man shall hate his brother. And many false prophets shall arise, and shall lead many astray. And because apostasy shall abound, the love of many shall wax cold. But he that endureth to the end, the same shall be saved.

"When ye therefore shall see the abomination of desolation spoken of by Daniel the prophet, he who said that it should stand in the Holy Place, then let them which be in Judea flee unto the mountains; and he that is upon the roof, let him not descend to take aught out of his house; and he that is in the field, let him not return to take his clothes. But woe unto them that are with child, and to them that are about to bear, and to them that give suck in those days! And pray ye that your flight be not in the winter, neither on the Sabbath: for then shall be great tribulation, such as there has never been from the beginning of the world until now, neither shall be after it. And if those days had not been shortened, there should no flesh be saved: only on account of the elect those days shall be shortened.

"Then, if any man say unto you, 'Behold, here is the Messiah, or there!' believe it not. Because there shall arise false Messiahs, and false prophets, and shall display great signs and wonders; that so they may bring about, if that were possible, the going astray of the very elect. Behold, I have told you. Wherefore if they shall say unto you, 'Behold, he is in the wilderness!' go not forth:

' Behold, he is in the apartments!' believe it not. For as the lightning goeth forth from the east, and is visible even unto the west; so shall be the coming of the Son of Man.

"Wheresoever the carcase is, there shall the eagles be gathered together.

"And immediately after the tribulation of those days shall the sun be darkened, and the moon shall not give her light, and the stars shall fall from heaven, and the powers of heaven shall be shaken: and then shall appear the sign of the Son of Man in heaven; and then shall all the tribes of the earth mourn, when they shall see the Son of Man coming in the clouds of heaven with great power and glory. And he shall send his angels with a trumpet, and a great voice, that they may gather together his elect from the four winds, from the heights of heaven to the extremities thereof.

"Learn ye the parable from the fig-tree. When its branch is tender, and the leaves sprout, ye know that the ripe fruit (*Qa'itz*) is nigh: so likewise ye, when ye shall see all these things, know that the end (*Qetz*) is near, even at the doors. Truly, I say unto you, this generation shall not pass away till the whole be accomplished. Heaven and earth shall pass away, but my words shall not pass away. Until that day, and concerning that hour, there shall be no man that knoweth, not even the angels in heaven, but my Father only. And as it was in the days of Noah, so shall it be at the coming of the Son of Man. For as they were in the days before the Flood eating and drinking, marrying and giving in marriage, until the day that Noah entered into the ark, and knew not until the Flood came, and swept them all away; so shall be the coming of the Son of Man.

"Then shall two be in the field; one shall be taken, and one shall be left. Two shall be grinding at the mill; one shall be taken, and one shall be left. Two shall be in one bed; one shall be taken, and one shall be left. Be ye alert therefore: for ye know not at what hour your lord cometh..."

Far into this night Jesus gravely taught his disciples many things in parables, while across the Kedron the vigilant Temple guard was posted at its twenty-four stations. And the admonition of the captain of the Holy House on that side was as the admonition of the Son of Man on this, "I say unto you all, Watch!"

Down the dark valley between there swept a wind, and in the wind an ancient spirit murmured, "The lord, whom ye seek, shall suddenly come to his Temple, even the messenger of the covenant whom ye delight in: behold, he shall come, saith the Lord. But who may abide the day of his coming, and who shall stand when he appeareth?"

CHAPTER XXII

Gethsemane

It was now the fourth day of the week, the 12th of Nisan, A.M. 3791, corresponding to Wednesday, April 25th, A.D. 31. The Passover in this year fell on a Sabbath, and this unusual circumstance created a difficulty which finds an echo in the Gospel records. The paschal lamb should be sacrificed on the 14th of Nisan "between the evenings." But if the 15th of Nisan was a Saturday, it would mean profaning the Sabbath which commenced at sunset on the previous day. This, at any rate, was the view held by the more conservative Jews, who regarded the slaughter of the paschal lamb as a private sacrifice, each animal representing a household. They therefore sacrificed the Passover on the Thursday (13th-14th Nisan) when the exceptional conjunction occurred. Many of the priests and Galileans adhered to this practice. Another and growing body of opinion, however, favoured by the Pharisees, would have it that the Passover was a public sacrifice, seeing that the festival was a national commemoration, and such sacrifices overruled the sabbatic law. They therefore found no just cause for changing the appointed time for the sacrifice even if the 14th did fall on a Friday.

Thus it came about that at this fateful Passover there was a slaying of lambs and an eating of the paschal supper on both the Thursday and the Friday, according to which authority was followed. Jesus and his disciples, being Galileans, observed Thursday as Passover eve.

Only one of the Twelve knew what were the plans of Jesus for that occasion, and he kept his own counsel and did not choose to reveal them to the rest: he was Judas the purser. The Master had called him aside, and told him to hire a guestchamber, and arrange for a guide to meet them near the valley gate and conduct them to the place quietly and secretly. It was late on this Wednesday that Judas set out for Jerusalem alone to carry out his instructions. The others remained with Jesus at Bethany; for it was too dangerous now for him to visit the city in the daytime. Not again would the authorities suffer him to escape them: he had gone too far to expect any clemency, and their methods, which he had experienced, had taught him that he was dealing with cunning and determined men. Even now, unknown to him, the Council was in session, debating how best to secure his person and put him to death. So far the only conclusion reached was, "We may not do this on the feast day, lest there be a great tumult among the people." Jesus himself believed that it was in the purpose of God that he should be delivered up to them, and that he should die the death of a political rebel at the hands of the Romans. He did not yet know how this would be brought about; but, with the symbolic and exemplary object he had in view, his principal concern was to protect himself from the risk of dying in any other fashion, and particularly in a hole-and-corner fashion to which no public attention would be drawn. It was for this reason that he pitted his wits against his enemies in devising stratagems to ensure that the desired result would be obtained. No suicide, intending to represent his end as murder, could more carefully have planned the manner of his death. If faith in the virtue of vicarious suffering is morbid, then Jesus was undoubtedly morbid; but none of the usual motives of the morbid, such as revenge or notoriety-seeking, was present. The only motives discernible are those of the purest benevolence, the intention to shock the conscience of his people into active repentance towards God for their own spiritual and physical salvation.

The motives of Judas for betraying his Master arc harder to discover. The meanest of all, that of avarice, has been ascribed to him, founded in part on his course of action, on his position as purser to the company, and on his financial carefulness. But this cannot have been his principal motive, if it was the motive at all, for the man was not base, and even the basest Jew will scarce sell blood for gold or silver. The transaction arose out of something deeper and more terrible. Let it be admitted that Judas, the son of a revolutionary, loved money and the good things of life as those may do who have only known to be poor and outcast and despised, that he had a warped mind, was cunning, miserly, even perhaps a thief: it may not therefore be assumed that he was something so infinitely degraded as has been suggested. A little while before he set out he had protested when Mary had poured a flask of precious oil upon the head of Jesus, saying, "To what purpose is this waste? For this oil could have been sold for much wealth, and given to the poor." It appears that the much wealth amounted to three hundred denarii, a matter of ten pounds. Moreover his sentiments had been echoed by the other disciples, Jesus had mildly remonstrated with them all, "Why do ye molest her? She hath wrought a good work upon me; for in that she hath dispersed this oil upon my body, she hath done it for my burial. And the poor will be continually with you; but I shall not be continually with you." Jesus did not imply that the thought for the poor was feigned. He did not say to Judas, "Thou hypocrite, thou carest nothing for the poor!"

On the other hand we may not whitewash the betrayer, and plead that he had discovered that the claims of Jesus to be the Messiah were false, and that he was determined to do his religious duty in saving the people from a deceiver by giving him up to justice.

We may repeat, indeed, what was said earlier in introducing Judas, that he was a man to whom bloodshed was most repugnant: this had prevented him from joining the Zealots as his father formerly had done. If he was out for gain, it was not by violence. One of the attractions of Jesus had been that he aimed at establishing the Kingdom of God through peaceful means.

We cannot be far wrong in holding that Judas had been steadily losing faith, that he had become increasingly and impatiently critical. His disappointment at the lack of response to the teaching of Jesus had been greater than he had allowed to appear. Most zealously had he assisted to spread the glad tidings as one of the twelve envoys. He was of those who expected the Kingdom of God to be established speedily. He trusted blindly in the beginning though there was much that he did not understand. Jesus would so frequently talk of the nearness of victory, and then at other times he would set forward the realization of his hopes to a more remote future. The confidence of Judas would wane, and would again be restored by a promise of high honour and possessions almost within reach. Latterly the Master had begun to speak about his death, yet he had allowed himself publicly to be acclaimed as Messiah. It was all so confusing and contradictory. His loyalty to Jesus had always been loyalty to his ideals rather than to the man.

The Master in several respects was too much like himself, sensitive, highly-strung, passionate, easily depressed, to win his love. The affinity had been laboured so strongly by Judas as to become through melancholia psychologically transformed into something resembling aversion. Judas knew and despised his own weaknesses, and admitted to himself that he was a failure; but it was gall and wormwood to have that failure and those weaknesses reproduced and exhibited to mock him in the leader through whom he had hoped to transform himself. The last thread of sanity had snapped when Jesus had told them all last night that further delay was inevitable. A few hours ago he had referred to his burial. He had mentioned often enough of late that he would be delivered to the chief priests and Gentiles, and that they would kill him. Well, if that was what he wanted and expected, why should he not have his desire?

The idea took shape in the brain of Judas as he walked towards Jerusalem. Everything favoured the design. He was alone, away from the others, and no one but himself knew the plans of Jesus. He had only to seek an interview with the chief priests, disclose his identity, and make a compact with them. A convenient opportunity would almost surely offer itself for him to carry out his part of the bargain. A bargain it should be: money was to be his professed object, lest the Council should doubt his story and ask why he was betraying his master. They had better send a strong detachment to make the arrest, for perhaps when the time came Jesus would not so easily submit to be taken as he suggested; he might change his mind and resist. If he was the Messiah—and Judas would not deny that he might be—he would ultimately triumph. And if his own fate was consignment to utter darkness and damnation, anything was better than the present agony and gnawing uncertainty....

So the poor unbalanced creature schemed as he went; and all the time the real truth was that it was not Jesus, but the Judas in Jesus, that he wanted to destroy. It was a case of transferred suicide, of self-destruction in an-other.

It is pertinent to remember that tradition has preserved the legend that Jesus did not die upon the cross, but that God made Judas look like Jesus, and he suffered in his stead.[70]

There was a buzz of excitement in the Council when word was brought that one of the disciples of Jesus was come, who wished to give valuable information. Had Providence delivered the enemy into their hands, just when they had given up all hope of dealing with him? Or was this some trick to put them on a false scent?

They received Judas coldly, though reassured by his obvious emotional distress. The wretched man looked wildly around at the stem faces regarding him interrogatively. Gladly would he have escaped from the presence of these mighty and unbending judges of his people, with his errand unaccomplished. But he was rooted to the spot. It was too late now to turn back. A mild but incisive voice reached him from very far away: "You have something to tell us, my son?" The voice, it was that of the high priest Caiaphas, released the strings of his tongue. Judas threw wide his hands, and burst out, "What will ye give me, and I will deliver him unto you?" It was needless to say who was meant.

Shortly after, the betrayer went out trembling, with a mina of silver (thirty shekels—about four pounds) in his pouch, an earnest of the sum which he would receive when Jesus had been apprehended.

The morning following Jesus called to him Peter and John, and said to them, "Go and prepare us the Passover, that we may eat."

"Where wilt thou that we prepare?" they asked.

"When ye have entered into the city, there shall meet you a man, bearing a pitcher of water; follow him into the house where he entereth in. And ye shall say unto the goodman of the house, 'The Master saith unto thee, Where is the guestchamber, where I shall eat the Passover with my disciples?' And he shall show you a large upper room furnished; there make ready."

Judas had carried out his secret instructions to the letter; and the two found everything as they had been told.

Stealthily, like a thief in the night, Jesus entered the city with his disciples, and they sat down to the *seder*, the Passover ritual supper. The nature and order of the service as performed in those days is not now exactly known; but in its broad features it did not differ materially from modem observance. There was the washing of hands, the eating of unleavened bread, the drinking of prescribed cups of wine, the dipping of bitter herbs, the sharing of a paste compounded of almonds, raisins and other fruits, and the chanting of the *hallel* group of psalms. Some of these rites preceded and some followed the eating of the paschal lamb.

Never had the ancient ceremonies been charged with such significance as was this evening imparted to them by Jesus in the upper room. Every word recited was filled with new meaning, every expression moved him deeply and called forth his comments, as he conducted the service. He had concluded the rehearsal of the story of the deliverance from Egypt, and the language of the devotions gripped him increasingly as he advanced towards the central part of the ritual.

> "Blessed art thou, O Lord our God, the King of the World, which has redeemed us and redeemed our fathers from Egypt, and hast made us to rejoice this night to eat therein unleavened bread and bitter herbs...

"How greatly have I desired to eat this Passover with you before I suffer!" he exclaimed with emotion.

He took the second of the four ordained cups of wine, lifted it, and said the blessing, drank, and passed it round, saying, "Take this, and divide it among yourselves: for I say unto you, henceforth I will not drink of the fruit of the vine, until that day that I shall drink it new with you in the Kingdom of God."

After this he washed his hands, and took the unleavened bread; and when he had said the blessing, he broke it, and distributed the pieces to his disciples with the strange words, "Take, eat: this is my body." He had marked the burning eyes and the distraught manner of Judas, and he had guessed the cause. Nevertheless his hand was steady as he dipped some bitter herbs in the bowl, and passed it on for each one to do likewise. But as it circulated, he suddenly said, "Truly, I say unto you, that one of you shall betray me." Narrowly he watched Judas to mark the effect of his words, and what he saw was sufficient to confirm his suspicions.

None of the others had noticed anything; they were too occupied with angry expostulation at the terrible suggestion. "Is it I? Is it I?" rose from all round the table, as the disciples tried to reveal the guilty one by a process of elimination. But Jesus would not help them. "It is one of the Twelve," he said, "that dippeth the hand with me in the dish. And surely the Son of Man goeth as it is written of him: but woe unto that man by whose hand the Son of Man is betrayed! It had been good for that man if he had not been born." The words were as bitter and sweet to the heart of Judas as the herbs and the fruit paste of which he partook. The sweetness was in the assurance that he was the instrument of destiny; the bitterness was at his own miserable fate. Would, indeed, that he had not been born! With an effort he controlled himself; but every morsel of the paschal lamb that passed his lips seemed as if it would choke him. Neither was his unhappiness helped by the conversation during the meal, which turned again on the question of who should be greatest in the Kingdom. What place could there be for him, the traitor and outcast?

Jesus reclined, apparently absorbed in his own thoughts; but when supper was ended, he rose decisively, divested himself of his robe, and took a towel and girded himself Then he poured water into the basin, and began to wash the feet of his disciples, and to dry them with the towel. "Lord, dost thou wash my feet?" cried Peter uncomfortably, when his turn came. Jesus answered, "What I do thou knowest not now; but thou shalt know presently." Still the humble fisherman resisted the menial service. "Thou shalt never wash my feet." Jesus said, "If I wash thee not, thou hast no part in me." "Not only my feet, then," replied Peter, "but also my hands and my head." Jesus told him, "He that is washed needeth not save to wash his feet, but is clean every whit: and ye are clean, but not all."

When he had finished his office, resumed his garments, and was again set down in his place, he gave them the awaited explanation. "Know ye what I have done to you? Ye call me Master and Lord: and ye say well; for so I am. If I then, your lord and master, have washed your feet, ye also ought to wash one another's feet. For I have given you an example, that ye should do as I have done to you.

The cup of wine was now filled for the third time, and the service continued. At the close of grace, Jesus stood up, and held aloft in his right hand the brimming cup, called "the Cup of Blessing." It was the climax of the ceremonial. Solemnly he gave thanks, drank, and handed on the cup, saying, "Drink ye *all* of it; for this is my blood of the New Covenant which is shed for many."

It was a horrible moment for Judas. He touched the cup with his lips, and passed it hurriedly to his neighbour. He could bear no more. In another moment he would have betrayed himself. The shadows veiled his agitation, as he turned away, and went silently out into the darkness.

When he was at the door, Jesus called after him, "That thou doest, do quickly." The words were an invitation, a prayer, and a brave covering of his exit. The obligations of the service had all been fulfilled: a point had been reached at which any of the company might leave with propriety; so that the rest thought nothing more than that Jesus had required their brother to buy what was needed for the feast, or to give something to the poor.

By a strange coincidence, in every Jewish home for hundreds of years the door has been opened at this stage of the Passover ritual.

In the upper room the celebrants concluded the service by singing the *hallel*, drinking the fourth cup of wine, and reciting the final thanksgiving.

The Fourth Gospel records that Jesus gave a farewell discourse. Through it there run threads of these closing praises. "Not unto us, O Lord, not unto us, but unto Thy Name give glory.... Blessed art Thou, O Lord our God, King of the World, for the vine, and for the fruit of the vine... Jesus said, "I am the vine, ye are the branches: he that abideth in me, and I in him, the same bringeth forth much fruit.... This is my commandment, that ye love one another, as I have loved you. Greater love hath no man than this, that a man lay down his life for his friends. Ye are my friends, if ye do whatsoever I command you. Henceforth I call you not servants; for the servant knoweth not what his lord doeth; but I have called you friends; for all things that I have heard of my Father I have made known unto you. Ye have not chosen me, but

I have chosen you, and ordained you, that ye should go, and bring forth fruit, and that your fruit should remain...

There in the upper room, isolated, cut off by the darkness outside in which inimical forces were already moving, the little group was brought into a new and intimate relationship. Yet as they prepared to take their departure, Jesus startled them for the second rime this evening, by asserting, "All ye shall be offended in me this night; for it is written, 'Smite the shepherd, and the flock shall be scattered.'"

"If they all shall be offended," said Peter sturdily, "I shall not be offended in thee."

Jesus shook his head. "Truly, I say unto thee, that this night, before cock crow, three times shalt thou deny me."

Indignantly, Peter still protested, "Even if I must die with thee, I will not deny thee."

And so said all the disciples.

Jesus appeared to accept their assurances. Nevertheless he asked, "When I sent you without purse, and scrip, and shoes, lacked ye anything?" "Nothing," they answered. "But now," he continued, "he that hath a purse, let him take it, and likewise his scrip: and he that hath no sword, let him sell his garment, and buy one. For I say unto you, that this that is written must yet be accomplished in me, 'And he was reckoned among the transgressors:' for the things concerning me have an end." Proudly they produced two swords. "It is enough," he said; and led them forth.

Of what use were swords to him, or scrip, or purse, who soon would have need of nothing in this world? But these, left without him, would have need of every human symbol of protection and support, to bolster up their courage and give them confidence. Poor orphans! He would pray the Father to send his spirit to comfort them.

Thus far Jesus himself had been marvellously sustained. Once he had become reconciled to the prospect of a tortured death, he had invested it with a halo of glory. The actual physical suffering faded out of the picture, leaving behind the vision of an emblem of cosmic significance adorned with a figure tremendous in purposeful repose. To that uplifted standard all Israel would rally in repentance, and then, in a moment, the emblem would become attenuated, transparent, and disappear, as the effulgence of the throne irradiated the landscape, and the former figure, now regal and majestic, blazed whitely upon it. Always there had been a to-morrow....

Perhaps it was the cool air blowing among the trees of the valley that affected Jesus with nostalgia. "When I am risen," he said wistfully to the disciples, "I will go before you into Galilee."

Now that the hour of his ordeal was so close at hand he began to grow depressed and dispirited. The horrors that he had put away returned with redoubled force, and his sensitive soul shuddered. Supposing that he should not be equal to the trial that awaited him? Suppose that what he was doing was all in vain?

Supposing he had been dreaming dreams, and now, too late, was awake?

Across the Kedron, on the slopes of Olivet, was a garden: it was part of the locality called Gethsemane (*Ge-shem-anim*—the fruitful vale), and Jesus had often resorted there with his disciples; for it was a peaceful spot free from pilgrim camps. Coming there now, he took Peter, James and John aside, telling the others, "Sit ye here, while I go yonder and pray." Sighing deeply, he confessed to these most intimate of his followers, "My soul is sorrowful even unto death: await ye me here, and watch." Going forward a little, he fell upon his knees, buried his face in his hands, and prayed, "O Father, all things are possible unto Thee; take away this cup from me: nevertheless not what I will, but what Thou wilt, be done." After a while, seeking human comfort, he returned to the three, and found them sleeping. With tingling nerves he demanded sharply, "Simon, sleepest thou? Couldst thou not watch one hour? Watch and pray, lest ye enter into temptation. The spirit truly is watchful, but the flesh is frail." Again he went away, and prayed the same words; and again he returned and found them asleep, drugged with sorrow. Yet a third time he went away, and prayed, "and being in an agony he prayed more earnestly; and his sweat was as it were great drops of blood falling to the ground."

Presently he grew calmer. The rapid bearing of his heart moderated, fear fled, and his mind became clear and tranquil. Satan had been routed triumphantly.

He came now to the slumbering trio with pity instead of vexation. "Ye have slept now, and taken your rest," he told them. "Behold the hour is at hand when the Son of Man shall be given into the hands of sinners. Arise, and let us be going. Behold, he draweth nigh that betrayeth me." Through the trees his watchful eyes had seen the gleam of torches trailing like a fiery serpent across the valley.

Barely had they time to rejoin the others when a cohort of troops appeared, led by Judas. The Council had taken no chances in case the betrayal should turn out to be a trap. But they need not have been concerned. Here was but a handful of helpless men. In conformity with the pre-arranged signal, Judas now indicated the person of Jesus by stepping forward and embracing him with the greeting, "Peace be unto thee, rabbi." The eyes of Jesus momentarily filled with tears, as he asked reproachfully, "Beloved, betrayest thou the Son of Man with a kiss?" With a groan of anguish Judas vanished into the darkness.

Malchus, representative of the high priest, was about to take formal possession of his man, when Peter, regaining the use of his paralysed limbs, drew his sword and struck at him. Jesus promptly stayed his hand. "Return thy weapon to its place: for all they that take the sword shall perish with the sword." And he added in kinder tones, "Thinkest thou that I cannot ask of my Father that He should send even now on my behalf more than twelve legions of angels? But how then shall the Scriptures be fulfilled, which declare that thus it must be?"

He turned banteringly to the captain of the guard. "Are ye come out, as against a brigand, with swords and clubs to secure me? Daily I was with you teaching in the Temple, and ye seized me not."

"Keep your speeches for the Council," replied the captain gruffly. "Away with him!"

Immediately they pinioned his arms, and led him away; and the disciples forsook him, and fled.

There were no other eye-witnesses of the arrest, unless it was a youth sleeping out on Olivet. Awakened by the clatter and the glare of the torches, he started up, hastily throwing his sindon about him. He was caught by the soldiers; but struggled free, and leaving the linen cloth in their hands, ran away naked. A tradition relates that Jesus subsequently handed this cloth to Malchus the high priest's representative, as evidence that he was risen from the dead.[71]

The instructions received were to bring Jesus directly to the high priest's palace in the Upper City. This was the family residence of Annas the son of Seth, head of one of the most powerful of the hierarchical houses, and one of the most high-handed and unscrupulous. Annas himself, and two of his sons, held at intervals the chief sacerdotal office, and the high priest at this time, Caiaphas, was his son-in-law. As individuals they were detested alike by the subordinate priests, the Pharisees, and the common people, and there was no love lost between them and the bullying Roman procurator.

Jesus had not been wholly deserted. Peter and another followed the escort at a safe distance until they entered the courtyard of the palace. The other disciple, being known there, got in without difficulty; and when Jesus had been taken inside, and the way was fairly clear, he returned, and said a word to the girl who kept the door, and introduced Peter.

The night was chilly, and a fire had been kindled in the portico. There Peter sat down among the menials to warm himself, and to wait for news. Presently one of the maids noticed him. She stared hard for a minute, and then came up to him accusingly, "Thou too wast with Jesus the Galilean." He shook his head violently, and moved further back into the shadows, muttering, "I know not what thou sayest, woman."

An hour passed, and still there came no word of what was passing inside. The others would be getting anxious.

Peter decided to abandon his post and come back later if he could. He was making for the door when another maid saw him and called out, "He also was with Jesus the Nazarene." Again he denied with an oath, "I do not know him." Now he dare not leave immediately; it would look too suspicious. He therefore hung about the door with as careless a manner as he could muster. But already some of those that stood by had their doubts, and a group approached and spoke to him. One of them, a kinsman of Malchus, declared, "In truth thou art one of them; for thine accent betrayeth thee." Peter was in a tight comer. He denied, and cursed, and swore, "I know not the man." Immediately a cock crew, and remembering the words of Jesus, he went out, and wept bitterly.

Hardly had he gone, when the captain of the guard clattered down the steps, spoke to one of the officials, called his men together, and marched away.

"What's going on inside?" someone asked.

"It looks as if they've uncovered a Galilean plot to bum down the Temple."[72]

"There!" exclaimed the maid who had first had her doubts. "I knew that horrid man was one of them. We might all have been murdered."

CHAPTER XXIII

Golgotha

Jesus stood before the high priest. For the first and for the last time the messenger of God and the representative of God were face to face. The hour was big with decision. The chamber was filled with members of the Council, chief priests of the houses of Annas, Boethos, and Pheabi, elders of the ruling Sadducean party, all of them committed to a policy of co-operation with Rome. The rustling of robes was the only sound that broke the silence.

What was required to be done was to obtain evidence that the prisoner had been guilty of a crime that in Roman Law, not Jewish Law, was punishable by death. It had already been determined that the procurator should be made to bear both the responsibility and the blame for the execution. In this way the odium of the Jewish masses would be deflected from the Council, and at the same time the hierarchy would be able to settle part of its score with Pilate for having seized the sacred Corban treasure by making him still more obnoxious to the people. The ignominious end of the nationalist prophet would also serve as a warning to all hotheads anxious to change the existing order. The case of Jesus of Nazareth had assumed an importance far beyond the question of punishing an insolent agitator and pretender; he had be-come a pawn in the game of power-politics.

The present assembly had no corporate authority other than that conferred by the status of its constituent members. It had not been duly convened as a judicial court either civil or religious; and if it had been, it was sitting at an illegal hour and in an illegal manner. It could conduct no trial, because there was no accusation. It had a prisoner neither of the Synagogue nor the State, but rather a suspect forcibly detained for inquiries. The only right that this Council had was the right to interrogate one from whom some immediate danger to the public peace and safety was apprehended and, if the result warranted, to remand him in custody for the proper processes to be set in motion.

The session began legitimately enough with the high priest, as president, questioning the prisoner concerning his disciples and his teaching. What sort of people were his followers? Were they many or few? What sort of doctrine was he propagating? Had it a political significance?

Jesus was not bound to incriminate himself, and he made the obvious answer. "I spake openly to the world; I ever taught in the synagogue, and in the Temple, whither the people always resort; and in secret have I said nothing. Why askcst thou me? Ask them which heard me, what I have said unto them: behold, they know what I said."

One of the attendants between whom Jesus stood, annoyed at his insolent manner, struck him sharply across the shoulders with his wand, saying, "Answerest thou the high priest so?"

"If I have spoken evil," protested Jesus, turning at the blow, "bear witness of the evil; but if well, why smitest thou me?"

"Summon the witnesses," ordered the high priest, shortly.

Unfortunately the most material witness, Judas, had failed to put in an appearance, and was nowhere to be found.

From this point the proceedings lost even the semblance of legitimacy. Not only had the assembly illegally constituted itself as a session of the Sanhedrin without proper notification; but the subservient rump went on to stage the mockery of a trial, which violated the code in every particular. The end was held to justify the means, and the end was to procure a conviction on a capital charge.

Even on the ground of ordinary justice Jesus was fully within his rights in refusing to recognize the jurisdiction of this court; but he had previously in the Temple conveyed a warning to the Council that he could not accept the competency of any court to try him.

The false witnesses suborned by the Council now came forward to testify; but they failed completely to agree in their evidence. Jesus did not deign to contradict the lies and calumnies that were uttered, or seek in any way to establish his innocence. To everything that was said, he maintained an obstinate silence.

At last two witnesses were found who were substantially in accord. One testified, "He said, 'I can pull down the Temple of God, and ere three days I can build it.'" The other claimed that the words used were, "I will destroy this Temple that is made with hands, and within three days I will build another made without hands."

So by a perversion of the language which Jesus had employed when he had attacked the stall-holders there was at last elicited evidence that could be construed as a plot to destroy the Temple. But of what value was it? Even had it been deemed that the crime was deserving of death, or lesser punishment, the Council was not there to find the prisoner guilty of any infringement of Jewish Law. Pilate could indeed endorse any death sentence which they might pass; but then they would have to carry it out, and this was exactly what they did not wish to do.

Imagine going to Pilate with the tale of a plot to destroy the Temple! How he would laugh, and possibly order the prisoner to be dismissed with a handsome gift.

They were getting nowhere.

Caiaphas rose up, and addressed the prisoner impatiently, "Answerest thou nothing at all concerning these things which they witness against thee?"

Jesus remained dumb.

On all sides it was felt that the issue now lay between the two principals. It was a dramatic scene. The high priest stood there with all the commanding majesty of his pontificate. The prisoner, not a whit abashed, met his look with a challenging directness, as he waited with calm and reposeful dignity. It was then that Caiaphas knew that the whole farce had been totally unnecessary. "This man," said an inner voice, "will convict himself." It came to him that, enemies though they were, they were both seeking to accomplish the same thing. Here was a self-deluded fanatic, but one who would carry through his fanaticism to the end.

Solemnly the high priest spoke, and it seemed as if all Jerusalem, the ends of the earth, and the unborn ages, were listening with silent intensity. "I adjure thee by the living God, that thou tell us whether thou be the Messiah, the son of the Holy One, blessed be He!"

Now there came an answer, quietly uttered, but ringing with a conviction that sang upwards to the stars. "I am. Wherefore, I say unto you, henceforth ye shall see the Son of Man, that sittcth on the right hand of Power, coming in the clouds of heaven."

Caiaphas nodded, an almost imperceptible gesture of thanks. Then the still air was tom with sound as he rent his robe, and cried, "He hath blasphemed. What further need have we of witnesses? Behold, ye have heard that he hath blasphemed. What think ye?"

"Death! He is guilty of death!"

The pent-up emotions were suddenly released, like the bursting of a dam, and gushed forth in a violence of physical expression. The councillors, in mass hysteria, swarmed upon the victim, buffeted him, spat in his face, covered his eyes, and shrieked at him, "Prophesy unto us, O Messiah, who it is that assailed thee." The servants emulated their masters....

But what was this blasphemy for commission of which Jesus had been found worthy of death? To claim to be the Messiah was no blasphemy in Jewish faith or Law. He had not spoken against God: he had not pronounced the holy Name of God: he had beguiled no one to worship other gods. Where was the blasphemy?

The blasphemy was not against God; it was against Caesar. These Jewish judges were such true Romans that they had convicted a fellow-Jew of the heinous crime of *loesa majestas*, of violation of the majesty of Tiberius, because he had claimed to be king in a Roman province. Here was the case to go before Pilate, a case to be dealt with promptly, and to end with the governor's order for immediate execution.

Thus did the disease that was blighting Italy overstep the seas, so that as Roman senators and knights, rather than as priests and elders of Israel, these unworthy sanhedrists for their own purposes became *delatores*, common informers.

"Among the calamities of that black period," Tacitus writes of this very year, "the most trying grievance was the degenerate spirit, with which the first men in the senate submitted to the drudgery of common informers; some without a blush, in the face of day; and others by clandestine artifices. The contagion was epidemic. Near relations, aliens in blood, friends and strangers, known and unknown, were, without distinction, all involved in one common danger. The fact recently committed, and the tale revived, were equally destructive. Words alone were sufficient; whether spoken in the forum, or amidst the pleasures of the table. ... Informers struggled, as it were in a race, who should be first to ruin his man; some to secure themselves; the greater part infected by the general corruption of the times."[73]

Terrible was the wrath of Tiberius against all found guilty of *majestas*, in Hebrew parlance, blasphemy. Only in A. D. 28, in the calends of January, Sabinus, an eminent Roman knight, had been seized in Rome, and dragged through the streets to summary execution on a feast day. The general murmur was, "Will there never be a day unpolluted with blood? Amidst the rites and ceremonies of a season sacred to religion, when all business is at a standstill, and the use of profane words is by law prohibited, we hear the clank of chains; we see the halter, and the murder of a fellow-citizen. The innovation, monstrous as it is, is a deliberate act, the policy of Tiberius. He means to make cruelty systematic. By this unheard-of outrage, he gives public notice to the magistrates, that on the first day of the year, they are to open, not only the temples and the altars, but also the dungeons and the charnel- house." The crime was blasphemy.[74]

What hope, then, was there for an insignificant Galilean carpenter on the feast of the first month of the Jewish national year, if he were charged with blasphemy before the arrogant Roman who administered Judea for his despotic master?

In the early hours of the morning the councillors met again. Their business was simple and brief: it was to draw up the accusation which informers were required to present. When this was completed they conducted Jesus without further delay to the palace of Herod, where Pontius Pilate resided when he came up to Jerusalem for the feasts. Having delivered their prisoner, the chief priests had the nicety not to enter the judgment hall lest they should be ritually defiled; but remained without in the paved courtyard, called Gabbatha, because of its elevation.

The buildings which figure in the closing scenes of the life of Jesus stood at a very short distance from each other ranged along the slopes of the highest hill on which the city stood. Here were the palaces and residences of the nobility, piled storey upon storey with supporting columns of stone and marble, climbing the hillside and fronting north. Before them at a slightly lower level, and at this part running almost due east and west, was the old wall, strengthened at the western and more exposed end by the three great fortress towers of Hippicus, Phasael, and Mariamne, built by Herod the Great. Immediately behind the forts was Herod's palace, protected again by walls thirty cubits high set with towers placed at regular intervals. The praetorium, occupied by a Roman garrison, was at the rear of the buildings. Coming from Caesarea, and entering by the western gate, the procurator did not have to pass through the narrow streets to reach his seat in the capital. Close by was the upper market to which the country folk could readily bring their produce for sale, and the merchants of the western world their merchandise.

The northern section of the old wall overlooked the Tyropoean, or Cheesemongers' valley, and beyond it, the houses and streets of the Lower City straggled up the lesser hill of Akra.

Following the valley eastward the wall reached the Xystus, and turning south-east by the Council building it approached the Temple hill, giving direct access to the south-western cloisters of the Sanctuary by bridges. It was behind and above this part of the wall that the palaces of the high priest and of the Hasmoneans were situated, enabling Caiaphas and Antipas with their respective retinues to cross over to the Temple without contact with the crowds in the lower ways and thoroughfares.

Further to the south of the Temple hill lay the poorer quarter of Ophel, abutting on the valleys of Kedron and Hinnom, and close to the Pool of Siloam. On the other side, to the north of the Temple and the Akra, stretched the new middle-class suburb of Bezetha.

It was in the Ophel, as in the poorer districts of other great cities, that the revolutionary and Zealot elements congregated. Somewhere among the labyrinth of passages in this neighbourhood was the house where Jesus had observed the Passover, and the dwellings where his disciples were now in hiding from the authorities.

Jesus had been brought by night from Gethsemane across the Kedron valley, up the main street of the Tyropoean, and through a gate in the old wall to the palace of Annas. It is not certain whether his examination took place there or in the adjacent Bouleuterion; but the nature of the proceedings makes it more probable that the councillors were summoned to the palace. In the morning he was taken the short step along the hill to be tried by Pilate at Herod's palace. From here he was returned, temporarily, to the palace of the Hasmoneans nearby, where Herod Antipas was in residence.

This topographical digression has been necessary in order to illustrate certain features of the narrative. One of

the most pertinent facts that becomes immediately evident is that the Jewish populace of Jerusalem was entirely
unaware of what was going on, and had no hand
whatever in the arrest, trial, or condemnation of Jesus.
Only the Galilean Zealots in the Ophel, if informed by
the disciples, could possibly have had an inkling of the
drama taking place within the heavily fortified and
guarded palace walls up there on Government hill, from
which they were entirely excluded. One day the outraged
masses, stirred up by the Zealots, would carry fire and
sword into those proud dwellings, and leave them in
smouldering and blackened ruin, while the remnant of
their aristocratic inhabitants hid trembling from their
vengeance in the vaults underground. But that time was
nearly forty years distant.

The procurator was considerably astonished, not to say
suspicious, when the Jewish government officials
brought him a prisoner with such urgency and with such
a body of authority. The fellow they had delivered to him
seemed to be a common man of no distinction. Why
bring the case to him, whatever it was; and why the
haste? He did not trust these scheming priests, who always concealed their real thoughts and intentions. They
might be Roman citizens, and loyal to the emperor; but
they were cunning Orientals for all that, and pastmasters
in the arts of intrigue. Experience warned him to be on
his guard, and to exercise the greatest caution. There was
no doubt more to this business than would appear on the
surface. Pilate went out to them, and asked casually,
"What accusation bring ye against this man?"

The prosecutors were hurt. The governor must realize that the matter was not to be treated lightly. "If he were not a malefactor we would not have delivered him up unto thee," they answered reprovingly.

"Take ye him, then," said Pilate peevishly, "and judge him according to your law." He made as if to go.

"It is not lawful for us to put any man to death."

Pilate started. So it was a capital charge. His suspicions were still further aroused. It was a curious thing that the Council should be bringing a fellow-Jew to be sentenced to death on the eve of their feast. He had no compunction about executing a Jew: he had strung up plenty of them. So far as he was concerned, the more of the stiff-necked race that suffered, the better. But why were they so anxious to get rid of this man? "What evil hath he done?" he inquired coldly.

"The informers presented their indictment. "We found this fellow perverting the nation, and forbidding to pay tribute to Caesar, saying that he himself is *Christos*, a king."

The crime was *loesa majestas*. The accusation was credible, but not coming from their lips.

Abruptly, Pilate turned on his heel, and went into the judgment hall. He called the most unregal-looking prisoner before him. "Art thou the king of the Jews?" he demanded, almost expecting an expostulatory denial.

It had become an irritating habit with Jesus to answer a question by asking another. He replied carefully, "Sayest thou this thing of thyself, or did others tell it thee of me?"

"Am I a Jew?" roared Pilate. "Thine own nation and the chief priests have delivered thee unto me. What hast thou done?" The business was getting beyond him.

Jesus explained patiently. "My kingdom is not of this present order. If my kingdom were of this order, then would my supporters have struggled, that I should not have been delivered up: but now is my kingdom not from hence."

This was talking in riddles. "Thou art a king, then?" persisted Pilate, trying to make the prisoner stick to the point. But Jesus remained evasive.

"Thou sayest that I am a king. To this end was I born, and for this cause came I into the world, that I should testify to the truth. Every one that is of the truth heareth my voice."

"What is truth?" Pilate was contemptuous. He sprang to his feet angrily: he hated mysteries. It seemed that he had to deal with a madman inside and rogues outside. He would be done with the whole affair. They could settle it among themselves. He strode out of the judgment hall, and stormed at the chief priests, "I find no fault in the man, no fault at all."

Immediately a fierce babble of protest broke out. "He stirreth up the people, teaching throughout all Jewry, beginning from Galilee to this place."

"Galilee!" exclaimed the governor, clutching at the opportunity. "Is the man a Galilean?" They said that this was so. Then let them take the prisoner to the tetrarch to whose jurisdiction he belonged. Fortunately Herod was at Jerusalem at the Hasmonean palace. How the prosecutors cursed themselves for the unlucky slip: but they had to put the best face they could on the situation, and departed, taking Jesus with them under escort, leaving the procurator inwardly congratulating himself, and mopping his perspiring brow.

The Fox was delighted to see Jesus. He bombarded him with questions, and hoped that he might see a miracle done by him. But Jesus refused even to speak.

Then the chief priests and elders stood and vehemently accused him. And still he would say no word. Tiring at last of such obduracy, Herod turned the prisoner over to his men-at-arms to have their sport with him. He meant to have some entertainment out of the encounter. The soldiers required no second bidding. Roughly they stripped Jesus, and robed him in a scarlet tunic, and encircled his head with thorns for a crown. He did not resist them, as they bound him to a pillar, and put a reed into his hand for a sceptre. Then they all gathered round, mocking him, and bending the knee, crying, "Hail, king of the Jews!" And they spat upon him, and took the reed, and struck him on the head.

When Herod had had enough of the horseplay, he ordered them to unbind him and clothe him in his own robe. Then he sent him back to Pilate with his compliments, and the finding that as far as he was concerned the prisoner was not guilty. That day Pilate and Herod, who had been at enmity since the affair of the aqueduct, made their peace with one another.

There is another tradition, however, the historical value of which is still indeterminate. It has been transmitted in several versions, with a common basis of agreement. Recently these have been collected in part, and investigated; and they are too weighty and circumstantial to be ignored in this or any future history of Jesus.[75]

According to this information, at a point in the proceedings Jesus temporarily obtained his liberty. One account says that Pilate set him free, having found him innocent of the charges laid against him; but that afterwards he took a large bribe from the chief priests, and had him re-arrested and executed.[76] Another account states that Jesus was released by the chief priests as part of the plot, so that in the interval Judas, their tool, might be able to turn the feelings of the people against him, as being guilty of a most serious crime against the nation.[77] A third account, and the most natural, would suggest that the disciples were not altogether quiescent in their refuge in the Ophel district; but learning that the Master was being judged by the tetrarch of Galilee in the Hasmonean palace, they raised some of the Galilean Zealots in the quarter, and made a demonstration in force outside the gate. Several hundreds collected, and when no attention was paid to their demands they began to volley stones and threaten the authorities, who were obliged to free their prisoner to prevent the spread of the outbreak, and a public riot. His followers bore Jesus off in triumph, but later he was caught in the Temple, and this time he was held securely.[78]

The canonical Gospels are silent about this episode; only Celsus, a second-century opponent of the Christians, assuming for the sake of his argument the guise of a Jew, reminds them that the object of their adoration, "after we had convicted him, and condemned him as deserving of punishment, was found attempting to conceal himself, and endeavouring to escape in a most disgraceful manner."[79] He points out that "these statements are taken from your own books, in addition to which we need no other witnesses; for ye fall upon your own swords."

Whatever be the truth, there appears to be no question that Jesus was brought again before Pilate, and that the chief priests were enabled to pursue their original plan to increase the unpopularity of the governor, and to exculpate themselves.

Once more the charge of *loesa majestas* was preferred and pressed, while the prisoner remained wholly passive. Pilate could make nothing of this extraordinary fellow, who let the stream of vituperation flow over him as if he did not hear it.

The procurator was convinced that he could establish his innocence if he chose. Why could not the man speak out, instead of being so deliberately unhelpful? "Hearest thou not the testimony which they witness against thee?" he urged. But Jesus answered him nothing.

So far Pilate had not tried the case at all: he had done everything to avoid trying it; for something told him that he did so at his own peril. He had not attempted to question the prosecution, or to ask for witnesses. He was still anxious not to be involved; but both the accusers and the accused seemed as if they were conspiring together to drive him into a comer. An inspiration came to him. "Ye have a custom that I should release unto you one at the Passover: I will therefore release him whom ye term *Christos*." But the prosecutors cried out, "Not this man, but Bar-Rabban." Now Bar-Rabban was in prison with others who had taken part in last year s riot over the Corban money. The governor began to get an inkling of the motive behind the accusations. He lost his temper, and ordered Jesus to. be scourged. Perhaps that would make the fellow talk.

He sat down again on the judgment seat to await the result. Then, to make matters worse, a servant delivered a confidential message from his wife, "Have thou nothing to do with that just man; for I have suffered many things in a dream because of him." Pilate believed in omens, and his superstition now came to reinforce his instinct. He recalled the prisoner, and inquired, "What is thine extraction?" Perhaps the man was a magus. Jesus made no reply.

The bully in Pilate again came uppermost. "Speakest thou not unto me? Knowest thou not that I have power to crucify thee, and have power to release thee?"

Weak from the scourging, Jesus at last opened his mouth, and answered wearily, "Thou couldst have no power over me, except it were given thee from above: therefore he that delivered me unto thee hath the greater sin."

Believing that the prisoner had reminded him that he was the representative of Tiberius, the governor grasped at his authority. He would not be coerced. He marched out purposefully and announced, "The case is dismissed."

Immediately there was an outcry. "If thou let this man go, thou art not Caesar's friend: whosoever maketh himself a king speaketh against Caesar."

Pilate was at the end of his limited resources. His last prop, the fear of Tiberius, was being used as a cudgel to beat him. One final appeal remained, an appeal so entirely at variance with his character and practice that he must have been hard driven to make it, the appeal to pity. He had Jesus brought out, bleeding from his wounds, and supported by two soldiers. "Here is your king!"

But the prosecutors were worked up to a pitch which excluded every tender feeling. The duel had been long drawn out, and nothing would stay their hand now that they saw themselves within an ace of victory. "Away with him," they cried. "Crucify him."

"Shall I crucify your king?"
"We have no king but Caesar."

The governor surrendered. It was nearly midday. *Matthew* relates that he publicly washed his hands as a symbolic expression of his innocence, and that the accusers willingly accepted full responsibility. If he did wash his hands, it was a confession of defeat; but for the accusers to have accepted responsibility meant that in the moment of their triumph they had overreached themselves, and fallen into the pit which they had dug. Their purpose had been to lay the blood of their victim at the door of the Roman. A higher justice required that this subterfuge should not save them, and that the blood of Jesus, which they had taken upon their houses, should rest there. In the eventual war with Rome justice was satisfied when most of the chief priests were slaughtered by the Idumeans, whom the Zealots brought into Jerusalem, and their bodies were cast out without burial.[80]

Bar-Rabban was released, and Jesus was delivered to be crucified, and with him two others, brigands or Zealots, lying under sentence of death.

There can be no doubt that Jesus was technically guilty of the crime of which he was accused. His claim to be the messianic king could certainly be construed as a violation of Caesar's majesty. But the trial was a travesty. Over his body a battle had been fought between the powers of government, the lordly priests and the governor, and the priests to all appearances had won. Beaten and shaken, the Roman wolf could still snarl at his tormentors. Oriental dogs: their triumph should be short-lived. They had insisted on this crucifixion. Very well, it should disgrace them, and their whole race. "Write out the titulus of accusation," he ordered. "Write it in Latin, Greek, and Hebrew, THIS IS JESUS OF NAZ-ARETH THE KING OF THE JEWS, and nail it to the cross." The scandalized priests protested. "Not, 'The king of the Jews,' but, 'He said, I am king of the Jews.'" "What I have written, I have written," snapped Pilate, and grinned at them malevolently.

Punishment had still to follow one other who had been intimately concerned in the sorry business. The crazed Judas, in a fit of remorse and temporary sanity, sought out the chief priests to return their silver, crying, "I have sinned in that I have betrayed the blood of the righteous." But they turned him away with the cold comment, "What is that to us? See thou to it." And he flung the tainted money into the Temple treasury chest devoted to the purchase of sin offerings. What his end was is not certainly known. One tradition makes him hang himself, another to be disembowelled by an accidental fall, and yet a third to die long after from a loathsome disease. [81] Whatever fate it may have been there remains associated with it the dread name of Chakel-Damah, the field of blood.

Jesus made his last exit from Jerusalem by the gate Gennath, in the neighbourhood of what is now the Jaffa Gate, where the old wall and the second wall joined on the west of the city. Thus he was spared the indignity and suffering of a long journey through the thronged streets. Nevertheless it was impossible that the procession could escape notice at this season, and the custom of supplying a retinue of wailing women for the condemned made it certain that a crowd would be attracted by the shrill lamentations, which could have only one terrible meaning. Weakened by the scourging, lack of food, and the awful ordeal so stoically borne, Jesus broke down beneath the weight of the cross-bar of the instrument of punishment. The soldiers therefore laid hold of a sturdy fellow named Simon of Cyrene, coming out of the country, and compelled him to shoulder the burden. The piercing cries of the mourning women added greatly to the distress of a soul so sensitive as Jesus. At last he turned to them, and exclaimed with prophetic insight, "Daughters of Jerusalem, weep not for me, but weep for yourselves, and for your children. For if they do these things in a green tree, what shall be done in the dry?"

The place of execution, called Golgotha, the place of a skull, lay to the north-east of the city; but not far distant. It seems to have been situated just beyond the line of the third wall commenced at a later date by Agrippa, in the locality nearly corresponding to the modem Jewish district of Mea Shearim. A reference by Josephus, the almost contemporary historian to the gardens in this neighbourhood, where Titus was in danger of being trapped, helps to determine the approximate position with tolerable accuracy.[82] Neither Gordon's *Calvary* nor the traditional site is correct.

A tortured end to a human existence can never be anything but deeply painful to describe; yet there was that in the death of Jesus which truly became his life. The soldiers stripped him of his robe and, with typical callousness, diced for it, leaving him naked except for a cloth about his middle. While they prepared him, and set up the cross, his only word was the noble sentiment, "Father, forgive them, for they know not what they do." He was offered the opiate provided by the charity of the wealthy ladies of Jerusalem; but when he had tasted he would not drink. He desired, if he might, to meet his end in full possession of his senses.

From about midday until three o'clock in the afternoon he hung upon the cross in agony, but with silent fortitude, while the soldiers, and the emissaries of his prosecutors, jeered at him, and invited him to come down, and they would believe that he was king of the Jews. His neighbour sufferers also reviled him in their torment.

But many of the people stood watching in misery and shame; among them some of his own followers, whom the dread tidings had reached. Tradition claims that his sorrowing mother was there, with his beloved disciple, and that once he spoke to commit her to his care.

At the time of afternoon prayer the torture drew from Jesus the cry, "Eloi, Eloi, lama sabachthani?" (My God, my God, why hast thou forsaken me?) Interested bystanders remarked, "He calleth for Elijah." Presently the wandering mind returned, and Jesus murmured, "I thirst." One of the men compassionately took the sponge, saturated it with the opiate, and reached it up on a reed so that he might drink. "Let be," said others, "and let us see if Elijah will come to save him."

Outraged nature could stand little more. Jesus felt himself going. "It is finished!" he was heard to say. The pious Jew's dying confession hovered upon his lips. "May my death be an atonement for all the sins, iniquities and transgressions of which I have been guilty against Thee—and for the sins of all Thy people Israel. Vouchsafe unto me of the abounding happiness that is treasured up for the righteous. Make known to me the path of life: in Thy Presence is fulness of joy; at Thy right hand are pleasures for evermore.... Father, into Thy hand I commend my spirit... He gave a loud cry: his head fell upon his bosom; and he was still.

Immediately, there broke out a terrible wailing. Many of the onlookers beat their breasts, and cried, "Woe unto us for our sins, for the judgment of Jerusalem has drawn nigh!" Even the centurion in charge could not help ejaculating, "Truly this was a righteous man."[83]

The tradition has it that the sky had darkened while Jesus hung upon the cross, as if the very orb of day would veil itself from the tragic sight. At the moment of his expiry the city was rocked by an earthquake, bringing down the massive lintel stone of the Temple,[84] and rending the curtain of the Holy Place as it crashed and shivered into pieces on the pavement. Thus the ministry which had opened amidst the reverberating thunders closed in like manner. The cycle was completed.

The scribes of the Galilean Nazarenes, playing with this wonderful theme, have been inspired to magnify the circumstances in their legends. The voice that cried, the darkness, the thunder, and the earthquake, recalled the scene at Sinai when the Law was given. This was not the end; it was in very deed the prelude to the Day of Judgment, and in token thereof the stones rolled from the mouths of the sepulchres, and many bodies of the saints, which were laid to rest, arose in the belief that the great resurrection morning for the just had already dawned. Had not the Voice which of old shook the earth promised, saying, "Yet once, it is a little while, and I will shake the heavens, and the sea, and the dry land; and I will shake all nations, and the Desire of all nations shall come: and I will fill this House with glory."

EPILOGUE

He is Not Here

To the life of no other man has there been appended so amazing a sequel as that which faith and history have combined to add to the life of Jesus. Those who are familiar only with the New Testament records have but a limited conception of the intricacy of the problem which confronts the historian; but even they to some extent are aware of the difficulties created by the doubt and the assurance, the conflict of testimony and the essential agreements, the legendary accretions and the fundamental truths, which together constitute the evidence for the tremendous proposition of the Resurrection.

The man for whom it is claimed that he was raised from the dead, not as an insubstantial ghost but with a tangible body of flesh and bone—and yet a body capable of transformation and de-materialization—believed implicitly in his lifetime that such a reward was in store for him: it was as much a Divine necessity as the suffering which had closed the first chapter of his messianic manifestation. Jesus had focused upon himself age-old hopes and prophecies: he had become intimate with a reality transcending the three-dimensional world of normal experience. He had served as a willing subject of time as a conscious preparation for the monarchy of eternity: he felt himself to be the symbol of regeneration, the herald, the promise, of a new order of physical being. He paid homage to death as the last act of obedience required of man born of woman: he expected to rise up as the first act of dominion granted to man bom of the Spirit of God.

The faith that Jesus had in his own resurrection, and the faith which his disciples had—and continue to have—in its accomplishment, cannot be affected by historical research or scientific criticism. It is not the faith, but the incidental happenings, some of which are, and some are not, external evidences for the central, dramatic, and mundanely inexplicable event, which may be the subject of investigation.

The biographer can, if he will, report the numerous posthumous appearances of his hero which are on record, as testimonies to the vivid personal impression left upon those who had known him intimately. He can dwell on the loyalty and devotion inspired by the man and his message, which assured the perpetuation of his memory and teaching. He can enlarge on the deathless qualities of the Master's spirit, which long afterwards could communicate to those who had neither seen nor known him a realistic sense of his presence in manifestations both consistent and characteristic. He can show how the dreams and visions of a true leader, tenaciously held and authoritatively expressed, can evoke such responsive confidence that the centuries are unable to diminish the certainty of his return to achieve their fulfilment. But when he has done all this he cannot fail to be aware that there is something more which defeats reason and makes it wholly inadequate.

Whatever else may be said, the unprejudiced mind must admit that the man of the appearances is identifiable, not only by the nail prints and the spear hole, but by all the marks of personality, mode of thought, mannerisms, and method of speech, with the very real and disturbing being whose activities over a considerable period have been sufficiently preserved and recorded. No theories of imitation or invention will cover the details given; for this "apparition" is as individual, as uncompromising, and as independent as the former Jesus of Nazareth. He remains as uncontrollable as ever: he neither says nor does the things which would enable a Church-building doctrine-formulating generation to profit by his authoritative endorsement. He is still the Master.

Only one burning problem is set at rest. The regretful "We trusted that it had been he which should have redeemed Israel," is characteristically answered by the emphatic, "O fools and slow of heart to believe all that the prophets have spoken! Ought not the Messiah to have suffered these things, and to enter into his glory?"

Apart from the mighty theme of the Resurrection, which the biographer is not called upon further to discuss, there remains a lower task that is both valid and significant.

It is in keeping with the scheme of this work that every ancient aid shall be enlisted which will help to shed light on the life-story of Jesus, and invest both the portrait of him and its background with a greater realism. The narrative must therefore be prolonged so as to include the strange things that happened between the time that he died upon the cross and the early hours of Easter Sunday.

The confused and fragmentary character of the material, and the conflict of testimony due to tricks of memory and later polemical and apologetic influences, make it impossible to ascertain the whole truth. But the traditions that will for the first time be assembled offer—at least so far as the body of Jesus is concerned—a physical explanation of the words, "He is not here," which will be new to most people.

The Jewish law was both rigid and merciful that those who were executed on a capital charge should not remain exposed overnight, but should be buried the same evening.[85] Sometimes the soiled and worn-out linen wrappings of the sacred scrolls were used as shrouds for such malefactors. They were interred in special cemeteries; but afterwards permission was given for the bones to be transferred to the ordinary burial ground or family sepulchre.

Crucifixion was not a Jewish mode of punishment; for the condemned rarely died the same day, and often continued for a long time in torment. The Romans commonly allowed the bodies to remain in position to be devoured by birds of prey. In the case of Jesus and his companions in suffering an exception was made at the express wish of the Jews, who petitioned Pilate, because the next day was a high day and the Sabbath, that the end of the condemned might be expedited, and that they might be buried before nightfall.

The petition was granted. The soldiers, therefore, according to the practice in these special circumstances, proceeded to break the legs of the crucified with mallets; but when they came to Jesus they found that he was dead already. So they forbore to break his legs; but one of the soldiers, to make certain, plunged his spear into his side.

In the meantime a wealthy Jew, a member of the Sanhedrin, named Joseph of Arimathea—said to be a secret disciple of Jesus, but certainly no friend of the prosecutors—went to the governor and begged to have the body. He was probably a Pharisee, and had been no party to the proceedings. Pilate could not credit that Jesus was already dead, and sent for the centurion in charge of the execution, who confirmed the fact: he therefore gave the required permission.

Golgotha was close to some gardens, one of them belonging to Joseph, and called after him. In it was a new rock-hewn tomb, where the councillor proposed to lay the body, at least until after the Sabbath, when the relatives and friends might wish other arrangements to be made.

Joseph took with him clean linen for a shroud, and the Fourth Gospel states that he was accompanied by Nicodemus, another supporter of Jesus in the Sanhedrin. Together they wrapped the body in the winding sheet with myrrh and aloes, and deposited it in the tomb. The other three Gospels, however, which know only of Joseph, claim that he took the body, and alone performed these pious offices. Moreover, some women of Jesus's company, who had stayed to see the end, followed to find out the place of his burial, and there now being no opportunity to anoint the body with spices before the Sabbath, they departed, purposing to return early in the morning of the first day of the week. Joseph then rolled the stone over the door of the tomb, and went his way.

These records alone establish that there was no fixed and settled tradition of what transpired. But they do not stand by themselves. The account which is closest to that of the canonical Gospels claims that the Jewish officials delivered the body to Joseph, presumably at his request, instead of attending to the burial, as no doubt they did with the two others who were crucified. The sepulchre was afterwards sealed on the instructions of the chief priests, and with the consent of Pilate, in order to prevent an anticipated attempt by the disciples to steal the corpse. A tent was then pitched, and a watch set to keep guard through the night. With the latter part of this tradition *Matthew* substantially agrees.[86]

There are other traditions, however. One states that when the Jewish authorities were seeking a place to bury Jesus they were approached by one of the gardeners, whose son the Master had healed, and who informed them that there was a tomb close to his vegetable plot, and that if they would lay him there he himself would keep watch over him. An alternative says that the tomb was actually in the vegetable plot. It was the intention of the gardener to visit the tomb when the road was clear, and to take away the body and anoint it with spices. The body was duly placed in the tomb, which was then closed with a stone, and sealed. After watching for a while the authorities departed. In the middle of the night—presumably Saturday night—the gardener went into the tomb and witnessed the resurrection.[87]

Another record relates that Jesus was buried in the usual way, but that the gardener, fearing that the disciples would come and steal the body, himself removed it, and conveyed it into his own garden. There he deflected an irrigation channel, buried the corpse in the bed, and brought the water back into its course.[88] A variation of this version makes the body to be buried in the garden, but to be taken away afterwards by the gardener because his vegetables were being trampled down by the crowds who came to see the tomb.[89] Of the canonical Gospels *John* alone speaks of a gardener, whom Mary Magdalene supposed the risen Jesus to be, and asked him if he had taken the body; and the *Gospel of Peter* mentions the multitudes who visited the sepulchre.[90]

These narratives give rise to questions, which, perhaps, must ever wait for an answer. Was there a real gardener, or is he an alias for Joseph of Arimathea? Was the corpse of Jesus removed by friend or foe from its first place of sepulture to another? Was it to the original tomb, knowing of no other, that the women and the two disciples came on Easter Sunday, and found it empty except for the grave clothes? It is well to state that the bulk of this material is from Christian sources.

Tradition has a final word. It reports that some of the guard at the tomb went to inform Pilate that the body of Jesus had been stolen. Thereupon the governor went in person to the sepulchre, accompanied by the elders. True enough, they found it empty. But on search being made, there was discovered in a disused well or cistern nearby the body of a crucified man. The elders claimed that it was Jesus. The governor, however, sent for Joseph and Nicodemus to identify the remains. Their verdict was that the grave clothes were his, but that the body was that of one of the robbers crucified with him. Pilate turned to the elders, "You believe that this truly is the Nazarene?" They answered, "Certainly." "Then," said Pilate, "it is but right to lay his body in his own tomb." The corpse was therefore conveyed to the sepulchre of Jesus. There a miracle was wrought. The corpse revived, and declared itself to be indeed one of the robbers.[91]

Such is the startling epilogue which tradition has delivered to the biographer of Jesus. It enables him, at any rate, to add this postscript: as with Moses, so with the prophet like unto Moses, NO MAN KNOWETH OF HIS SEPULCHRE UNTO THIS DAY.

Notes and References

1 These nativity legends are to be found scattered over the pages of numerous ancient works, including the *Talmud* and *Midrashim*, the Palestinian *Targum*, *Antiquities* of Josephus, Biblical *Antiquities* of Pseudo-Philo, the *Pirke de Rabbi Eliezer*, *Book of Jasher*, and the *Chronicles of Jerahmeel*. See Schonfield, *The Lost Book of the Nativity of John* (T. Sc. T. Clark), and S. Baring-Gould, *Legends of Old Testament Characters*.

2 The names of Mary's parents are given in the *Book of James*, where it is also stated that Joachim was a farmer. Reference is made to the plot of land which descended in the family by Eusebius, *Eccl. Hist.* bk. iii, ch. 20, where it is said in the time of Jude's grandchildren to have consisted of thirty-nine acres, and to have been worth about £275.

3 See Schonfield, *According to the Hebrews*, pp. 140-3 (Duckworth), on Josephus, the Quran, and other traditions.

4 *Antiquities*, XVII, vi. 2-4.

5 *Book of James*, xvii. 2.

6 *Book of James*, xviii. i; xix. 3.

7 Josephus, *Wars*, I, xxxiii. 6.

8 Josephus, *Wars*, II, i. 3.

9 Josephus, *Wars*, II, vi. 2.

10 Josephus, *Antiquities*, XVII, x.

11 *Gospel of Thomas*, xii. I.

12 *Gospel of Thomas*, vi: -vii.

13 *Gospel of Thomas*, ii. 3.

14 *J. Taanith*, ii. I (ed. Greenup).

15 *Gospel of Thomas*, ix. and xvi.

16 Josephus, *Antiquities*, XVII, xiii. 2.

17 On the history of the Baptist, see Schonfield, *The Lost*

Book of the Nativity of John.

18 *Gospel of Thomas,* xix. 4.

19 *Shir HaShirim Rabba* on *Cant.* ii. 9.

20 *Odes of Solomon* (Ode 36).

21 Josephus, *Wars,* II, ix. 2-3.

22 *Gospel of the Hebrews.* Quoted by Jerome, *Dialogue against Pelagius,* iii. 2.

23 *Gospel of the Hebrews.* Quoted by Jerome on Isaiah, xi. 2. See also *Odes of Solomon* (Ode XXIV. 1.)

24 Reference is made to the fire on the Jordan by Justin Martyr, *Dialogue with Trypho,* lxxxviii, and in old MSS. at Matthew, iii. 15.

25 In the *Gospel of the Hebrews.* The reference is by Jerome on Ezekiel, xviii. 7.

26 Enoch, xciv. "Woe to you ye rich! for ye have trusted in your riches and from your riches ye shall depart, because ye have not remembered the Most High in the days of your riches.... Woe to you sinners! for ye persecute the righteous; for ye will be delivered up and persecuted.... Woe to you! who devour the finest of the wheat and drink the power of the source of the fountain, and tread under foot the lowly with your might."

27 *Baba Bathra,* fol. 3b.

28 *Targum of Jonathan, in loc.*

29 *Sanhed.,* fol. 64a.

30 *Testament of Levi,* xiv. 5-6.

31 *Psalms of Solomon,* viii. 8-14.

32 *Ecclus,* xxiii. 9-12.

33 *Sanhed.,* fol. 36a.

34 *Sanhed.,* fol. 63b.

35 *Meg.,* fol. 6a.

36 *Gitt.,* fol. 57a.

37 *J. Taanith,* fol. 2a.

38 *Baba Bathra,* fol. 9b.

39 This is the form of the Hebrew text of Matthew vii. 1-2, which exhibits the original parallelism. See Schonfield, *An Old Hebrew Text of Matthew's Gospel* (T. & T. Clark).

40 *Baba Bathra,* fol. 15b.

41 When Fadus was procurator of Judea, a certain

imposter, whose name was Theudas, urged a great part of the people to take their effects with them, and follow him to the River Jordan; for he told them he was a prophet, and that he would, by his own command, divide the river, and afford them an easy passage over it: and many were deluded by his words" (Josephus, *Antiquities*, XX, v. 1). In Felix's time "there came out of Egypt to Jerusalem, one that said he was a prophet, and advised the multitude of the common people to go along with him to the Mount of Olives... for he said he wished to show them from thence, how, at his command, the walls of Jerusalem would fall down, through which he promised to procure them an entrance into the city" (*Antiquities*, XX, vii. 6).

42 The translation of the quoted passages from the Sermon on the Mount are from the Hebrew text.

43 The interpretation that Jesus was referring to his new doctrine as compared with the old doctrine quite misses the point.

44 Codex Bezae at Luke, vi. 4.

45 *Gospel of the Hebrews,* quoted by Jerome on Matthew xii. 13.

46 The word floor is given in the Hebrew text of Matthew viii. 20. The reference is to the cheapest form of lodging at the village khan, where a paved recess was provided raised a foot or two above the level of the courtyard where the cattle were tied.

47 "My secrets are for me, etc." A saying of Jesus quoted in the *Clementine Homilies,* xix. 20, and by Clement of Alexandria, *Strom.,* V, 10, 63. See also *Odes of Solomon* (Ode VIII, xi).

48 *Toldoth Jeshu,* cod. Wagenseil.

49 *Toldoth Jeshu,* cod. Strasburg, iii. 19. For the complete translation from Hebrew of the whole incident see Schonfield, *According to the Hebrews.*

50 *Toldoth Jeshu,* iii. 16; *Gospel of Thomas,* ii. 2-5; Quran, sura iii.

51 Quran, sura v; Celsus, quoted by Origen, *Contra Celsum,* 1, lxvii- lxviii.

52 Reported by Papias, and quoted by Irenaeus, v. 33. See also *Apocalypse of Baruch,* xxix. 5-6.

53 *Letter of Aristeas,* 141 (ed. H. St. John Thackeray).

54 *Kethub.,* fol. 110b.

55 The story of the Syro-Phoenician woman is given in the *Clementine Homilies,* xix-xx.

56 As above (note 2).

57 This seems to be the most ancient reading. See *Odes of Solomon* (OdeXXII 12) "And that the foundation for everything might be thy rock: and on it thou didst build thy kingdom." The Odes are a primitive Christian hymnary.

58 *Erub.,* fol. 19a.

59 *Midrash. Tehill,* 39a.

60 *Apocalypse of Esdras,* Vision VI (xiii. 1-12).

61 *Gospel of the Hebrews.* Quoted by Origen on John, ii. 12, and also on Jeremiah, xv. 4.

62 This reading of Matthew, xvii. 27 is in *Codex Algerines Peckover.*

63 *Gospel of the Hebrews.* Quoted by Jerome, *Dialogue against Pelagius,* iii. 2.

64 Josephus, *Wars,* ii, ix, 4.

65 Josephus, *Antiquities,* xviii, v, 2.

66 Josephus, *Antiquities,* xx, ix, 1.

67 *Gospel of the Hebrews.* Quoted by Jerome, *Of Illustrious Men,* 2.

68 *Shabb.,* fol. 62b.

69 *Gospel of the Hebrews.* Quoted by Pseudo-Origen on Matthew, *in loc.*

70 See Schonfield, *According to the Hebrews,* pp. 170-2.

71 *Gospel of the Hebrews.* "Now the Lord, when he had given the linen cloth to the servant of the priest..." Quoted by Jerome, *Of Illustrious Men,* 2.

72 *Gospel of Peter,* vii. "We (the apostles) were sought after by them as malefactors, and as thinking to set the Temple on fire."

73 Tacitus, *Annals,* Book VI, vii.

74 Tacitus, *Annals,* Book IV, lxx.

75 These traditions are given in full in Schonfield, *According to the Hebrews.*

76 Slavonic Josephus, following *Wars,* II, ix. 3.

77 *Apocryphyon of Joseph of Arimathea,* ii. 1-4.

78 *Toldoth Jeshu,* iii. 40-3.

79 Quoted by Origen, *Contra Celsum,* II, ix.

80 Josephus, *Wars,* IV, v. 2. "But the rage of the Idumeans was not satiated by these slaughters... they sought for the high priests, and the generality went with the greatest zeal against them; and as soon as they caught them they slew them.... Nay, they proceeded to that degree of impiety, as to cast away their bodies without burial."

81 Reported by Papias. Quoted by Apollinarius and Ecumenius on the *Acts of the Apostles.* "Judas walked about in this world, a great example of impiety, his flesh blown out so much that he was not able to pass even where a wagon might pass easily... and he suffered from foul discharges of matter and worms."

82 *Wars,* V, ii. 2. "Now it was here impossible for him (Titus) to go forward, because all the places had trenches dug in them from the wall, to preserve the gardens round about, and were full of gardens obliquely situated, and of many hedges." A full description of his position is given in the context, which should be compared with a modem map of the same area.

83 *Gospel of Peter,* vii. and Curetonian Syriac version at Luke xxiii. 48.

84 *Gospel of the Hebrews.* Quoted by Jerome, *Letter to Hedibia,* 8, and elsewhere. "In the Gospel that is written in Hebrew letters we read, not that the veil of the Temple was rent, but that a lintel of the Temple of wondrous size fell."

85 Josephus, *Wars,* IV, v. 2. "The Jews used to take so much care of the burial of men, that they took down those that were condemned and crucified, and buried them before the going down of the sun."

86 *Gospel of Peter*, viii.

87 *Book of the Resurrection of Christ by Bartholomew the Apostle*. See M. R. James, *Apocryphal New Testament*, p. 183.

88 *Toldoth Jeshu* (cod. Strasburg), v. 10. See Schonfield, *According to the Hebrews*.

89 Amulo, *Epistola contra Judaeos*, quotes a Jewish tradition that Jesus was buried in "a tomb in a garden full of cabbages." Tertullian, *Against the Jews*, "or the gardener abstracted that his lettuces might not be damaged by the crowds of visitors."

90 *Gospel of Peter*, ix. "There came a multitude from Jerusalem and the region round about to see the sepulchre that had been sealed."

91 *Gospel of Gamaliel* and *Arabic Life of Pilate*. See M. R. James, Apocryphal New Testament, p. 151.

Note: Regarding the extra-canonical traditions of Jesus contained in ancient Christian and non-Christian documents, the author has dealt very fully with the question of what elements are likely to be historical in his book *According to the Hebrews*. He has been forced to conclude, on the weight of evidence, that much genuine material is embedded in works usually dismissed as entirely legendary. Traditions in the East are extraordinarily tenacious, and when they are found cropping up in quite unexpected places in very similar forms, often where verbal or literary contact is excluded, the burden of proof lies with those who hold that they are unworthy of credence. It is for the sound investigator to take the advice of Jesus (in an authentic uncanonical saying): "Be ye approved money-changers," rejecting the spurious, but retaining the true.

Index